Devotion in Motion

# Devotion in Motion

PILGRIMAGE IN MODERN MEXICO

*Edward Wright-Ríos*

*The University of Chicago Press    Chicago and London*

The University of Chicago Press, Chicago 60637
The University of Chicago Press, Ltd., London
© 2025 by The University of Chicago
For more information, contact the University of Chicago Press,
1427 E. 60th St., Chicago, IL 60637.
Published 2025
Printed in the United States of America

34  33  32  31  30  29  28  27  26  25      1  2  3  4  5

ISBN-13: 978-0-226-84081-9 (cloth)
ISBN-13: 978-0-226-84083-3 (paper)
ISBN-13: 978-0-226-84082-6 (e-book)
DOI: https://doi.org/10.7208/chicago/9780226840826.001.0001

Library of Congress Cataloging-in-Publication Data

Names: Wright-Ríos, Edward N. (Edward Newport), 1965– author.
Title: Devotion in motion : pilgrimage in modern Mexico /
Edward Wright-Ríos.
Description: Chicago : The University of Chicago Press, 2025. |
Includes bibliographical references and index.
Identifiers: LCCN 2024043608 | ISBN 9780226840819 (cloth) | ISBN
9780226840833 (paperback) | ISBN 9780226840826 (ebook)
Subjects: LCSH: Christian pilgrims and pilgrimages—Mexico—
Oaxaca (State) | Christian pilgrims and pilgrimages—Social
aspects—Mexico—Oaxaca (State) | Juquila, Nuestra Señora
de—Cult—Mexico—Oaxaca (State) | Christian shrines—
Mexico—Oaxaca (State) | Social media—Mexico—Religious
aspects—Catholic Church.
Classification: LCC BX2320.5.M6 W75 2025 | DDC
263/.0427274—dc23/eng/20241123
LC record available at https://lccn.loc.gov/2024043608

♾ This paper meets the requirements of ANSI/NISO Z39.48-1992
(Permanence of Paper).

*Para mis hermanos/as, Juanito, Caro, and Betsy*

# CONTENTS

# *En camino*—In Transit, November 2016

We wake up with a start to the keening whistle and unnerving boom of fireworks. It is perhaps 3 a.m. We are a relatively small group, some twenty-five pilgrims, comprised mostly of vendors from Oaxaca's Mercado de Abastos (a vast, urban market on the edge of the state capital), Mike (an unflappable photographer), and I (a groggy historian). A few of us sleep on the sidewalk; others doze in the bed of an empty fruit truck or amid fellow pilgrims strewn in clumps across a small-town plaza.[1] Alone or in small groups we amble over to a house selling access to toilets, sinks, showers, and mirrors. In clusters, still shrouded in darkness, pilgrims sip sweet coffee or *champurrado* (a thick, chocolate-and-corn-based hot drink), nibble on prepackaged cookies or stale *pan dulce* (pastries). Swallowing is a challenge. Myriad support vehicles, jigsawed together for the night about six hours earlier, sputter-grumble to life and begin to maneuver cautiously. Each time the drivers put their rigs in reverse they add to the strident chorus of back-up alarms swelling the mounting din. Slowly, individual trucks escape and lumber down the road, heading to the next stopover. Diesel fumes remain with the mustering pilgrims and mix with the sulfur stink of spent rockets—*huele a fiesta* (it smells like festival).

Gradually, shaking off the previous day's aches, the throng of devotees snakes its way out of town; hundreds of bobbing headlamps and flashlights delineate the trail, fore and aft. Across rivers, up hillsides, down ravines, and then climbing and climbing still more: up into mountains, where the vegetation shifts from pastures and broad-leaved trees to pines anchored in rocky white dirt, up . . . up into the clouds.

Night lingers and distinct pilgrim groups, like flocks of starlings, mingle, merge, swell, fragment, and come back together, over and over. Individuals huff and puff; walking sticks clatter on stones. Some pilgrims play devotional music on their cell phones, a candy-sweet praise pop providing a surreal soundtrack as dawn approaches: a remix of synthe-sizers, string machines, drum tracks, and saccharine vocals amid the tramp and murmur of sleepy devotees. Sadly, waste—abandoned plas-tic bottles, bags, wrappers, and even human excrement—also appear in clumps and piles next to the trail. A large group from Ocotlán, an an-cient Zapotec town in Oaxaca's southernmost Central Valley, struggles on their second day of walking. There may be fifty or ninety of them all told—they are so spread out that it is hard to tell. Their matching shirts announce that they have made the journey every year since 1974, and they bring together teens in hoodies and Chuck Taylors (or, more likely, pirated Chuck Taylors), patterned athleisure, and school-kid backpacks, alongside *señoras* in the traditional long skirts favored by some Indige-nous women in Oaxaca and many adults in their pueblo workday attire, jeans, T-shirts, and sturdy shoes. Flitting past their laboring colleagues, grizzled, sinewy men and adolescents from Acatzingo, a town in Puebla over two hundred miles away, materialize from the mist. On their tenth day walking, with hushed patter of, "compermisito . . . comper' . . . ," they request permission to pass. There is something awe inspiring about their speed and discipline, in combination with the tinkling little bells attached to the delicate, wood-and-glass custom-built case (*vitrina*) housing their copy of the Virgin of Juquila. Like most groups, they take turns carrying her on their backs—she and her ethereal chimes lead the way.

We try to stay together following our own *Virgencita*, without success. She usually resides in the back of Silvio's *bodega* (a large, permanent, wholesale fruit stall) in the market, behind the carefully arranged, tall piles of fruit in an attractive, homemade altar. Lacking her own vitrina, she travels tied to an unfinished wooden chair retrofitted with leather straps. Like so much in the pilgrimage, do-it-yourself ingenuity and a make-it-work attitude takes center stage: simple, practical bodega fur-niture is transformed, and a stout backpack litter emerges, accessorized with red and white plastic lilies and LED bike lights (my contribution). The lights, also red and white, blink, blink, blink as we hike, always out of synch. Members of the group take turns carrying our Virgencita (see plates 1 and 10).

Sunrise gradually catches us in a field at the foot of a looming ridge. Clouds and cook-fire smoke envelope congregating, exhausted devo-tees. Pilgrims lie strewn across the surrounding grass, catching their breath, attending to blisters. A sterilized needle and thread do the job: puncture the side of the blister and pull the steel spine through the entire pocket of fluid; make sure you leave the thread in the blister, trimming the excess but with a little sticking out on each side to help it drain; apply mescal.

We gather at an improvised restaurant, a testament to Mexico's inexhaustible entrepreneurial creativity, with handmade, stump-and-plank benches for seating and plastic sheeting fluttering above us, held up by an array of quickly cut and fashioned wooden poles. Pilgrimage: the original pop-up dining experience. Fires blaze under large *comales*—the ubiquitous and unrivaled round, red clay Mesoamerican cooktop. Coffee or champurrado again. We order *huevos al comal*, eggs fried on the hot clay griddle. The cooks are slow, so the women in our group muscle their way to the glowing stoves and take charge. Scraped off the comal and nestled in soft large tortillas, salted and smothered in fresh salsa, the eggs are fantastic (see plate 6). We relax . . . for a time: twenty more miles must be covered by nightfall.

Pilgrimage, for many of us, is merely a metaphor, a concept connected to travels of seeming importance, actual or ironic. Perhaps we have visited a famous shrine, but, for the most part, we have no idea what pilgrimage really entails. Getting there requires entering pilgrimage's enveloping atmospherics. In other words, to feel, watch, smell, and hear pilgrimage means to embrace a disorienting, unrelenting, and unforgettable ordeal.

How many participate in pilgrimage in Mexico, and how many go to Juquila? I've learned that most statistics offered deeply flawed estimates. Claims of more than ten million annual pilgrim visits to the shrine of the national patroness, Our Lady of Guadalupe, are common.[2] News outlets often suggest that perhaps 2.5 to three million visit Oaxaca's most famous image of Mary each year.[3] Citing calculations from archdiocesan officials in 2020, the state government claims that approximately one million devotees visit the basilica each year and spend at least one night in Juquila, and they estimate that the figure surpasses two million visitors when counting those who arrive and depart the same day. The state also asserts that 731 local jobs are directly dependent on the shrine economy, and the annual flow of devotees sustains an additional 1,882 workers indirectly.[4] These figures are certainly plausible. Even a casual observer can see that the pilgrimage anchors the local economy.

But how would one count all the devotees streaming in along different routes, at different times of the year, and by different means? Church administrators at the basilica measure the flow by the special Masses devotees contract and pay for at the shrine's offices ("Mass intentions," dedications of the grace emerging from the service to a specific need or commemoration). Oaxacan tourism officials develop their estimates from voluntary hotel surveys (which proprietors may falsify to escape higher taxes) and imprecise assumptions about occupancy (six people per room).[5] But many visitors simply can't afford special liturgies or hotels. An accurate assessment would require a careful metering of devotees' arrival by various means, which no one seems willing to finance.

My interest in Juquila's pilgrimage took shape almost by accident, although seasoned *peregrinos* (pilgrims) doubt serendipity is a factor when the Virgencita is concerned. I am not motivated by Marian devotion or a middle-aged quest for meaning and renewed purpose. I grew up in the Catholic Church, a child of a religious, Mexican American family, but Mexico's baroque popular traditions reverberated only faintly in my upbringing. Coincidentally, my great-grandmother, Beatriz, was from Oaxaca, and my great-grandfather was a Oaxacan priest, although his identity remains a mystery. No one in the family seems to know if this individual's violation of his priestly vows and my great-grandmother's pregnancy stemmed from forbidden love or sexual assault, but it was clearly scandalous. Beatriz, while still quite young, left Oaxaca and moved to Mexico City. Subsequently a birth certificate bestowed upon her newborn son an apocryphal last name, "Ríos," and she claimed he was an orphaned nephew. My grandfather, apparently, didn't learn the truth until adulthood.

We, the Wright-Ríos clan, however, were North American, suburban, Vatican II Catholics, embracing the relaxed religious norms and ecumenical ethos of the era. We sometimes attended Spanish-language services, which my mother helped establish in our parish, but, mostly, we were mainstays of the 1970s folk Mass—services that were younger, trendier, and "more American." They also started on time, were comparatively brief, and required less obligatory socializing afterward: this matters a great deal to children. My older brother, a twelve-string guitar strapped to his body, anchored the choir, and the rest of us followed his lead. Some of the repertoire, particularly compositions by the Saint Luis Jesuits, still lilt through my memories from time to time. We were square (not "counterculture," by any stretch), although I remember a blue jean–covered Bible in the house, and my father sported lamb-chop sideburns and even put flowers on his white VW Beetle. Inculcated in notions of a "common good," we embraced the progressive Catholic social teachings that predominated among guitar-Mass parishioners and inspired a sentimental (although not ideological) affinity for aspects of liberation theology in Latin America, my brother excepted. He went there, as it were, imbibing its social justice teachings, living in community with fellow activists, and taking part in years of protest to support human rights campaigns in Central America.

Close relatives who remained in Mexico, however, chose a different path, following the conservative ideas, traditional gender norms, and the austere rhythms of the Opus Dei. Both realms, it bears mentioning, remained resolutely bourgeois. In short, I grew up in a very Catholic family, but we did not attend popular religious festivals, show interest in sacred images, or partake in pilgrimages alongside Mexico's devout working class. Those practices were vaguely construed as archaic. Race played a mostly unspoken role. My grandmother was prone to declarations that began, "Para la gente decente" (Among decent people), an old Mexican turn of phrase denoting social precedence and a Hispanic, "civilized," cultural orientation. Naturally, such a stance remains at odds with Mexico's unapologetically kinetic, predominantly nonwhite religious traditions. But devotion represents an arena where such distinctions can emerge sharply.

So, for families like mine, effervescent practices like Juquila's pilgrimage remained mostly invisible or characterized as security risks when crowds jammed the streets and plazas. Mexico's famed images and public pious traditions functioned like sepia photographs of long-dead forebears none of us had known personally. In other words, we rarely thought about pilgrimages and the traditional nine-day *ferias* (feast-day celebrations) of the culture's myriad religious icons—Mary, Christ, and famous saints—scattered across the liturgical calendar. Images of Mary inhabited our home, but more as mementos than as the focus of devotion. My mother perched a small, gilded Virgin of Zapopan near the front door—a reminder of her high school years in Guadalajara—but she never invoked the image. She also never took us to Zapopan's basilica, perhaps a twenty-minute car ride from the city center, despite multiple visits to see relatives nearby.

Notwithstanding this upbringing, as a teenager I concluded that I had no faith whatsoever, and I've avoided church services ever since, unless a wedding or funeral was in the offing. But I made religion in Mexico my scholarly specialty, and so I remain distant by some measures and close by others. In truth, my enduring ties to a varied cast of devout Catholic relatives serves me well. It reminds me that life suffused with observances, obligations, prayer, and the certainty of a palpable divine presence are, in fact, quite common, both historically and in the present day.

I stumbled across Juquila while working in Oaxaca's archdiocesan archives over twenty years ago. In retrospect, this represents a pitiful admission. I had been to Oaxaca many times and spent months researching its religious cultural history, yet, I had failed to notice her, even though her devotion pervades everyday life. Stickers, magnets, T-shirts, statuettes, caps, and pictures bearing her likeness move through traffic

ceaselessly on cars, buses, cabs, and devotees' bodies. She graces posters, photos, and altars in stores and private homes. Textual testimonials,
like the common *Regalo de Juquila* (Gift from Juquila), appear stenciled
across windshields and dashboards. Butchers, bakers, printers, mechanics, and countless shopkeepers honor her in naming their businesses—
for example, Carnicería Juquila (Juquila Butcher Shop) and Farmacia
Juquilita (Juquila Pharmacy). I just wasn't yet paying attention.

At the time, I was interested in how different Indigenous communities responded to modernizing religious reforms during the late nineteenth and early twentieth centuries. In simplest terms, I researched
the Oaxacan archdiocese's efforts to Westernize Indigenous Catholicism, and I tracked how native parishioners defended their own ideas
about the nature of their faith and local configurations of modern religiosity. I found that priestly authority was not sufficient to reshape
local religion. Change emerged from gradual, sometimes conflictive
negotiation and organically driven innovations. Devotions that centered on images of Mary or Christ, and the miracles attributed to them,
often appeared as the apple of discord. This is how I came across the
Virgin of Juquila and her pilgrimage. Oaxacans sustained many different devotions, the archives attest, but she was clearly more popular
than most others.

Newly aware, I saw her everywhere, and I made plans to attend her
festival in 2001. Her feast day remains December 8, the official celebration of the Immaculate Conception, although because of her surging
popularity devotees plan their visits throughout the year. Juquilita is
an Inmaculada (Mary Immaculate), a distinct advocation, and hence
different from Dolores (The Virgin of Sorrows), Asunción (Our Lady
of the Assumption), and the famed Virgin of Guadalupe. Dolores represents the anguished Holy Mother during the crucifixion and thus her
limitless maternal love and compassion. Asunción depicts the resplendent Queen of Heaven miraculously exiting the mortal world and metaphorically representing the Catholicism's ultimate apocalyptic victory.
The Virgin of Juquila is a small one-foot-tall (30 cm) wooden statue.
Her exact age is unknown, but a study by Mexico's National Institute
of History and Anthropology deduced that the image was carved in the
late sixteenth century and is therefore over four hundred years old.[6] She
embodies the dogma stating that Christ's mother remained a virgin,
chaste and without sin, and thus symbolizes unimpeachable purity and
unquestioning, obedient faith. Her name, Juquila, comes from the town
where she has resided since the early 1700s. Before this, she was known
as the Virgin of Amialtepec, after the small Chatino Indigenous village
where her devotion began, perhaps twenty miles from the present-day

basilica. In truth, she likely had a distinct Indigenous name among her original devotees.

Guadalupe, the official Catholic patroness of both the nation and the entirety of the Americas, is the most popular of all image devotions in Mexico. Every year her shrine draws millions of pilgrims, and particularly during massive pious convergences at her shrine in the days leading up to her feast on December 12. Emerging from stories of her sixteenth-century apparition before an Indigenous peasant on a rural hillside outside Mexico City and her image's miraculous manifestation on his cloak, she has been the subject of sustained, often aggressive promotion since the 1600s. The slightly darker hue of her skin in the venerated image has also made her a symbol of Mexican mixed-race nationalism. These characteristics and her widespread popularity have led to Guadalupe's periodic conflation with Mexican national identity. But history isn't all love and roses: the invocation of miscegenation reveals that within nearly all Catholic traditions born in Mexico lurk tensions rooted in colonialism, racialized subjugation, and coercive evangelization.

For non-Catholics the abundance of different images and attendant pomp can be bewildering. A strict Protestant or Muslim could be forgiven for seeing the profusion of figures and fiestas as idolatrous. Outsiders may find the elaborate festivals and flamboyant decorative practices disconcerting, too, but pious splendor enjoys deep doctrinal and cultural roots among Mexican Catholics.[7]

In church teaching, Mary is singular (there is only one Virgin Mary), even though the varied, seemingly personalized, image-centered pageantry and ritual can suggest otherwise. The institutional church and common believers categorize Marian images by location, famous apparitions, or iconographic elements linked to the Virgin's legendary biography. Some are relatively new (like Our Lady of Lourdes and the Virgin of Fatima), but in many cases centuries of devotional tradition surround these likenesses and the seemingly endless copies of famous images belonging to churches and individuals. The church argues that the Virgin Mary is venerated, not worshipped, as a model of piety, humility, purity, and unfailing obedience to God. Doctrine, moreover, holds that Mary, as the universal mother of mankind, retains a deep and abiding love for the humble laity and hence advocates for them before her son, Christ.

This, according to Catholic tradition, is how Marian miracles happen. Devotees, through acts of penitential zeal and devotional fervor, seek Mary's support in alleviating suffering, curing illness, finding work, overcoming personal problems, and securing celestial protection for loved ones. Devotees' pleas are granted thanks to the Virgin's intercession on their behalf: essentially, she convinces God to reward meritorious requests. Images, in church teaching, are merely representations.

But elaborate feasts and performative shows of deference amid coronations, processions, opulent garments, and vibrant folklore undermine doctrine. In other words, the cultural practices, and the array of emotions and ideas conveyed through them, treat famous images as individuals. The dynamics of devotion, moreover, can be quite tender and moving. Devotees often frame devotion in intimate familial terms. They trust that Mary, their *Madrecita* (literally, little mother, meaning beloved), will hear them and help them if they demonstrate honest motives, openhearted dedication, and unflagging faith. Particularly in the context of considerable hardship and need, the doctrinal classifications of veneration, worship, and intercession appear to be of scant interest among fervent supplicants; many devotees believe that Juquila grants miracles directly.

In any case, in December 2001, knowing a fair amount about the history of Mexican religion but little about the nuances of pilgrimage, I booked a room and purchased a ticket on one of the overstuffed minibuses shuttling passengers between Juquila and Oaxaca. My fellow passengers were devotees. The man sitting next to me spoke of many visits to Juquila and testified to the extraordinary role she played in his life. He had visited the shrine every year since 1975. A middle-aged woman in the van also spoke to me of how Juquila granted pious requests. She assured me that if I asked the Virgencita for something on my next visit, I'd experience her miraculous grace. As we passed the town of El Vidrio, the turnoff for the shrine, perhaps forty minutes from Juquila, an older woman announced that she would begin reciting the Rosary: "If you're willing, you can provide the responses."[8] The handful of women present took part, filling the van with the repetitive, almost murmured, call-and-response cadence characteristic of this Marian prayer. They shifted to singing hymns as we got closer, like the waltz "Viva el Rosario" (Long Live the Rosary) and the classic devout corrido "La Guadalupana," which they sang with special intensity: "Desde el cielo una hermosa mañana . . . la Guadalupana bajo al Tepeyac" (From Heaven one beautiful morning . . . the Virgin of Guadalupe came down at Tepeyac). Midway through the song, a man joined in, immediately enriching the sound with his resonant baritone. The van thrummed with expectation. It was an impressive moment. It gave me a sense for what devotees seek on these journeys: a collective experience, a harmonious joint purpose.

However, what seized my imagination still more was the sheer density of pilgrims in the shrine town. They choked the roads, the plaza, the market, the church atrium, and, of course, the basilica. At night, exhausted devotees bedded down on every inch of sidewalk and open space, and at 4 a.m. fireworks exploded and bells began to ring announcing the pending dawn Mass. By 5 a.m. tired pilgrims had shaken off their slumber and crowded into the basilica to celebrate the *Mañanitas de la Virgen* (a sunrise service on her feast day, December 8), packing the sanctuary so tightly that burning votive candles occasionally singed bystanders' braided hair, seeding the air with acrid wafts. Every few minutes impromptu *conjuntos* (musical groups) began singing devotional rancheras or the serenade standard, "Las mañanitas." At intervals, individuals unleashed *gritos* (a characteristic Mexican shouted cheer), "Viva la Virgen de Juquila!" inspiring a fervent response from others, "VIVA!" The event also featured a brilliant, perhaps ancient bit of liturgical theater: the Mass commenced with devotees streaming into the sanctuary in darkness and culminated as the great main doors opened to let a resplendent dawn pour into the sanctuary. Mentally tipping my hat to the shrine's priests, I resolved then and there to pay better attention to Juquila and her followers.

This book represents the belated outgrowth of that decision. On one level, it seeks to foster an immersive, nuanced understanding of pilgrimage in a particular setting—southern Mexico. I hope to impart a sense for the "doings" and "feelings" centered on devotional travel to the Virgin of Juquila's shrine and lifetimes of votive religiosity. But my intentions go beyond merely convincing readers to care about religious Mexicans and their ideas and experiences. The realization that individuals and societies reveal themselves in all their messy, contradictory complexity amid religious practice was what drew me to religious movements and cultural processes many years ago. Devotion, celebration, ritual spaces, and even religious institutional culture convey understandings of power, truth, value, merit, and accomplishment. They also provide settings for voicings of joy, hope, fear, desire, and despair.

Most everyone pondering pilgrimage imagines that the practice of ritual, long-distance travel is ancient. What is less understood, however, is how it remains a dynamic facet of present-day cultures, a living practice woven into the lives of people who are very much part of the modern world, where religion, work, school, politics, and economics are simultaneously in tension and intermingled. It is not, by any means, static. Pilgrimage is many things at once and constantly in flux. In fact, the value in studying it resides not in understanding "tradition," but rather in appreciating the complexities of change.

Researching this book continually reminded me of the importance of two interwoven dynamics. First, there is no enduring devotion without a history of promotion. A pilgrimage takes shape gradually over time and develops as individual devotees, communities, and institutions (religious and secular) publicize miraculous narratives about the sacred image and mythic stories about the journey, create and maintain attractive devotional spaces, shape understandings of pious expression, and market notions of transcendent experience. Likewise, pilgrimage devotions are also subject to stagnation and decline at times. Past popularity and centuries of tradition are no guarantee of endurance, let alone fluorescence. Second, pilgrimages develop in tandem with complex shrine economies and in constant connection to broader social transformations. This means that devotions remain sensitive to wider changes and instability; they evolve alongside unflinching earthly conflicts over resources and efforts to control profits and power generated by the flow of pilgrims. That doesn't mean that the entire endeavor is cynical. It simply means that various less-than-devout interests are key shaping forces.

As I learned, tracking Juquila's devotion over time exposes the interweaving of faith and commerce, local and regional struggles to control and shape religious culture, competition between towns and social groups, and long-standing conflicts rooted in complex tensions between the Catholic Church and Indigenous communities. In other words, Mexico's colonial legacies remain palpable.

This book, moreover, is neither a traveler's how-to guide nor a wistful portrayal of a uniquely devout people and unalloyed faith. Nor does it chronicle a subculture that holds itself apart from society. On the contrary, this is about integration: the integration of men, women, and children who are caught up in the rhythms of modern hectic existence and technological change but who embrace pilgrimage as part of that existence. It is also about another kind of integration, a deliberate, inventive incorporation and recombination of practices, traditions, innovations, technologies, and customs in *our* time. In other words, sustaining pilgrimage doesn't represent a purist, preservationist crusade. *Devotion in Motion* is about how common people adopt practices they find attractive and make them their own. It explores the "use" of custom, how people reconfigure it with new meaning, new expressive fashions, new ways of organizing, and new technologies; devotees constantly enliven and reshape pilgrimage as they re-embed it in evolving, contemporary cultures. In short, *Devotion in Motion* offers both a descriptive and a visual testament of how a "tradition" remains highly adaptable, flexible, and thus vital. It reveals that pilgrimage, in fact, isn't old at all.

In a sense, I've patterned this book on pilgrimage, and thus it remains idiosyncratic and episodic. I begin with descriptions of people, practices, and the past before setting out for the shrine. But it is impossible to fully encompass the range of devotee motives, ideas, practices, and

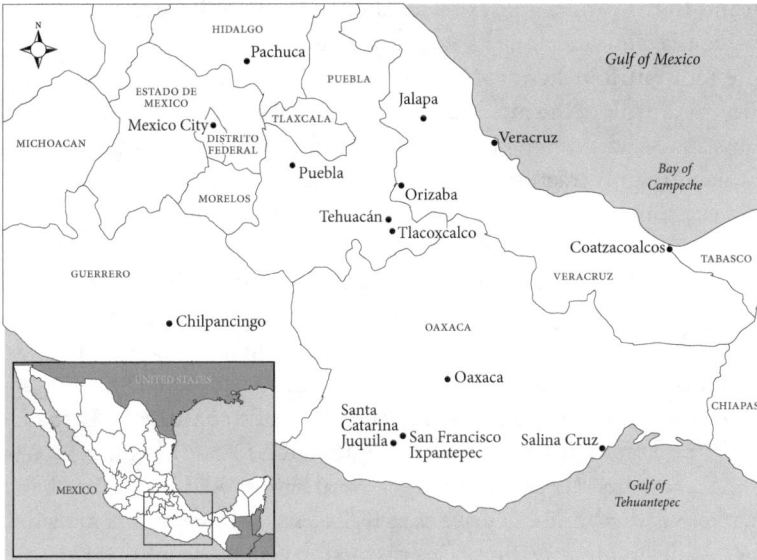

Figure 1. Southern Mexico, Oaxaca, and Juquila. Map by Tracy Ellen Smith.

Juquila experiences. Individuals I met by chance, and others introduced to me by friends, shaped my portrayal with their memories, explanations, and stories. Likewise, the simple fact that two pilgrimage groups welcomed my participation when others ignored messages or responded coldly impacts the course and scope of my observations.

Some readers may wonder if I talked to the "right" pilgrims and imagine that there are "pure" or "traditional" approaches to Juquila's devotion that have remained untouched by the passing of time. Pilgrimage, I would argue, doesn't work that way. It doesn't belong to a single group. It is dynamic, because each generation of practitioners adapts and re-interprets it amid new social contexts and cultural pressures. There are no hard and fast rules to break, and no single way to *do* pilgrimage. In other words, its adaptive genius resides in its malleability, the absence of firm strictures, and the ease with which devotees can give it intimate personal meaning.

I begin with personal stories of devotion among present-day pilgrims and a sketch of pilgrimage scholarship to give readers unfamiliar with Mexican Catholicism and image-centered practice a sense for its rhythms, patterns, and logic. I also convey how Juquila's followers intertwine their autobiographies and cherished relationships with the episodic histories of shrine visitation. Naturally, I use pseudonyms to protect their privacy. I then journey into the past, tracking the history of the shrine and famed image, examining an eighteenth-century promotional campaign designed to foment long-distance pilgrimage to Juquila, and sketching historical practices surrounding this humble, one-foot-tall, four-hundred-year-old likeness of the Virgin Mary. Along the way, I explore the interwoven dynamics of shrine development and devotion amid shifting political and social conditions. In addition, the available, highly fragmented evidence suggests long periods of political and economic turmoil that brought on contraction and meager endurance in the first half of both the nineteenth and twentieth centuries.

Subsequently, I introduce the reputedly corrupt but savvy priest who presided over Juquila's extraordinary resurgence in the 1950s, and I attend to devotees' oral histories that shed light on the pilgrimage's evolution and expansion since the 1960s. Here again, I stress that Juquila's devotion appears to ride the rails of domestic commerce. As roads, trade, and technology increasingly integrated Oaxaca within the national economy, the pilgrimage appears to have spread among truckers, market vendors, and cab drivers, as well as small-town middlemen and merchants in other regions. This discussion also reaffirms that devotee narratives of religious commitment and ritual travel take shape as stories of opportunity, family, friendships, movement, and faith.

I then pause the chronicle of pilgrimage history and move into the virtual realm of social media. Between the time when I first noticed Juquila's pilgrimage in 2001 and when I began researching the topic in earnest in 2015, Facebook and YouTube emerged and rapidly evolved into vital spaces of devotee expression and crucial tools for those leading pilgrimage groups. These online platforms, and the volume of pilgrimage-related content published on them, have only increased in importance in subsequent years as many devotees document and share their experiences online. In addition, institutional and commercial interests hoping to stimulate visitation and channel the shrine economy have emerged as active producers of Juquila-related content. Finally, with these foundations in place, I accompany pilgrims to Juquila, interweaving the journeys of the walking pilgrims of Oaxaca's central market and a cycling group from Actazingo, Puebla.

# CHAPTER 1

# The Virgin Moves You

Josefina, Doña Fina, was an alert, thoughtful woman in her mid-sixties with curly, salt-and-pepper hair and sturdy, round glasses when I met her in 2016. After describing my research to a Oaxacan friend, he suggested I speak to the woman who cleaned and cooked for his family and invited me to his home to meet her. Taking a break from her work, she recounted her history of devotion while sitting at the dining room table wearing a no-nonsense apron, the ubiquitous, locally made *delantal*, the practical accessory for many working women throughout Mexico. They are available in a few different styles—the button-in-the-back, two-pocket, quasi-house-dress classic; the over-the-head, side-tied, sandwich-board variety; and variations on the loop-around-the-neck, bistro apron. They can be dressed up with piping, lace, ruffles, Disney characters, or scalloped fringes, or set ablaze with gingham-versus-flowers juxtapositions. Alternatively, they can be toned down with muted colors and brawny, even waterproof, fabrics. Fina's (a button-in-the-back apron) provided near full coverage, enlivened by a subtle yellow floral print: a sensible choice for someone who has cooked and cleaned in other people's homes for almost fifty years.

Fina's life had been lonely and hard. Or, as she deadpanned, harsh realities shape the existence of many humble people in Mexico, those whose lives are constrained from the start, "por ser feo, pobre, y no tener" (for being ugly, poor, and without).[1] Hope, purpose, connection, and companionship, however, emerged from her abiding devotion to the Virgin Mary, especially Our Lady of Juquila. She was born in the small town of San José del Paso during the 1950s. Located at the far eastern edge of the Oaxaca's Central Valleys, it lies within Mitla's municipal jurisdiction, an area famous for uniquely beautiful Zapotec ruins and artisanal mescal. In her recollection, she lived an idyllic youth: a rural, agricultural existence, finding joy in family, the soil beneath her bare feet, and the different herbal flavors and aromas of each season. Over time, though, the rains failed, and the harvests shrank. Fina, as well as her ten siblings, sought work elsewhere, in construction, weaving, embroidery, baking, and domestic labor. For her, childhood joys gave way to a difficult, seminomadic adolescence and young adulthood, working briefly as a maid in Mexico City before settling into years of toil within the homes of various families in Oaxaca's state capital. Like many other domestic workers, she labored in the city and lived apart from her family in the countryside: first, to support a daughter, whom she left with her parents; and, more recently, to support her aging parents. When time allowed, she took the bus to San José, carrying with her the medicines they needed and foods they appreciated. Back and forth, she walked a tightrope between meager wages and abiding obligations. Marian devotion, enmeshed in her closest relationships, gave her solace and purpose and helped her process the past.

As far back as she could remember, family and neighbors periodically set out for Juquila. She calculated that she had "visited the Virgencita" eight times, guessing that her first trip took place in the early 1980s. Fina did not walk, run, or cycle; she always made the journey in a vehicle of some sort. Each trip, however, was distinct, and she remembered them fondly. In her youth, all the devotees she knew walked. They had no access to support trucks or extra money for transportation. They set out carrying everything they needed on an eight-day trek across the mountains, believing that Juquila would take care of their needs and grant any request if they beseeched her "con fe verdadera" (with true faith). Living almost thirty miles to the east of Oaxaca City, they did not follow the route established by the colonial-era church. Instead, they trod a more direct, rugged path, linking up with the "official" itinerary perhaps at the halfway mark, and then walked home along the same path.

There are still pilgrimage groups that make their way to and from Juquila in this manner. In 2022, I spoke with a small, cheerful group from the Zapotec town of San Juan Teiticpac, eight men and an eleven-year-old girl. This group of devotees doesn't keep a count of their journeys to the shrine or have T-shirts made. They don't make posters, fundraise, recruit, or advertise. At the center of their pilgrimage resides family. Everyone is related: fathers, brothers, cousins, sons, and a daughter (the most avid hiker in the group). Two men serve as guides. One of them surmised that he had made the journey eighteen times, inheriting the role from his father; the rangy girl claimed it was her fourth pilgrimage. Like Fina's family in previous decades, they walk both to the shrine and back, improvise, and travel light. They prefer the simplicity and flexibility this affords, although they acknowledge that nearly all present-day pilgrimages employ support vehicles.[2]

Fina recalled her uncles making the trip at least every other year during the late 1950s and early 1960s, a period of dramatic expansion for Juquila's devotion. Sometimes their wives joined them. But the pilgrimage tradition wasn't shared throughout her family. Some of Doña Fina's siblings never visited the shrine. Among believers, pilgrimage devotion is a choice, a decision.

For Fina, however, the firmness of her devotion emerged early, when a miraculous cure secured through the kindly mediation of one of her pilgrim uncles cemented her bond with Juquilita. In her telling, chronic, hypersensitive, painful dermatitis plagued her youth. Doctors were no help. At one point a burning, horribly inflamed rash on her arm drove her to the edge of desperation. Seeking relief, she began coating the area with lemon juice and placing hot stones directly on the sores, leaving her skin blackened and rubbery, yet the painful, prickling sores kept returning. Noting her despair, her mother recommended seeking help from the Virgin of Juquila. Her father reached out to a *compadre* (godparent) whose sons made special devotional candles from virgin wax, and he brought one home for Fina. Her parents then cleaned the burning, itching portion of her arm and gently rubbed the candle over the discolored, inflamed lesions. Subsequently, her uncle—Fina's devotional go-between—carried the candle on his journey to Juquila. After his arrival at the shrine, he lit the candle at three in the afternoon. At the precise hour, Fina claimed, as the candle burned alongside other offerings, she began to feel better although she was over one hundred miles away.

Eventually, all signs of the festering rash disappeared. Upon his return from Juquila, her uncle presented her with a small, framed print of the Virgin, which remained on Fina's parents' altar for many years. She tried to keep a candle continuously lit in front of the image, although it was often impossible. At the very least, she made sure one burned there every Sunday, resting beneath a wall hanging of the Virgin of Guadalupe, next to the Santo Niño de Atocha (a popular representation of the Christ child), and in the company of several other images and candles. Today, no scars mar her forearm, but devotion to Juquilita marks her life.

Doña Fina offered a subsequent life history in veritable chapters framed by an evolving and deepening connection to the Virgin Mary and characterized by cycles of fervent supplication, perceived intercession, and testimonial gratitude, which usually included a trip to Juquila. By necessity she sustained a flexible approach to her expressions of appreciation and obligation. Her personal life and economic precarity didn't allow her to join a pilgrimage group every year, but she believed

Juquila accepted her devotion and humble offerings in whatever time frame circumstances allowed.

An intimate, rite-of-passage pulse drives her devotional biography: the Virgin Mary has helped her through every age and its challenges. For example, barely beyond adolescence, and after only eight months working in Mexico City, she found herself pregnant, alone, and heartbroken. Far from Oaxaca and Juquila, she made her way to the Virgin of Guadalupe's shrine on the outskirts of the nation's capital, and she begged the national patroness to expunge the aching feelings for the man who had abandoned her. Indeed, gradually, and Fina believed miraculously, she found peace.

Outside her brief time in Mexico City, Fina found Our Lady of Juquila more approachable than the Virgin of Guadalupe. She sought her assistance in relatively mundane, basic needs, as well as in larger, more pressing concerns. Once, lacking even a modest space to store her few belongings, she dreamed of building a small room for herself on her parents' land, but she couldn't imagine how she could transform this hope into reality. With little in the way of money or time, she visited Juquila with a group of close female friends and asked for help. Certain of support, Fina began building even before she had secured the proper materials. Borrowing, scavenging, and unsure how she would finish, she nonetheless found that every obstacle evaporated as the room took shape. Proud and grateful, Fina returned to the shrine to give thanks as promised.

Flashing a grin, she described refusing to leave her candle at the Pedimento, the large votive chapel on the outskirts of Juquila that has been central to the devotion for the last forty years or so, because she had noticed laborers throwing away the amassed offerings left by other devotees. Indeed, the large piles of devotional waste on the slopes below the chapel remain impossible to ignore. Fina wondered, if the candles and testimonials become mere garbage, what does that say about the hopes of supplicants? She couldn't bear the thought of her candle moldering in one of these heaps. Instead, on this visit, she lit her candle and explained to Juquila her intention to take the taper home and relight it on the family's altar. The Virgencita, she argued, understands.

Getting to Juquila remained a perennial challenge. Sometimes Fina paid for a seat on one of the minivans that careen between the shrine town and Oaxaca. When possible, she rode with others. For a time, Fina joined employees from a local grocery chain (Piticó) on their store-sponsored annual bus pilgrimage. Her daughter worked at the store for twenty years, and, at one point, Fina made and sold lunches in the parking lot outside. As a result, she developed close ties to the store's workers and managers, and they invited her to join the Piticó pilgrimage, which took place every January, after the shrine's peak season. The devotees pooled money to buy food, charcoal, and a grill (*anafre*) for cooking beside the road. They also shared the cost of hotel rooms in Juquila, where they spent a single night after visiting the shrine. Except for four or five men, women made up the entire group. A female accountant, who did most of the organizing, also led the Rosary and Marian songs as they traveled. Fina cherishes the memory of these pilgrimages with her daughter and like-minded women.

When I spoke with her in 2016, Fina had recently found herself newly in Juquila's debt. A dear friend was battling cancer, and the two of them, as well as others, prayed to Juquilita. According to Fina, the Virgin places knowledge and medications at the disposal of doctors and nurses, and hence she described her friend's treatment as a miraculous liberation from cancer. Subsequently, with cancer in remission, the friends began planning a visit to Juquila without urgency. Pondering work and family commitments, Fina anticipated that opportunities would present themselves as they always had. She was waiting for Juquila to clear the calendar, put the means at her disposal, and, perhaps, arrange a ride.

## The Big Picture

In the most basic sense, pilgrimage is simply a journey to a sacred location, yet in Mexico the most popular pilgrimages carry a deeper meaning in which Mary is seen as a powerful intercessor. Those embracing this kind of devotion tap into a deep reservoir of customs centered on nurturing a personal bond with a particular representation of the Virgin. Pilgrimage, however, is unique because of its emphasis on physical movement over the landscape (imbued with meaning by previous generations of pilgrims and a shared folklore) and its intertwining of the personal and collective (see plate 2). On one hand, pilgrimage emerges from individual belief and action. On the other hand, its fame stems from a charged social experience: a shared struggle involving a particular group of pilgrims and taking place within a festive convergence that draws many thousands of fellow devotees, often traveling in their own groups.

Nonetheless, in the Catholic tradition it remains anchored in understandings of personal sacrifice and an almost contractual relationship between the individual believer and the sacred figure in question. In simplest terms, devotees seek a personal, emotional tie to a heavenly advocate; and, in exchange, they offer unflagging commitment. Humbling the self and seeking both understanding and purification through exertion, penance, and abnegation are crucial to many participants. In this context, many devotees embrace the opportunity to walk, bike, or run for several consecutive days, incorporating an array of rituals as they travel. Although traveling for hundreds of miles is common, neither speed nor distance is the point. Pushing past one's personal limits, seeing pain and exhaustion as both penance and offering, is often a central facet of the pilgrim ethos that many participants talk about.

I should point out, however, that thousands of devotees, perhaps a majority—especially women and older pilgrims—prefer safer, less physically taxing modes of travel. They organize caravans, drive on their own, or arrive together in tour buses, and they trust that Juquilita understands their approach and knows the depths of their faith. In other words, following devotees I prefer to define pilgrimage broadly.

Religions the world over include ritual journeys among their most venerable customs. In all likelihood, pilgrimage took shape alongside the earliest human conceptualizations of uniquely sacred places long before recorded history. Networks of shrines branch out across regions and religious calendars knitting together landscapes and cultural traditions in places as diverse as Europe, India, and Mexico. Some of Juquila's pilgrims understand their actions as extensions of ancient traditions and biblical history. For example, according to Don Carlos, the aging leader of a walking group from Coscomatepec, Veracruz, he and his colleagues emulate the Jewish people's flight from Egypt and Mary and Joseph's journey to Bethlehem.

Juquila's devotees, therefore, are part of a much wider phenomenon. In fact, seeking out "traditional" pilgrimage has become something of a global fad. Of late, faith-centered travel fuels a burgeoning industry marketing a sliding scale of amenities for those who wish to experience famous shrines and holy places.[3] Some opt for luxury religious tourism, and others embrace a mix of exotic adventure, volunteering, outdoor activity, and sightseeing. Such is the high profile of Marian shrines that *National Geographic* featured the phenomenon as its cover story and aired a television special *The Cult of Mary* in December 2015.[4] Pilgrimage memoirs also emerge periodically, offering a combination of accessible church history, narratives of self-discovery, and travel writing.[5]

For the time being, Oaxaca's Virgin of Juquila is not part of the international shrine circuit. This pilgrimage attracts few foreigners—not many well-to-do Mexicans take part, either—but its current popularity in Mexico, particularly southern Mexico (the states of Puebla, Tlaxcala, Veracruz, Guerrero, and Oaxaca) is undeniable. A quick search on YouTube (*peregrinación Juquila*) yields hundreds of clips offering a variety of do-it-yourself video mementos, and a healthy number of them

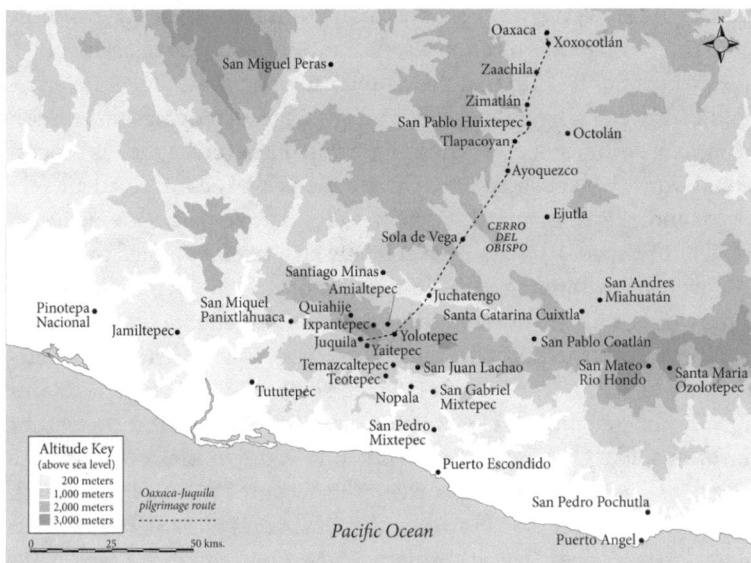

Figure 2. The "official" pilgrimage route (but not the only route) to Juquila. Map by Tracy Ellen Smith.

document pilgrimages from Mexico City and Puebla, over two hundred miles away. Many celebrate traditions surpassing thirty to forty years. Juquilita also has an oft-visited Facebook page, run by a Oaxacan organization promoting religious tourism to the shrine.[6] Not surprisingly, Oaxacan immigrants in the United States also celebrate her feast day, December 8, in such places as Gilroy, California.[7] Some of these transplants also name their new businesses after Juquila, as they do in many parts of southern Mexico. Thus, in Appalachian towns like Morristown, Tennessee, where US Immigration and Customs Enforcement carried out a controversial raid on a meat packing plant in 2018, you can buy traditional Mexican pastries at Juquilita Bakery, Panadería y Pastelería.[8]

The Catholic Church has always taken the practice of pilgrimage seriously, although with occasional trepidation due to the combination of unfiltered, individual fervor and unfettered, mass celebrations common at many shrines. Many priests, especially in regions like Oaxaca, approach popular devotion and practice with ambivalence due to misgivings about the unorthodox or independent nature of Indigenous Catholicism. Still, pilgrimage has remained symbolically available as a powerful allegorical reference for the Catholic Church as a devout collective "on the move," stubbornly advancing, triumphantly facing adversity. Thus, in the nineteenth century, it frequently appeared as a metaphor when the institutional church was battling liberal nation-states and secular notions of modernity. However, most prelates didn't simply want more devotions; amid their own modernization efforts, they promoted large-scale collective professions of faith that defied secularizing trends and anticlerical politics. Speaking figuratively about pilgrimage, deploying it as a mobilizing expression, and organizing pilgrimage-like events (such as processions) proved effective because these actions evoked imagined ancient fervor and offered dramatic public spectacles when throngs of believers filled public spaces. Often, large collective happenings linked these acts to debates surrounding religion and national identity. Pilgrimage, in other words, sometimes rhetorically stood for pro-church protest action.

Historically, the point for the church leaders wasn't simply to celebrate tradition for its own sake; in fact, some of the most popular, politically charged pilgrimages were inspired by new, nineteenth-century devotions, like Our Lady of Lourdes in France.[9] In Mexico, it was the Virgin of Guadalupe that the clergy kept center stage as the church tacked toward militancy. However, the same set of ideas were at work at many lesser shrines. The church promoted some devotions regionally, particularly if priests could assert a semblance of control over the celebrations. At others, where free-form piety and traditional trade fairs predominated, priests managed the shrines, celebrated Masses, and tried to overlook the concurrent profane revelry. Of course, referring to the Catholic Church as a whole as the "Pilgrim People of God" perpetually serves as an emblematic flourish.

Professional scholars only began to scrutinize pilgrimage in the 1970s, and for a time the topic attracted attention as its collective, uninhibited festivities seemed to echo the cultural currents emerging from the 1960s. In some ways, the academy's examination of pilgrimage takes place in a parallel universe. Scholarly interpretations usually don't reach the parishes and pueblos where image devotion thrives. Researchers carry out their fieldwork and then proceed to debate each other, sometimes for years, with little thought to broader engagement. In the 1970s Victor and Edith Turner's very influential interpretation idealized pilgrimage as a culturally enshrined "time-out," a temporary escape from rule-bound society, and they argued that the practice strengthened deep social bonds tested by competition and status hierarchies in daily life.[10] This approach, however, didn't stand up to scrutiny: narrow human interests within shrine communities and among pilgrims received no attention, and tensions embedded in gender, race, and class remained unexamined. In addition, this analysis offered little sense of historical evolution.[11]

In societies like the United States, where religious pilgrimage is relatively uncommon, the most abiding image of the practice is as a quest of self-discovery. North Americans, for example, tend to recall things they've heard about the Camino de Santiago (The Way of Saint James) in Spain. In addition, best-selling memoirs and films depicting long-distance travel, feats of stamina, and personal transformation form the basis of perceptions. Many of us, in other words, understand pilgrimage as sweaty therapy. To a certain degree, this is also true in Mexico, where the practice remains popular. As a result, shrine devotion conjures an array of experiential ideas about time, exertion, space, spirituality, truth, authenticity, and the self. Indeed, the ability of "pilgrimage" to encompass simultaneously the transcendent, the social, and the personal has much to do with its popularity.

Or, to put it another way, extraordinary elasticity characterizes pilgrimage. Such is its flexibility that scholars question the merit of distinctions between tourism and pilgrimage.[12] Currently, they are much more likely to approach pilgrimage by focusing closely on individual participants (rather than "societies" or "cultures"). Eduardo Chemin, a sociologist and philosopher of religion, eloquently takes us in this direction:

> To walk on a perceivably ancient pilgrimage route, to smell, see and touch an imagined past, favors a relocation of the self into imagined landscapes produced by various means of cultural reproduction, such as literature, art, cinema, and theater. Indeed, such journeys reflect issues that are at the center of consumer society and culture and issues about identity. Pilgrimage, as such, embodies not only a preoccupation with aesthetics (of body and place), but also ideas about mobility, aging, changing social roles, politics, social class, gender and sexuality, health and, of course, religion and spirituality.[13]

As Chemin suggests, notions of history, personhood, perception, and identity are in dynamic interaction among pilgrims. In our consumer culture's understanding of well-being, pilgrimage brings together interconnected symbolic acts linked to consumption and representation. These, in turn, mix within modern messages that focus on the individual and the body while still being fused to older ideas about devotion and sacred space. Pilgrimage remains religious, but its place outside institutionally controlled ritual makes it adaptable and easy to appropriate. It offers a loose cultural script ready for reinterpretation and reenactment.

In part, because pilgrimage's fame centers on transit from an everyday life and locale to a legendary sacred place, individuals bring with them an assortment of ideas and beliefs (not all of them religious). Gender roles are often in play. The voyage may offer settings where individuals imagine remaking their identity as a man or woman, and ideas about pilgrimage's life-changing potential can be the catalyst for reimagining

one's place within a social group. To put it another way, many participants believe that pilgrimage allows them to tap primordial values, inner
strengths, and personal insights, which can facilitate a reimagining of
the self.

It is important to emphasize, as Chemin does, that pilgrimage also
activates symbols, plotlines, and themes from film, media, and literature. As humans, we remain addicted to stories, and we devour narratives of movement. We find travel at the core of most stories, even if only
metaphorical. Be it self-help books, romantic novels, cinematic dramas,
or scholarly writings, we build narratives around mobility, and we measure change amid exile and exploration. Thus, steeped in narratives of
transformation and movement, individuals often enact pilgrimage as if
they were stepping into an artistic, even legendary, epic setting.

These insights shed light on how pilgrimage remains dynamically
connected to present-day culture as ritualized, personally meaningful
travel. In the idealized sense, the point is to take the same path over and
over: preferably, a fabled, ancient path. Thus, pilgrimage provides spaces
that are given special significance within the landscape: at emblematic
crossings, near natural landmarks, amid grueling climbs, in the stories
retold on the fly, and in the climax of achievement and commitment
celebrated before the venerated image (see plate 7).

The key is plasticity, the way pilgrimage's loose nature facilitates
appropriation and experimentation. Participants can adapt their concerns to specific locations and expected (or unexpected) feelings within
a devotional journey. Furthermore, this mode of devotion is socially
acceptable, even laudable, in places like Mexico: a sojourn framed as a
timeless pursuit of renewal can bolster a sense of purpose while securing
the approval of others.

In this context, over the last few decades scholarship has pivoted
to analyzing pilgrimage routes and shrine sites as settings where devotees *create* meaning (see plate 8). Likewise, scholars typically stress
that shrines remain fully connected to contemporary social hierarchies and cultural trends. Devotees, from this perspective, structure
experiences in which they believe they can attain idealized states, or,
perhaps, discover new identities.[14] Thus, some studies describe shrines
and the sacred images housed within as screens upon which the faithful project their hopes, beliefs, and visions, or, alternatively, as vessels
into which fears, faith, and redemptive narrative can be remixed and
symbolically imbibed anew.[15] These interpretations can appear dismis-
sive of devotee belief, although that is not their intention. Once again,
scholars, finding little evidence to support the oft-repeated claim that
pilgrimages occupy a separate, egalitarian social space fostering mass

collective identity and creativity, have shifted their focus toward individual meaning-making.

Quite recently, in 2021, anthropologist Simon Coleman stepped forward to offer a broader, innovative synthesis and ask new questions.[16] For Coleman a more fruitful approach involves focusing on pilgrimage's "articulation" within a wide array social activities and processes, including those we deem wholly secular. Pointing to very complex, sometimes overlapping, blurred or interconnected linkages, he argues that pilgrimage remains particularly suited to the foggy cultural crossroads and gray areas where the institutional, religious, economic, political, and personal interact, and even drive each other, amid complex tensions and synergies. According to Coleman, pilgrimage's extraordinary flexibility and its tendency to connect religious and secular processes lies at the core of its remarkable endurance and modern global florescence.

Devotees see things differently, naturally. Many of them would likely find scholarly approaches off-putting and presumptuous. They might also detect a whiff of class and cultural prejudice in our arm's length analyses. Devotees, for the most part, embrace "enchantment." They keep it personal, as it were. As pilgrims often say, it is about faith in Juquila, plain and simple: *her* town, *her* temple, *her* image, *her* mercy, *her* grace, and their repeated efforts to reach *her*. It is about getting there to *cumplir la manda* (fulfill their devout vow).

Mexico's unique history, however, suggests we also need to keep additional factors in mind. For example, one way to think about Juquila's devotion today is to imagine a pilgrimage catchment area that encompasses almost all of southern Mexico. This geographic framing leads to another important topic embedded in Juquila's history: southern Mexico is home to the greatest density and diversity of the nation's Indigenous peoples. It is a region where native practices and Indigenous cultural sensibilities remain prominent and palpable. Therefore, we might ask to what degree do non-Western ideas and customs permeate Juquila's devotion?

There isn't a simple answer. We can't just observe Juquila's pilgrimage and identify distinctly Indigenous elements, except in a few instances. For example, a few groups travel to the shrine with traditional dancers in tow, and occasionally you can see individuals pause at special locations along the route to perform distinctly Mesoamerican purification rituals (*limpias*). Likewise, it is not uncommon to see Maya pilgrims from Chiapas wearing traditional clothing and Oaxacan women from well-known Indigenous communities attired in long skirts and embroidered handmade tunics (*huipiles*). On another level, Juquila's devotees put considerable energy into imbuing the landscapes they traverse with spiritual

and moral significance and often frame their pilgrimages in terms of reciprocity. Both dynamics have deep roots in Indigenous practices.[17] But
traditions emerging from the hybrid cultural legacy of colonial history
also remain cherished and vibrant. In short, Mexico's Mesoamerican
heritage remains ingrained across the spectrum of practices taking place
during the pilgrimage, and yet impossible to easily separate from other
facets of the devotional culture.

In truth, it is impossible to do this topic justice here. Even a cursory
foray pushes us toward the work of the generations of scholars analyzing centuries of religious change among Mexico's Indigenous groups
and within the broader populace.[18] But anthropologist Kristin Norget
provides perhaps the most concise synthesis in her analysis of an enduring and ever-evolving "Indigenous Catholicism."[19] As she points out,
centuries of interaction, coercion, exploitation, and ongoing hybridity
have produced an intricate blending of native and Catholic traditions
that varies considerably while permeating life in southern Mexico. According to Norget, it thrives among working-class and humble Catholics appearing most distinctly in group rituals, devotions to household
images, and unscripted celebrations beyond the Catholic liturgy. It
isn't, however, wholly independent of institutional Catholicism. In fact,
movements within the Catholic Church, such as the Pastoral Indígena or
"New Evangelization" of the 1980s, sometimes target these customs for
reform. But such initiatives, although episodically impactful, eventually
lose steam. They can influence practices to a degree, but what endures is
the adaptable, effervescent core religiosity tethered to devotees' pressing
personal needs intertwined with image devotion. As Norget contends,
Indigenous Catholicism remains "integrated in the everyday; multi-
textured, sensuous, deeply affective, and embodied."[20] There is hardly a
more apt encapsulation of Juquila's devotional ethos.

## Staying True

When I first contemplated researching pilgrimage, I imagined walking
as the "real thing" and regarded the jogging relays and cycling groups
as idiosyncratic yet valid improvisations. Simultaneously, without serious thought, I identified the scores of individuals packed together in
pickup trucks, personal vehicles, and charter buses as mere tourists. I
assumed that Juquila's followers saw sustained physical exertion and
walking as the defining characteristics of pilgrimage. My thinking was
likely an outgrowth of relatively recent (often secular) understandings
of the Spain's Camino de Santiago, which emphasize the trail over the
shrine and frame trekking as the "authentic" experience.[21] Spending time

with an array of Mexican devotees explodes such assumptions. There is no such thing as a typical pilgrim or standard pilgrimage, although many commonalities connect them. Sustained conversations dash neat categorizations of beliefs, interpretations, and behaviors. Even within close-knit groups boasting decades-long pilgrimage histories, understandings vary considerably. On another level, individuals often enact profoundly personal approaches to devotion, which they rework over time. In other words, it isn't up to outsiders to define "pilgrimage."

It isn't up to Catholic Church authorities, either. Priests sometimes lecture devotees about the appropriate way to venerate Juquila. Likewise, when pilgrimage organizers visit the shrine's offices to schedule (and pay for) special Masses in advance, church staffers hand them official packets in glossy folders, spelling out the shrine's guidelines regarding belief, behavior, and even pilgrim motivations in a series of handouts. As far as I could tell, most devotees don't bother to read them. The president of Acatzingo's cycling pilgrimage simply handed his packet to me on the eve of the pilgrimage in 2018. It had been in his possession for several months, yet it remained in careful presentation order, seemingly untouched. To some it represents the height of presumption for clergymen to school devotees on the proper pilgrim mindset. Priests rarely accompany devotees on their journeys. Few have climbed the ridges, ridden bikes in the sun, cooked their meals on the side of the road next to their bus, or slept on the sidewalks and plazas in small, noisy towns along Mexico's roadways. In contrast, many pilgrimage organizers have visited the shrine with their respective groups over twenty times, and some make the voyage annually: Lalo, Acatzingo's reigning pilgrimage record holder, didn't miss a single cycling pilgrimage during his lifetime. He took part in forty of them, from the inaugural sojourn in 1979 until 2019.

Lalo was a joyful, buoyant presence amid the bustle and hard work required of large pilgrimages on the road to Juquila's shrine in 2018. He enjoyed the festive camaraderie and was quick to laugh and joke with the young male cyclists. In addition to being a devotee, Lalo was also a long-standing member of the organizing committee, one of fifteen to twenty veteran pilgrims who managed the logistics and meals, drove the support vehicles, and solved whatever problems emerged during the journey. He didn't need be told what pilgrimage meant or how he should understand devotion.

Pilgrimage, Lalo told me, is about commitment—staying true. Juquila takes care of her followers. He then shared a personal anecdote. When he was too broke to take part one year, Juquilita arranged for an unexpected, last-minute windfall: a group of strangers appeared, unannounced, and paid cash for his entire crop of prickly pear paddles (*nopales*), the central ingredient of a popular side dish accompanying many meals, particularly carne asada. Cash in hand, he kept his pilgrimage streak intact. In his view, Juquila looked out for him; she wanted him to make the trip and therefore removed obstacles. As he described it, there was something like a pact between them. She responded to his pleas and protected him, so he didn't fail her, either.[22] For individuals like Don Lalo or Doña Fina, it isn't about set rules, precise rituals, a particular approach to veneration and devotion, or the means of travel—it is about making time, making sacrifices, making do, and making it happen. It isn't complicated.

Still, Lalo's approach isn't instinctively understandable to many observers, especially those unfamiliar with Catholic devotional traditions. Even in Mexico, where Catholicism seems ubiquitous, there is considerable misunderstanding. It is not uncommon to hear offhanded comments about "fanaticism" in reference to pilgrims clogging the roads and carrying large, heavy, penitential items like crosses, statues, and framed images as they travel. There is a long history of these attitudes as well. As far back as the eighteenth century, colonial and later national officials, and even voices within the church, critiqued the humble Indigenous and mestizo populace as innately superstitious, caricaturing them as smitten by effusive display, miraculous expectation, and raucous celebration. Conflations of "backwardness" with nonwhite ethnicity have long been common. Modernizing reformers of the nineteenth century blamed the clergy, arguing that they cynically exploited humble Catholics and sought to keep them ignorant and thus in thrall. Conservative Catholics, in turn, pointed a finger at secular liberalism, which they argued recklessly blocked the priesthood's effort to finish the moral, educational, and civilizing mission begun by sixteenth-century evangelists. Of course, we don't need to look too deeply to perceive upper-class insecurities rooted in racial inequalities forged amid colonial domination. Sensitive, open-minded examinations of popular religiosity were rare until relatively recently. Few have bothered to ask Mexicans like Fina and Lalo about their motivations, how they understand devotion, and what it means to them.

Most pilgrims I've met profess belief in the power of the Virgin and other sacred figures, but so do many Mexicans who do not take part. Only a subset of Catholics embraces pilgrimage for a variety of reasons. Perhaps parents or aunts and uncles modeled this kind of piety and took them along as children, or maybe they joined up with friends and co-workers at some point. From the outside, we often imagine a kind of traditionalist inertia, an involuntarily commitment to ancient customs. But devotees have options: within families long involved in pilgrimage, some individuals are outright skeptics. Still others may have abandoned Catholicism altogether, or simply don't practice actively. Additionally, many observant individuals prefer a staid religiosity focused on the sacraments and Mass attendance, as priests frequently promote. Either of these directions is more mainstream and less tinged by stereotypes about "superstition." Thus, it is not that uncommon to hear Mexicans voice some version of "I'm Catholic, but not that kind of Catholic" when they comment on pilgrimages and popular festivals. Others, frustrated by crowds of devotees slowing traffic, sneer at them as *anafreros*, a classist slur referring to the simple braziers many pilgrims use for roadside cooking.

After spending a considerable amount of time with pilgrims, I realized that most of them have made a conscious choice. They expect inconvenience, discomfort, even pain, but they enjoy the experience. They crave the camaraderie, the break from work, and a temporary escape from everyday daily tasks and family drama. They've learned that the hours or days en route to the shrine foment unique bonds with their fellow pilgrims. Some label fellow members of their group as their *familia peregrina* (pilgrim family). On a personal level, they believe in the value of sacrifice and penance and find special meaning in the emotions generated amid exertion. In other words, during the pilgrimage they learn things about themselves—things they like. Their faith is also more complex than we might imagine, and their notions of pilgrimage take shape unburdened by the romantic traditionalism outsiders suspect. I also quickly noticed that those walking, running, and cycling are mostly male. Female pilgrims often prefer to arrive by charter bus, truck, or car.

Women, for good reason, are security conscious. In addition, traditional gender norms in Mexico do not encourage working-class women and girls to take up athletic pursuits. Well-organized, safety-conscious walking groups often include many women, at times comprising half the pilgrims. In my own observations they often appear to make up perhaps 20 to 30 percent of the walking participants.[23] At night women are more likely to sleep in the support vehicles than on sidewalks or in open spaces, like many men and boys. Running groups—typically organized as torch-bearing relay teams—always seem to include a handful of young women. In cycling groups, however, female riders are rare, although many women take part in support duties. Others simply arrive by vehicle to rendezvous with the mostly young male riders from their hometowns and to take part in celebrations at the shrine alongside them.

Juquila's followers are not of one mind about pilgrimage, and their explanations may evolve over time. Pilgrimage for Cecilia, a twenty-one-year-old, first-time pilgrim, stems from a simple youthful quest, "to have an experience."[24] Her father, Don Ezequiel, the owner of a vegetable stand in Coscomatepec, speaks of fervent gratitude: "I owe the Virgin a favor . . . and I promised to walk from my house to the soles of her feet."[25] Only completing the full, fourteen-day walking pilgrimage will suffice, he stresses, despite generous attempts to send him on the bus: "They've paid for my ticket, like twenty times, my family and other friends. But I've never wanted to . . . because my goal . . . was to pay her in sacrifice along the way."[26]

For Alicia and her husband Francisco, taking part in pilgrimage represents a long-term spiritual and personal investment: a handful of days of struggle and sacrifice in exchange for deeper understanding and greater perspective. As Alicia says, "Walking to go see the Virgin not only increases our faith, or makes us see what faith truly is, it also helps us emotionally: to see things in a positive manner. . . . There you understand brotherhood. . . . When you return to reality, to work, to family, all problems seem smaller."[27]

Seasoned pilgrims, especially organizers, often describe Christian altruism as their inspiration. Don Carlos, who leads the Coscomatepec, Veracruz, group, started out as the quintessential novice who didn't even think to bring bedding and whose cheap shoes fell apart only three days into the two-week journey. He simply couldn't fathom what it meant to walk twenty to thirty miles day after day. Carlos found himself forced to accept the charity of more experienced companions who pooled their resources to outfit him properly. Most of us, he jokes, "We are like the garden hoe, everything pulled towards us, and nothing goes the other way."[28] For him, pilgrimage first teaches humility, to accept the help fellow devotees offer. Subsequently, it inculcates the importance of giving, to be of service to others. This feeling or commitment, he suggests, drives his efforts to lead others to the shrine every year.

But Carlos cautions that walking isn't for everyone, even though he tosses out the common pilgrim refrain, "When faith is great, the road is short."[29] Taking his emphasis on belief a raspy, salty step further, he adds that grit and mental fortitude are crucial too: "Here you don't walk. Here your faith walks, and this is mental. Psychologically, if you say I can do it, you'll get there. But if you're going along with the idea that 'Eeew, I can't get there . . . ,' you've already screwed yourself. You may as well get in the car because you're not going to get there. But if you say, 'I promised [the Virgin of Juquila] to arrive,' you'll make it."[30] It is his job, he asserts, to help the various devotees in his group fulfill their vows.

Juan, one of the mainstays of the Mercado de Abastos pilgrimage in 2016, has a somewhat different approach. His efforts are an extension of his role as a catechist, a teaching mission, as it were. Pilgrimage, he says, shouldn't be about suffering for a week, or year after year, and he downplays miracles and devout vows. For Juan, organizing his fellow pilgrims represents enacting a pious mandate to embrace and model a service-oriented life.[31]

On another level, as I met more devotees, I realized that the practice sometimes marks individuals socially, and, in some instances, garners respect and prestige. Leaders and organizers take on a distinct public role within their communities. They set aside time to travel the route, seek out donors, recruit pilgrims, and make complex arrangements for food and lodging months in advance.

Simple participants may not be carrying the logistic burdens, but they must convince their employers to release them from work. For example, another Coscomatepec pilgrim, Javier, works near Mexico City and described begging his boss for twenty days off so he could first travel to his hometown in Veracruz, two or three hundred miles distant from the shrine, and then begin walking to Juquila from there.[32] Clearly for devotees like Javier, pilgrimage is important: he sets aside almost three weeks each year to "visit the Virgin," he forgoes wages, and he even risks dismissal.

For Alicia, her involvement with Juquila's devotion is still more complex. Since she has embraced pilgrimage, friends have begun approaching her amid their personal crises or when some long-sought goal seems unattainable. They ask her to carry a special candle to the shrine for them and to explain their plight to the Virgin. She acts as a go-between or advocate before Juquila. She has also sought Juquila's intervention in her parents' health problems. In other words, Alicia has become a human intermediary to the sacred intermediary. She sometimes leaves behind symbolic representations of others' pleas, *milagros*: a tiny tin kidney for renal problems, miniature metal eyes for diabetic complications, or a doll for a friend struggling to get pregnant. Essentially, Alicia serves as a liaison to miraculous grace.[33]

## Petitions and Promises

Literary scholar Frank Graziano, among the most thoughtful individuals analyzing Mexican popular religion, refers to the piety Fina and Alicia practice as "petitionary devotion." He also underscores how personal histories of devotion can function as a form of serially revised autobiography.[34] In a broader sense, historian Paul Vanderwood refers to the religious ethos of humble nineteenth-century Mexicans as "practical religion," a religiosity focused on the immediate, earthly needs of common people.[35] In other words, notions of salvation, biblical texts, and liturgical observance remain somewhat distant concerns. It isn't that devotees reject institutional norms of belief and practice, but basic human necessities and desires inspire efforts to secure celestial help and protection "here and now."

As is evident in these stories, the foundations of image devotion reside in a lasting, personal relationship with a sacred figure, and an exchange-driven, quasi-contractual bond anchors this connection. The devotees address the image, often detailing their perceived needs and requesting Mary's help. These needs, for the most part, coalesce in three broad categories: home, encompassing the quest for shelter, safety, stability, and harmony within families; health, spanning disease, disability, mental and emotional challenges, and accidents; and well-being, a broad range of socioeconomic concerns, including jobs, land, livestock, tools, food, goods, education, professional advancement, and commercial success. Some concerns, like grief and loss, the professed need for a romantic partner, fertility, marital strife, transnational migration, and personal improvement, bridge these categories. There are also many petitions for overarching protection, a devotee hedge against all uncertainties, or, as Graziano notes, a seeking of spiritual "insurance/assurance."

Pleas can be expressed out loud, textually, and with symbolic objects, visual images, miniature models, or a combination of these methods. As we will discuss in considerable detail (chapter 10), the Pedimento chapel near Juquila offers an extensive, often moving, showcase of petitionary expression. As Fina's memories reveal, along with their pleas, devotees often leave offerings, which can be anything deemed of value or symbolic importance. Flowers and candles are the most common.

Crucially, vows (traditionally called a *voto*) accompany devotee requests. In exchange for Juquila's protection or miraculous aid, the devotee promises to carry out a devout act, often publicly, and perhaps even commit to personal transformation. The vows range widely, ranging from modest and simple to elaborate and difficult. Pilgrims, like Fina, often promise to travel to the shrine and express their appreciation in person. Many pilgrims commit themselves to a symbolic trinity of pilgrimages. It is this tradition of pleas and promises that produced the somewhat clumsy Latin term *ex-voto* to describe the narrative objects left at shrines attesting to a plea answered or a miracle granted. The most famous of these are painted pictures, often called *retablos* among North American collectors and enthusiasts. They typically represent a devout request and often include a few sentences briefly describing a desperate moment of supplication and the resultant miracle: for example, a sailor on a ship beset by a storm fervently prays for rescue; a suffering patient pleads for a miraculous cure; or an individual waylaid by knife-wielding assailants cries out for the Virgin's aid. Some, reaching back to the colonial period, appear in large oil paintings. In the nineteenth and early twentieth century, simple, primitive votive scenes painted on tin became popular. All of them, incidentally, have become valuable among collectors and folk-art aficionados. In addition, devotees often leave behind items connected to the miracle received, like crutches for a leg ailment cured, a diploma for exams passed, or a wedding dress for a marriage secured.

Graziano reminds us of another factor in these petitionary offerings and mementos of gratitude left behind in Juquila: they symbolically extend the pilgrim's presence. Long after the devotees have gone home, their testimonies remain, reiterating their requests and declaring their gratitude days, weeks, or even years later. Today the representational options and expressive media are much more extensive. The hopes and sentiments, however, remain quite stable.

# CHAPTER 2

# A Past in Fragments

Ideally all discussions of Juquila's devotion in the distant past would begin with a confession. An impressionistic threading together of disparate fragments and a discussion of likelihoods is all that I, or anyone else, can offer. Quite simply, when it comes to popular devotions there is rarely much in the way of a historical record. Priests, political officials, and journalists mentioned pilgrimages from time to time, but ordinary devotees (the historical pilgrims) rarely left behind even a trace of their thoughts and experiences. Occasionally we find evocative hints in the rare pious offerings that remain. These tend to be brief, poignant narrations of divine intercession, conveying fervent hopes pinned on life-changing miracles. Institutional archives, in contrast, offer us page after page and box after box of administrative boilerplate salted with transitory references in reports, letters, and receipts. For example, shrines hire laborers, artisans, musicians, and additional priests during the peak periods of visitation, and they purchase building materials, furnishings, and decorations.

Ideally, we would have accurate statistics on Juquila's devotion in different eras, but I've yet to encounter trustworthy figures. Some sources contain estimates offered by observers marveling at fervent crowds. In the present day, shrine officials extrapolate from fee collection, and tourism officials generate projections based on suspect hotel data. But the crush of pilgrims wending their way to the shrine in the present day is undeniable, and the statistics attesting to Juquila's recent growth underscore the devotion's expansion. According to federal census data, the municipality's population increased 26.8 percent between 2010 and 2020, reaching 18,654 inhabitants.[1]

Sometimes we can access church-sponsored histories promoting a pilgrimage. As luck would have it, an extraordinary book published

in 1791 chronicles Juquila's devotion, Father Joseph María Ruiz y Cervantes's *Memorias de la portentosa imagen de Nuestra Señora de Xuquila*
(Memories of the wondrous image of Our Lady of Xuquila).[2] It represents the best available foundations of this history, even though it appeared two centuries after the devotion's legendary emergence. Equal
parts guidebook and marketing gambit, the text offers chronicle, folklore, history, maps, observations, and illustrations. It is a remarkable
gem: a detailed portrait of an emergent long-distance pilgrimage in late
colonial Mexico when few others existed. Pondering pilgrimage as an
innovative rarity represents a surprise for scholars, observers, and devotees. We assume that the practice was always a fixture of Mexican culture
because of its deep Iberian history and tantalizing evidence of ancient
Mesoamerican pilgrimage sites. However, in his exhaustive study of colonial shrines and devotions, historian William Taylor stresses that there
is no record of large, long-distance devotional journeys in Mexico before
1800.[3] Shrine visitation, image devotion, and widespread attendance at
festivals (*romerías*) provided the heartbeat of colonial culture, but these
practices remained local. Cities and towns celebrated cherished images
of Christ and the Virgin Mary with great fanfare, and the entire society
took part in religious processions and performances. But Taylor maintains that devotees only traveled short distances.

In this light, Ruiz y Cervantes's book represents a pioneering media
campaign. According to Mexican historian Mario Sarmiento, Juquila's
devotion emerged as a centerpiece of the reform vision promulgated by
Oaxaca's high clergy in eighteenth century.[4] After decades working to
replace the missionary friars in the Mexican countryside with diocesan
priests, the image, recently brought under diocesan management and
housed in a new basilica, could be promoted as an official pilgrimage.

To this day thousands of pilgrims—those approaching Juquila from
Oaxaca City—follow a path nearly identical to the one traced on *Memorias'* maps. However, it was never true that the pilgrimage featured a
single traditional route (see plate 4). Padre Joseph admits as much when
he gushes about the kaleidoscopic diversity at Juquila's festival and notes
pilgrims' disparate origins. It is also evident in the present-day testimony
of devotees from Mitla (an ancient town at the western fringes of Oaxaca's Central Valleys), in interviews with devout cyclists from the Pacific
coast, and in a do-it-yourself YouTube documentary filmed among pilgrims from the Oaxacan Mixteca.[5] Pilgrims, both historic and contemporary, generally seek the safest, most direct route from their respective
communities. But promotors trumpet a single *ruta*, which conjures an
aura of ancient and fixed traditions, merging throngs, towns, legends,
and landmarks.

Padre Joseph lived and worked in a key town along the pilgrimage route. He was the pastor of Zimatlán, an important Zapotec parish nineteen miles south of Oaxaca City, and he probably visited the shrine a few times during his career. In *Memorias* he describes consulting records and

Figure 3. The Virgin of Juquila, eighteenth-century print. From Joseph Manuel Ruiz y Cervantes, *Memorias de la portentosa imagen de Nuestra Señora de Xuquila* (Mexico City: Felipe de Zúñiga y Ontiveros, 1791). Image provided by the Bancroft Library, University of California, Berkeley.

account books, as well as interviewing elders and pilgrims in Juquila. He even claims to have held the famed image on one occasion.[6] He implies he was on hand for the Virgin's festival at least once, and he mentions preaching at the shrine in 1785.[7] In sum, Ruiz y Cervantes offers us a unique eyewitness account at a pivotal moment in Juquila's history.

Still, we must engage *Memorias* with caution because it remains an artifact of devotional propaganda. In simplest terms, Ruiz y Cervantes champions a pilgrimage centered on a Marian image that local priests had pried away from Chatino devotees a five decades earlier. Commandeering popular images, however, represented an established practice of the colonial church. In this case, it led to renaming the image and repurposing an Indigenous devotion as an officially promoted Marian cult.

Padre Joseph was not alone in his crusade. *Memorias* emerged from a prestigious Mexico City press, and he secured important backers, as evidenced by the ecclesiastical imprimatur and publication licenses from important officials accompanying the text. Even the viceroy proffered his approval. In other words, *Memorias* spearheaded a campaign to consolidate priestly control and foment broad participation. It is no coincidence that builders finished Juquila's first basilica in 1784, and Ruiz y Cervantes's book appeared in 1791. Indeed, as Sarmiento suggests, the Chatina Marian image that became known as the Virgin of Juquila was a priority for a series of Oaxacan bishops.[8] The top-down management and marketing context, however, does not disqualify *Memorias*. Although legends and church-sponsored narratives pretend otherwise, large pilgrimages do not emerge organically. They require investments in infrastructure and marketing. In truth, approaching Ruiz y Cervantes's book as part of a promotional campaign makes it particularly intriguing.

## Histories and Memories

Pilgrimage traditions often celebrate mythic origins. They offer straightforward, pious narratives anchored in notions of divine grace and inherently sacred space. In some cases, like Mexico's Virgin of Guadalupe, stories of a miraculous apparition and the Virgin's request for a shrine at the site center the pilgrimage. In many others, miraculous events take place around a particular image, resulting in claims that the location is of unique spiritual importance. In these narratives, devotees then simply coalesce in large numbers around the seer or image, begin deploying the customs associated with petitionary devotion, and clamor for the construction of a shrine. In most cases, the realm of historical fact recedes as we approach, and stories spring from a time beyond proof. We find nebulous invocations of distant forefathers, no-longer-existent manuscripts, and casual assumptions of continuity across centuries. In addition, we encounter stock characters, settings, and recurring plotlines in different shrines' folklore.

At the heart of Ruiz y Cervantes's *Memorias* resides a classic colonial conflict. A simple battle pitting Spanish attempts to impose Christianity in the face of Indigenous acceptance or resistance is not what historical evidence usually reveals, particularly after the first century of colonial rule. Instead, we find that native peoples sought to shape Catholicism in their own communities and pressed clergymen to accept Indigenous understandings of devotion. They sustained elaborate traditions of festive pageantry, image-centered ritual, performative piety, and a diversity of saints and sacred figures complete with elaborate iconographies, penitential rites, and liturgical calendars. In many ways Indigenous Catholics embraced Christian practices that echoed pre-Christian traditions. European ideas like individual sin and salvation often translated poorly, whereas notions of collective ritual obligation linked to pressing social needs made more sense within Indigenous cultures.[9] Given that there were few priests in many areas, Mexican religious traditions molded by Native American sensibilities developed deep roots over the centuries. Communities founded religious brotherhoods, in keeping with Spanish law and tradition, to manage image devotions (their finances, the practices surrounding them, and celebrations in their honor), and these institutions often included prominent individuals.

In a nutshell, colonial religious culture and its social foundations were quite complex and typically entangled in prevailing hierarchies. This was true at the Spanish and urban elite level and within Indigenous towns and villages. Once well established, and in some cases functioning independently for generations, attempts to alter customs or assert priestly control could spark intense resistance, even violence. At the center of many disputes, we find images. If they enjoyed a sizable following, it meant that some individual or group was collecting donations, organizing festivities, and allocating funds. Success drew the attention of church authorities and accusations of malfeasance and unorthodox worship. *Memorias* reveals that precisely this kind of struggle took shape around the image that would become known as the Virgin of Juquila.

Ruiz y Cervantes conjures the early days of Oaxaca's sixteenth-century evangelization in his musings about the image's mythical past. He alleges that a famed missionary of the Dominican Order—Fray Jordán de Santa Catalina—gave the image to an assistant from Amialtepec, who subsequently hosted her devotion in his own home independent of priestly oversight of any kind, but offers no concrete evidence. In fact, presently Juquila's priests acknowledge that Jordán never visited the region. Without mentioning any sources, the literature handed out to pilgrims at the shrine's offices postulates that perhaps one of Jordán's assistants elsewhere was originally from Amialtepec and carried the image back to his hometown.[10]

By simply underscoring the independent nature of the Virgin's devotion, Padre Joseph activates prejudices about Indigenous piety: few questioned the fervor of Mexico's native people, but many Spaniards and Creoles assumed that they remained prone to idolatry and superstition. In addition, priests and colonial elites believed their Indigenous neighbors to be morally weak, and hence prone to impious excess, irreverent debauchery, and corrupt profiteering. They also believed that autonomous Indigenous devotion took place in unseemly settings.

Although he affects paternal understanding, condescension pervades Ruiz y Cervantes's narrative when he imagines the Virgin's first devotees. The image's original owner remains a nameless wretch, an "indio desvalido" (destitute Indian) hosting devotion in his "negro xacale" (black hovel).[11] In addition, he muses that the Virgin doled out miracles because Indigenous people were too stubborn and dim to learn otherwise.[12] In doing so, Padre Joseph reiterates the prejudices peppering centuries of parish administration documents in regions like Oaxaca. What present-day scholars view as evidence of the energetic local initiative, colonial priests criticized as obstinacy and superstition, or even stupidity. Most likely, the image's emergent local fame both alarmed and interested the Juquila's pastors well before Ruiz y Cervantes's birth. He breezily alludes to tasteless extravagance and deploys hackneyed rationalizations, criticizing "superstitions" and undignified settings to justify the Virgin's seizure. Moreover, Juquila's pastors likely felt that any alms or valuable offerings should be consigned to their stewardship. In other words, perhaps the wealth generated by devotion represented the chief bone of contention.

Ruiz y Cervantes offers no concrete dates until 1633, when, he asserts, Juquila's pastor began seeking the relocation of Amialtepec's Inmaculada. Devotees resisted. Again, Padre Joseph relies on stereotypes as he describes the "pious resistance of the tender Indian." He even offers a cloying explanation: we are all "like Indians" when it comes to cherished images—that is, childlike and irrational.[13] Still, he reveals, Juquila's pastor at the time only secured a half-measure: the Virgin's transferal to Amialtepec's church. Thereafter Ruiz y Cervantes retells the oft-repeated story of this chapel's destruction in a fire and the image's miraculous emergence from the ashes, singed but otherwise unscathed.

We don't need to see this as a factual account. What we are dealing with is an established tradition—a narrative genre—with its own conventions.[14] The fact that similar stories appear over and over is part of the construction of devotional authenticity. In other words, the trial-by-fire legend fits patterns that devout audiences expect to encounter, be it the eighteenth or twenty-first century. It makes Ruiz y Cervantes's version "sound right," as it were. From a broader perspective, *Memorias* suggests that Juquila's devotion developed gradually in the seventeenth century like many other famous images in Mexico. Indeed, from the final decades of the 1500s to the first decades of the 1700s an extraordinary fluorescence of religious culture unfolded amid the interactions of In-digenous, Spanish, African, and mix-raced members of society.[15] There are good reasons for Ruiz y Cervantes's narrative approach: it suggests that divine grace arrives among Oaxaca's native converts through heroic, missionary efforts. In other words, he positions the church and its min-isters as the transmitters of sacred truth.

But the alternate history endures. Residents of Amialtepec maintain that the tiny image of Mary appeared miraculously in their humble In-digenous village. No missionaries were involved. Many present-day dev-otees repeat this story and visit the town to see the alleged apparition site. It has even made its way into devotional *rancheras* (songs), which can be heard in YouTube videos, on compact discs, or streamed on Spo-tify: "Pueblito de Amialtepec . . . donde vino a aparecer mi madrecita del cielo, una fresca mañanita en este humildito pueblo" (Little town of Amialtepec . . . where my dear mother from the heavens appeared on a fresh morning in this humble town).[16] This version of events has its own logic, a logic common in other apparition narratives. If the Virgin "chose" Amialtepec, then she "wants" to be there, and her shrine should reside within the community. Father Joseph ignores their claims and tacitly asserts that the ecclesiastical hierarchy is the sole arbiter of reli-gious questions.[17]

Ruiz y Cervantes reveals, nonetheless, that the relocation and renam-ing of the image remained contentious. On more than one occasion, after seventeenth-century priests carried the Marian statue to Juquila's church, she vanished and reappeared in Amialtepec. The villagers, he notes, proclaimed her return miraculous, yet Ruiz y Cervantes impli-cates conspiratorial sacristans. Finally, he tells us, in 1719, by order of the bishop, Juquila's pastor transferred the Chatina Virgin to the parish seat definitively. For a time, the devotion's local management fell to a lay brotherhood (*cofradía*) named for "Our Lady of Amialtepec," but when the sodality went through a diocesan-directed reorganization and ele-vation to Archicofradía in 1769, its members, led by prominent citizens of Oaxaca City, appeared as devotees of "Our Lady of Juquila."[18] During this transition period, Ruiz y Cervantes notes, some individuals pressed

Figure 4. The first Juquila shrine, circa 1786. From Joseph Manuel Ruiz y Cervantes, *Memorias de la portentosa imagen de Nuestra Señora de Xuquila* (Mexico City: Felipe de Zúñiga y Ontiveros, 1791). Image provided by the Bancroft Library, University of California, Berkeley.

for her relocation still closer to Oaxaca City. They argued that devotees from the Central Valleys were responsible for most of the alms donated to Juquila and therefore should enjoy easier access to the image. However, a diocesan decree put an end to such schemes in 1783, and a new temple dedicated to the now renamed image opened in 1784.[19]

Still, Amialtepec won't give up. They have erected signs along the highway to Juquila broadcasting their claims and inviting pilgrims to visit. In 2016, with a sigh of resignation, Juquila's exasperated director of tourism, sounding much like Ruiz y Cervantes, attributed the legend's staying power to stubborn ignorance.[20] Essentially, the secular institutions that have fully embraced the pilgrimage as the town's engine of growth and prosperity promote a simpler, single storyline. They present the shrine town (Juquila) as a unique sacred locale of harmonious fervor, rustic beauty, and calm. Contestation surrounding the image's origins only muddles their messaging.

From a historical perspective, it is somewhat remarkable that Juquila's secular officials and the town's priests have become tacit allies, given the many historical instances when the Oaxacan church countered politicians trying to tap the shrine's wealth. Presently, although differences remain, both encourage Juquila's popularity. In fact, in 2019, the archdiocese and municipal authorities celebrated the tricentennial of the

Virgencita's polemical relocation in 1719, oblivious to the heavy-handed colonialist reverberations of the anniversary.

Amialtepec's story, however, still reaches Juquila's far-flung devotees. I even heard pilgrims in 2022 theorizing that the original statue of the Virgin probably remains in the Chatino village. Possibly, they surmise, the basilica merely harbors a copy.[21] Of course, fact-checking origin stories is usually a waste of time, and such things hardly trouble devotees. What matters is Juquilita's miraculous reputation, the testimony of people they know, and stories about the Virgin's ability to aid and comfort her followers.

But the dueling narratives lay bare the cultural, political, and economic ramifications of pilgrimage. It is not uncommon for several generations to elapse before a "tradition" appears consolidated. In other words, although it is common for priests and devotees to talk about the Virgin of Juquila's sixteenth-century origins, her pilgrimage, in the sense of large-scale, devotional travel to a distant shrine, stems from the church's appropriation and energetic promotion of the devotion in the eighteenth century.

Ruiz y Cervantes's history is most convincing for the mid-to-late 1700s, the era he witnessed.[22] This period coincided with Oaxaca's increased integration in the wider economy, particularly in terms of the trade in cochineal (a natural, red dye).[23] According to him, twenty-three thousand devotees and 1,500 merchants converged on Juquila during the festival he witnessed in the 1780s, nine days of celebrations culminating in the Feast of the Immaculate Conception on December 8. Residents, he tells us, deserted Oaxaca's Central Valleys and coastal pueblos alike as they flocked to the shrine. Such was Juquila's popularity, he suggests, that the pilgrimage brought the full panorama of colonial society together: "blacks, mulatos, Indians, and all the mixed-raced groups we have in our America, alongside with the infamous rabble of Oaxaca."[24] Many devotions in the colonial period tended to map on to specific cultural groups and their separate communities. Peninsular and Creole elites focused on particular images and controlled the brotherhoods managing them. Simultaneously, Mexico's African-descended and Indigenous communities sustained separate intuitions and devotions. But here, the idea was to foment an elite, clerically controlled Marian pilgrimage attracting all of society. With palpable awe, Padre Joseph portrays a dizzying array of distinctive Indigenous clothing and the clamor of prayer in different languages. He also notes the presence of Black pilgrims from the nearby Pacific coast. Even upper-class city dwellers, trailed by luggage-laden mule trains, mixed with the humble masses. The real miracle, he quips, was that the confusion of classes did not trigger violence.

On another level, Juquila's feast served as a key annual opportunity for economic exchange, where traders from the Pacific coast met their counterparts from Oaxaca's more populous Central Valleys. In this sense, the devotion and the Virgin's annual feast day each December 8 functioned as many pilgrimages have historically. The confluence of pilgrims drew merchants, and thus the religious gathering doubled as a regional trade fair.

Like historians today, Padre Joseph uses financial records to gauge participation but admits that he only enjoyed access to the shrine's account books from 1746 to 1785.[25] As a result, he can offer a detailed portrait of only four decades—a remarkable contribution but not a full history. For example, he cites figures for the Mass intentions (fees charged for special dedicated Masses) and alms collected during this period: an impressive 112,372 pesos and six reales. He also points to material culture as a measure of devotional intensity, asserting that pilgrims purchased nearly twenty thousand prints of the Virgin and two thousand rosaries annually, while leaving behind approximately two thousand wax and tin milagros (small offerings symbolizing different needs or ailments). Wealthy devotees, he asserts, left silver milagros, 482 of them between 1765 and 1785.[26] Priests treated valuable offerings like silver as the Virgin's capital, which they allocated for things they felt dignified the image, such as decorations and accessories. In fact, a century later Oaxaca's archbishop decreed that miscellaneous silver ornaments and milagros at the shrine be carefully inventoried, weighed, and then melted down to craft the Virgin of Juquila's new throne.[27]

Ruiz y Cervantes asserts that other kinds of offerings were equally important, such as vegetables, grains, fruit, jewels, cloth, fine altar linens, baskets, silk, flowers, cochineal, coconut oil, small paintings, staffs, crutches, and hundreds of pounds of wax. In addition, he claims that the quantity of rosaries, medals, scapulars, and *medidas* (ribbons cut to approximate the Juquila's height) offered to the Virgin was so vast as to remain incalculable. According to Padre Joseph, the shrine's *mayordomos* (stewards) could not keep up, leaving piles of offerings amassed inside the sanctuary. Not surprisingly, he also describes moving scenes of penitential fervor, desperate weeping, and shouted appeals.[28]

Incongruously, when it comes to Juquila's famed miracles Ruiz y Cervantes avoids specifics. He claims they were so many, and so varied, that to list them would require too many pages.[29] His reticence almost certainly stems from the fact that although many devotees proclaimed personal experience of miraculous intervention church authorities never verified them. It was one thing to recount mythic events from the past, like the image's trial by church fire, and quite another to research and certify claims made by Juquila's followers. This also reveals that, despite assertions about greater liturgical splendor, the devotion depended on unsubstantiated acclamations of Juquila's grace. In this context, Ruiz y Cervantes gestures to "many miracles" without having to defend circulating popular narratives.

In the end, however, such was the value and quantity of offerings left behind at the shrine that Padre Joseph concludes that a great deal of wealth may have disappeared suspiciously. He even suggests that additional account books at the shrine were kept hidden from him because they exposed corrupt management. Musings about malfeasance should not surprise us even though he offers no proof: misgivings about fraud at pilgrimage sites remain common, and they emerged scandalously in Juquila during the mid-twentieth century. Quite simply, amid the frenzy of festival commerce, the lavish vestments and sumptuous décor, the elaborate liturgies, the cacophonous profligacy of fireworks, and the heaps of offerings, observers imagine bottomless wealth and assume the worst. Allegations of venality, in other words, remain as central to shrine sites as candles and flowers. But only rarely does concrete evidence emerge. The irony, of course, is that preventing "abuses" served as the justification for taking the image away from the Virgin's original Indigenous devotees.

## The Tides of Devotion

*Memorias* implies expanding fervor at Juquila after the diocese requisitioned the image in 1719 and built a suitable shrine in the 1780s. As he promoted the renamed Virgin in the late 1700s, Padre Joseph and his superiors likely assumed that favorable conditions would endure. The colonial order seemed secure, and Mexico's vibrant religious culture, although occasionally fractious, showed no signs of flagging. Perhaps they imagined that Juquila would elevate Oaxaca's reputation and draw devotees from other parts of the colony. *Memorias* certainly gives that impression. But very difficult years were in the offing. Violent struggles for political independence rocked Mexico from 1810 until 1821, leaving behind an impoverished, unstable new nation, and a deeply divided populace—conditions that likely endangered the pilgrimage's survival.

At its core, then, independence was a three-way struggle: a powerful, mostly nonwhite, agrarian uprising against Spanish rule, racialized exploitation, and increasing precarity; a battle between Creoles (European-origin elites) seeking independence against their royalist brethren and Spanish officials; and a ruthless civil war prosecuted by the viceregal state and Hispanic elites against popular efforts to overthrow the social order.[30] Beginning in September 1810, rebels enjoyed success and seemed poised to oust their rulers. They sacked towns, burned haciendas, and defeated hastily mobilized royalist militias. But inexplicably they failed to capitalize on their advantage and take Mexico City. The crown's supporters regrouped and routed the insurgents in a string of subsequent battles, capturing and executing many leaders and scattering the remaining combatants in early 1811. Subsequently, rebels reorganized and gained control of some parts of Puebla and Oaxaca during 1812 and 1813. But Spanish generals and the mostly Mexican-born royalist army eventually gained the upper hand thanks to brutal counterinsurgency tactics. By 1820, scattered insurgent bands in remote areas had been reduced to guerrilla tactics.

Ironically, Mexico's eventual independence emerged from a conservative military coup, not an anticolonial revolution. Tiring of Spain's instability and its cycles of liberal constitutionalism and absolutist restoration, officers of the royalist militia conspired with the remaining insurgent leaders, deposed the viceroy, and declared independence in 1821. The resultant government, unsurprisingly, blocked transformative visions of society. The end of colonial rule, in other words, did not bring significant improvements in opportunity or equality to Indigenous and mixed-race peoples. For many communities, political independence worsened conditions. The chaotic new order empowered opportunistic actors who used their positions to appropriate resources and restrict democracy.

Independence, in other words, did not resolve the explosive legacy of colonial rule. Deep grievances festered within an impoverished and divided society. Many of the nation's mines and farms lay in ruins, and some towns had been ravaged repeatedly. In addition, no social or political consensus emerged. Economic depression persisted as racial and ethnic enmities deepened due to the widespread social violence. Under these conditions, conspiracies and coups hobbled a series of short-lived governments. Armed groups led by strongmen carved out regional fiefdoms; fiscal crises followed one after another, making the young nation easy prey for US expansionism in the late 1840s (resulting in the alienation of the nation's vast northern territories); and then French imperialist intervention and yet another round of fratricidal civil war beset Mexico in the 1860s.

In sum, sustained unrest upended Juquila's emergent pilgrimage only twenty years after Father Ruiz y Cervantes published *Memorias*. But the devotion endured, and so did Padre Joseph's book. Almost all subsequent publications about the pilgrimage lean heavily on his narrative even if they fail to acknowledge him. In addition, *Memorias* established the "official" route, a six-day trek originating in the city of Oaxaca, a path symbolically connecting a regional center of Hispanic culture to Oaxaca's Indigenous heartland. Ruiz y Cervantes's itinerary, in other words, maps Mexico's eighteenth-century cultural continuum: from a colonial urban space dominated by the stately convents of the missionary orders and the lavish homes of wealthy merchants, through the bustling Zapotec agricultural towns in the southern Central Valley, and then up into the remote mountains of the Sierra Sur, where humble Chatino villages predominated. War and subsequent turmoil, it appears, put this vision on hold.

Pilgrimage, like most large-scale collective practices, remains sensitive to social unrest and economic recession. It is difficult to move thousands of people and merchandise across the countryside amid civil strife. Then as now pilgrimage requires an array of expenses, be they for the shrine's managers and traders frequenting the festival, or devout travelers. In addition, as the mid-1800s approached the Catholic Church shifted its focus in the face of reformist efforts to modernize the economy and secularize society. In simplest terms, independent Mexico began quarreling over the nature of Catholicism, its status as a state-sanctioned religion, and religious institution's considerable wealth and influence.

It pays to pause and consider Catholicism's omnipresence in colonial life. Religious orders, dioceses, and parishes managed nearly all educational institutions and social welfare organizations (e.g., hospitals and orphanages), and the liturgical calendar defined the rhythms of daily life. A dense network of brotherhoods raised funds to sustain devotions and organized festivals, and the fees these events generated supported the priesthood.[31] Furthermore, thanks to pious bequests and institutional investments, Catholic entities functioned as the colony's bank and biggest landlord, lending capital to well-connected families and collecting rents. But the Wars of Independence progressively gutted church finances. The crown extracted contributions from religious institutions during the fighting, and the sheer destruction left many properties in ruins, and many renters and donors bankrupt.[32]

Outside of the violence and destruction, ideological challenges to the Catholic status quo were not unique to Mexico. They formed part of the modern zeitgeist spreading across Europe and the Americas. For some ultra-conservative Catholics, the threat originated in a satanically inspired grand conspiracy emerging from the French Revolution.[33] Historians tend to frame these conflicts in terms of liberalism versus conservatism, but the clash was much more complicated than a simple two-sided debate, and, moreover, polarization developed gradually.

Figure 5. Colonial map of the pilgrimage route from the city of Oaxaca to Juquila. From Joseph Manuel Ruiz y Cervantes, *Memorias de la portentosa imagen de Nuestra Señora de Xuquila* (Mexico City: Felipe de Zúñiga y Ontiveros, 1791). Images from the Biblioteca Nacional de España.

At first only a few radical reformers and impassioned reactionaries defined the poles of debate. Many priests, in fact, supported moderate liberalism. The question, naturally, was how far to go in restructuring society. Should the new nation declare religious freedom and separate church and state forcefully, or was some middle ground possible? In the past, the colonial government enforced mandatory tithing and Catholic regulations on religious practice. Should the government secularize education and the documentation of births and deaths? And, more ominously for the church, should Mexico force religious institutions to sell off their holdings to encourage the free circulation of property and broader landholding?

In short, amid the aftermath of the Wars of Independence, debates centered on how much to modify an entrenched order. The Catholic Church, although never monolithic, formed a crucial bulwark of Spanish rule, but it was not the only institution in the crosshairs. Indigenous villages with their communal landholdings and intertwined religious and political cultures also emerged as targets for reform. The clash became much sharper, however, as the nation struggled to establish a functional, stable political system and economy. Factions embraced more extreme positions as clashes intensified and foreign countries preyed on the unstable nation. Conservatives argued that sustaining the traditional order was the only way to guarantee stability in a society characterized by a vast nonwhite underclass (a group vilified as the cause of upheaval). In this formulation, a strong and protected church served as a guarantor of stability. Radical liberals, for their part, argued that traditional elites and the high clergy simply wanted to protect their preeminent status and parasitic dominance. From their perspective, Mexico would only achieve stability when all vestiges of colonialism had been expunged. Liberals, in other words, argued for democracy, both social and political, although they too viewed Indigenous peoples and the nonwhite poor as second-class citizens, or worse.[34]

In the 1850s and 1860s, church-state conflict was at the center of coups and outright civil war while remaining moderate Mexicans watched in horror amid paroxysms of violence. Catholic institutions frequently backed conservative forces financially, but this support often emerged from extortionist tactics rather than a deep commitment to individual leaders. Radical liberals increasingly argued that the clergy represented an antinational, reactionary force that had to be neutralized. In a moment of ascendency, this faction pushed through the constitution of 1857 enshrining the reformist vision, but the resultant conservative coup and two years of war halted implementation. Armed conflict, in turn, stoked polarization. When radicals returned to power they adopted even more draconian measures, expropriating all church property (often sold off to well-connected speculators), disbanding religious brotherhoods and orders (scandalously evicting nuns from their convents), banning religious celebrations in public spaces, declaring full religious tolerance, and mandating strict church-state separation. This, however, proved a mere intermission. French troops with conservative backing invaded Mexico in 1861 and installed a Habsburg prince (Ferdinand Maximilian Joseph) as emperor of Mexico in 1864. Civil war continued until French troops withdrew in 1866 and liberal militias defeated the remaining conservative forces and executed Maximilian in 1867. Now firmly in control, liberals reinstated and strengthened the raft of anticlerical provisions in the new constitution.

In sum, a decidedly less favorable atmosphere for pilgrimage spread across Mexico during the first half of the nineteenth century. The Catholic Church, fearing for its survival amid political, financial, and cultural crisis, had little time or energy to promote long-distance devotional practices. What we find regarding Juquila is mostly silence with some exceptions. In the early 1830s, the Archicofradía (brotherhood) of Our Lady of Juquila issued regulations detailing the level of pomp and splendor for her December festivities, suggesting an enduring appetite for the celebratory standards of the late colonial era.[35] However, mid-nineteenth-century edicts, pastoral letters, and parish reports broaching local customs don't mention pilgrimage.

We should not, however, equate a lack of documentation with a lack of devotion. Buried in archdiocesan collections are reports from the latter half of the nineteenth century and receipts, small slips of paper recording expenditures on building maintenance, stipends for visiting priests, and fees charged by musicians and fireworks maestros. In fact, nearly every box in the archdiocesan archive storing parish administration files from 1860 to 1900 includes receipts and reports from Juquila.[36] For example, not long after liberals emerged victorious in 1867, the shrine's pastor reported modest but steady revenues from 1868, 1871, and 1873.[37] This evidence of fiscal activity suggests that Juquilita's feast-day celebrations on December 8 (the traditional peak of the pilgrimage) endured as a modest local tradition. Indeed, the devotion's persistence underscores another dimension of pilgrimage's legendary elasticity: the ability to shrink and withstand adverse conditions.

Likewise, it shouldn't surprise us that Our Lady of Juquila experienced a comeback when more auspicious conditions emerged. The decades marked by the autocratic administration of Porfirio Díaz, 1876–1910, brought relative stability and renewed economic growth. The president cultivated regional bosses and allowed them to exploit their respective turf if they kept the peace, and he promoted a cadre of loyal military officers to key posts. In addition, Díaz welcomed foreign investment to foment economic modernization, such as the construction of a new railroad network. Crucially, he soft-pedaled constitutional provisions targeting the church, allowing a resurgence of Catholic institution building with the tacit understanding that conservative groups and important clergymen would muzzle criticism of his government.

For this era, we are again dependent on records that speak to the material culture of devotion. For example, in 1887, Juquila's pastor ordered nine thousand prints of the Virgin to sell at the festival, and, in 1889, he increased his order to thirteen thousand copies, in addition to hundreds of printed prayers and novenas, and scapulars (a small devotional necklace made from two patches of wool cloth).[38] These purchases hint at an increasing demand for devotional merchandise. It is logical to assume, therefore, that more devotees were attending Juquila's festival. Confirmation of this interpretation appeared in the Oaxacan press a decade later. In 1899, a Catholic newspaper, *La Voz de la Verdad*, published a journalist's anonymous description of a trip to Juquila.[39] The author echoes Ruiz y Cervantes, gushing about the throngs of devotees converging on the shrine and the tender, multilingual supplications of the Virgin's diversity of followers. He depicts upward of thirty thousand pilgrims, a bustling commercial encounter, intense popular fervor, and (once again) a boisterous, multilingual mix of the region's peoples. For our anonymous journalist it represented a touching time-travel-like experience. He imagines a return to the fervent dawn of evangelization, a time unsullied by modernity.

Additional evidence of the pilgrimage's waxing popularity appears in another realm of print commerce. In the late nineteenth century, Oaxacan presses began printing new editions of Ruiz y Cervantes's *Memorias*: for example, the Imprenta de Lorenzo San Germán's version (1878) and the Imprenta de La Voz de La Verdad's printing (1900). Printers' actions, in other words, point to surging interest in Juquila's pilgrimage as the twentieth century approached, as they pivoted to meet increasing demand for the century-old text.

The renewed attempt to sell Ruiz y Cervantes's book, however, remained regional. Mexico City's presses and the ecclesiastical hierarchy did not embrace Juquila's promotion in the late 1800s as they had in the late 1700s. In addition, this resurgence occurred while Oaxaca's religious authorities promoted other devotions (Our Lady of Guadalupe and the Sacred Heart of Jesus) suggesting that lay initiative and ingenuity— alongside improving conditions—powered the devotion's growth. The extension of a rail line to San Pablo Huixtepec, a town considerably closer to the shrine than Oaxaca City, also facilitated visits to the Chatina image. Apparently, during this era, many pilgrims took the train to this town and walked or traveled on rented horses and mules from there.[40]

Eulogio Gillow y Zavalza, Oaxaca's late nineteenth-century archbishop and conservative modernizer, had other goals, we could say. He was one of the leaders of a Vatican-inspired reform effort that sought to bring the predominantly Indigenous regions like Oaxaca in line with Rome's new standards, a more measured, individual piety centered on priest-mediated sacraments (like Confession and Communion) and active participation in priest-led lay associations. Rome hoped to generalize the bourgeois norms of European Catholicism and fuse practice to pro-church political action. Juquilita's humble devotees did not fit the picture of an obedient, militant flock.[41] The Oaxacan archbishop, therefore, sought to harness and channel local devotion, sustaining its intensity but moving it away from the boisterous fiesta ethos on display in Juquila. Pilgrims, most likely, gave little thought to these institutional interests.

Thanks to Gillow's diaries and decrees, we know that the archbishop visited Juquila in 1894 and 1898, but he does not describe the festivities. His focus remains administrative. Implying that considerable sums are in question, Gillow worries about local politicians bent on tapping shrine funds. Municipal and district authorities searched for ways to tax donations flowing into the Virgin's coffers and sought justifications for impounding property "belonging" to the image. Laws against collective property holding, for example, could be used to denounce and expropriate land or livestock managed to support ritual and shrine expenses. Gillow, in his decrees, attempts to demonstrate Juquila's orderly, scrupulous management and thus preempt accusations of corruption that could be used as a pretext. But his designation of set stipends for extra priests and missionary preachers during the annual pilgrimage suggests that more devotees were converging on Juquila. He discusses how best to use the quantities of wax and silver milagros devotees left at the sanctuary. However, the prelate never praises the pilgrimage or the devotees; instead, he emphasizes improved management, proper accounting, and ecclesiastical authority.

Regardless of archdiocesan initiative, the Virgin of Juquila's following expanded, which suggests that economic and social factors catalyzed growth. Devotees likely increased their shrine visits and promoted the devotion independently, sharing personal stories of Juquila's miraculous grace, displaying tokens of their devotion, beseeching the Virgin to help loved ones, giving shrine souvenirs to others, and inviting friends and family to accompany them in the future. It is impossible to prove that such things took place, but it fits present-day patterns we can discern in oral histories, like Doña Fina's, and the earnest recommendations I received while sharing a minivan with devotees in 2001. In short, Juquila's late nineteenth-century followers probably coordinated their own pilgrimages and spread news of Juquila's miracles. This echoes the rural, small-town religious culture that clergymen often complained about in the late nineteenth and twentieth centuries: common Catholics, particularly Indigenous Catholics, often kept their pastors in the dark about their devotions. Priests found it particularly irritating when parishioners treated them as service providers—like musicians and carpenters—requiring compensation, not consultation.[42]

Whatever the precise dynamics, the available documentation points to a new phase of expansion for the Juquila pilgrimage toward the end of the nineteenth century. If recent history is a guide, devotion spread along trade and transportation networks. In this era the Mexico Southern Railroad reached Oaxaca City, connecting the region to Mexico City, Puebla, and Veracruz, and spurs within Oaxaca's Central Valleys bolstered commercial agriculture and mineral exploration and facilitated pilgrim travel.[43] Locally, the rugged slopes of the Sierra Sur had begun to draw non-Indian coffee entrepreneurs to the region in the late nineteenth century.[44] For a time, it appeared that this export crop and new mining ventures might catalyze modern development in Oaxaca. But alas, social upheaval would again complicate matters.

# CHAPTER 3

# The Polemical Priest

Whenever I visit Juquila I find a seat on the central plaza's benches, if any are unoccupied, or I linger on the edges of the shrine's busy churchyard to observe the ebb and flow of pilgrims. For me, this serves as a pulse check. Large groups in their matching T-shirts and tracksuits emerge from the crowded main street lined with vendors and their makeshift stalls. Devotees carry their images and standards, symbolically bringing them to visit the Virgin too. Individuals typically bear personal offerings for Juquilita and recently purchased souvenirs that they hope to get blessed before the trip home. Speakers positioned at the foot of the sanctuary project the lilt and drone of Mass into the plaza. There liturgy merges with the brash horns and insistent percussion of bands accompanying the steady stream of pilgrims. Portrait photographers work the crowds, hoping to convince devotees to surrender a few moments and a few pesos. Normally, depending on crowd size, Juquila's followers slowly squeeze through the cast iron gates and crowd the basilica's main entrance. There they wait for a chance to enter the sanctuary.

Few, however, pause to contemplate a modest, off-kilter gravestone in a corner of the churchyard, the final resting place of Father Cornelio Bourguet, the controversial former pastor of the shrine who died in 1987. Some juquileños and critics of the Catholic Church characterize him as a merger of two stock Mexican villains: the *cacique* (small-time, rural tyrant) and the debauched, greedy village priest. But other locals view him as the architect of the devotion's revitalization in the latter half of the twentieth century. This faction, presumably with the support of the archdiocese, interred his body in the basilica's churchyard. He is the only priest honored in this manner.

Bourguet managed the shrine from the 1941 to 1980, a pivotal phase in the pilgrimage's history. His era began amid the Mexican Revolution's extended aftermath when the devotion seemed to teeter on the verge of collapse. It ended when popular protesters unceremoniously ousted him from his post and chased him out of town. By then the pilgrimage was beginning to attract many newly formed groups of devotees from beyond the state of Oaxaca. Is this a simple story of avarice, power, and exploitation? Or can the career of a controversial shrine manager shed light on the complexities of modern pilgrimage?

## Another Revolution

Like the Wars of Independence a century earlier, the Mexican Revolution of 1910 put Juquila's pilgrimage to the test. Ironically, the same independent streak in the Oaxacan faithful that sometimes irked rural clergymen proved to be the Catholic Church's greatest asset when the new revolutionary government expropriated all church property (like their liberal predecessors), curtailed public celebrations, and limited the number of priests in many regions.[1] Essentially, Oaxacans maintained their religious traditions in the face of lasting unrest and official policies designed to alter popular culture, even when pastors abandoned their parishes due to federal threats and legislation. To put it bluntly, the devout populace didn't need priests to sustain the faith. Oaxacans, particularly in Indigenous communities, had centuries of experience safeguarding their beliefs in the face of external pressure—pressure from an array of outsiders, whether clergymen, civil authorities, non-Indigenous neighbors, or mestizo entrepreneurs.

The revolution in Oaxaca was complex, although never a central theater of the conflict. It began elsewhere, with the most powerful popular mobilizations of Emiliano Zapata's peasant and Indigenous followers in the state of Morelos (close to Mexico City) and a more amorphous and socially varied constellation of uprisings in the semiarid northern sierras. In truth, the revolution wasn't a single movement; it was a loose agglomeration of local revolts that overwhelmed the government, forcing President Porfirio Díaz to flee in 1911. Subsequently, politically moderate efforts to replace the autocratic leader and dampen popular mobilization failed miserably. Instead, Mexico faced a brief yet brutal military regime that fell to a coalition of revolutionaries, and then a disastrous "war of the winners," as insurgent leaders fought each other in 1914 and 1915.[2] Tragically, for the general populace this meant widespread, sustained violence and the flight of refugees to the southwestern United States. In the end, Mexico suffered another catastrophic loss of 10 percent of its population as it had during the Wars of Independence. By 1917, the "Constitutionalists" led by Venustiano Carranza had emerged victorious and begun consolidating power, although they, too, would turn on each other in 1920. Indeed, the emergent order remained tenuous amid internal power struggles and resistance in various states. Stability only gradually took hold in the 1930s.

Oaxaca's internal politics had long been fragmented, with an essentially conservative elite running the state capital and small-time strongmen dominating chunks of territory and constellations of towns in the countryside. Revolutionaries of distinct stripes crossed into Oaxaca from the neighboring states, and local factions sought alliances with them, while adapting long-standing local interests to received militancy, new ideologies, and streams of reformism.

Oaxaca was also a region that had long worked to keep federal power at bay. In 1915, as battles raged elsewhere, some politicians attempted the impossible: isolation.[3] Fearing an externally imposed transformation of Oaxaca's political order, they decreed the state a separate sovereign entity until a legitimate federal order returned.[4] They failed. Troops allied with Carranza brushed aside Oaxacan resistance and occupied the state capital in 1916, although holdouts remained in the countryside. Despite these clashes, Oaxaca never experienced the large battles that devastated other regions, yet simmering factional violence endured. Far from Oaxaca City, the mountainous region surrounding Juquila remained volatile for much of the 1910s and 1920s, and economic stagnation lingered for many years afterward. Various armed groups took turns occupying and plundering the shrine town.[5]

Juquila's pastor throughout this period, Father Ausencio Canseco, showed himself to be a shrewd steward at a difficult moment. He cultivated relationships with local supporters and found ways to hide money and valuables that "belonged" to Juquilita and sustained his ministry. The Virgin's feast endured on a reduced scale in this climate. We have almost no data on shrine visitation beyond Canseco's report to his superiors stating that he collected only thirty-eight pesos for Masses celebrated at the festival in 1914.[6] Although we lack information on the subsequent years of Canseco's tenure, these figures point to a sustained low point for the pilgrimage. For comparison, Bourguet would report in 1941 that he collected 3,800 pesos for Masses, as well as 8,298 pesos in alms, wax, and milagros.[7]

Nonetheless, despite instability Juquila's festival remained important economically. A Oaxaca City newspaper commented on its centrality in livestock and horse trading in the 1920s and called for increased troop patrols to safeguard the pilgrimage.[8] As in the colonial period, the Virgin's feast brought residents from the Central Valleys, the mountains, and the coast. Specifics from that time are rare, and although Juquila today is known for its bread and artisanal sweets, presumably a range of products were also on offer: tools and textiles produced in the nation's cities, tropical fruits and horses from the coast, sheep and goats from the nearby Mixtec region, and perhaps grain from the Central Valleys. Apparently, Juquila was even known as a place to purchase parrots, birds once common in the Sierra Sur and the forested slopes leading to the Pacific.[9] As a result, early twentieth-century authorities sought to safeguard the *feria*, promising to protect travelers along the route to the shrine in the 1920s. They even temporarily lowered taxes in 1928 to encourage merchants and traders.[10]

The spike in anticlericalism (antichurch legislation and policy) that accompanied revolutionary centralization ignited another cycle of violence in the mid-1920s and enflamed tensions around the shrine town.[11] Antirevolutionary uprisings, particularly in states like Jalisco and Michoacán, deployed the battle cry of "Long Live Christ the King" and made sizable chunks of countryside ungovernable from 1926 to 1929. In Oaxaca armed resistance was not as strong, but small groups proclaiming their defense of the faith skirmished with government forces near Juquila too.

Considerable conflict, centered on tapping the wealth generated by the Virgin's devotion. In keeping with new federal legislation in 1926, Father Canseco ceded the parish church and sanctuary control to a commission of town representatives. However, he succeeded in packing this body with eight supporters, although he warned that the two remaining individuals were known enemies of the church, and he requested that the archdiocese use its influence in the state capital to have them replaced. Canseco also worried that his allies, whom he condescendingly characterized as gullible "inditos" (little Indians), could be intimidated or duped by his antagonists.[12]

Canseco described a double-locked, sealed room in the shrine where Juquila's valuables remained but identified the relentless municipal president as the shrine's chief threat. This politician, apparently, had plundered the shrine's stores of wax and cash and begun using church furnishings for civic events. In addition, he pressured the Virgin's mayordomo (the leader of the lay brotherhood organizing her festival) to surrender additional moneys. As Canseco warned, his nemesis sought to reallocate donations to pay municipal legal costs related to land disputes. Some locals also wanted to use shrine funds to buy instruments for Juquila's brass band and to pay public school teachers. Still others lobbied to use the shrine's wealth as municipal loan capital. His opponents' goal, Canseco alleged, was full secular control of the Virgin's festival and the flow of alms.

Anthropologist James Greenberg's oral history of twentieth-century violence in Juquila describes an even broader plundering of the shrine's wealth.[13] Armed groups, politicians, and rapacious individuals simply looted the basilica. Some of them, apparently, managed to track down where Canseco had buried some of the Virgin's money. Others simply stole and sold off the image's vestments and decorative accessories. Even ostensibly pro-church rebels pillaged the shrine as they passed through town.

We have almost no information on the pilgrimage in the 1930s, but the region remained unstable. Making matters worse, a powerful earthquake in 1931 badly damaged the basilica. Then Father Canseco drowned crossing a river near Sola de Vega in 1933; several years of careless management ensued.[14]

## Padre Cornelio

Finally, in 1941, the archdiocese named Cornelio Bourguet as Juquila's pastor. He had already been working in the region for several years, and likely enjoyed a reputation as a capable manager. Juquila was not a good post for unproven priests. Archival evidence shows, he was a conscientious record keeper, although the statistics he provided may not be fully trustworthy. As we will see, his letters and reports reveal that Juquila's festival remained small during his early tenure and teetered on the verge of collapse in the late 1940s as regulations and economic changes undermined the festival's traditional foundations.

Thanks to Bourguet, however, we have a rough picture of the ebb and flow of pilgrims. For the first twenty years of his tenure, in the weeks before the Virgin's festival, he would send letters to his superiors asking them to publish promotional announcements throughout the archdiocese. Then, in the days following the Juquila's feast day (December 8), he would remit a report describing the celebrations and an account of donations and fees collected during the festival. He almost always reminded his superiors that the figures provided represented gross income; he had yet to subtract costs. He made it clear that remittances to the archdiocese would be somewhat less than what he was reporting.

As with Ruiz y Cervantes's observations from the 1780s, we must derive our conclusions about devotion and participation from these kinds of records. At the beginning of the 1940s, Father Bourguet generally collected between ten and twelve thousand pesos annually through fees for Mass intentions, cash and wax donations, and the sale of devotional merchandise such as rosaries and scapulars. There were also noncash donations; for example, Juquila's bus and package delivery company gave the Virgin of Juquila a clock and a generator to power forty lightbulbs in the sanctuary in 1950.[15]

However, in 1947, Bourguet canceled the festival when the government refused to grant a license for a public religious event. Laws stipulating such a license had been on the books for years, yet locals often ignored them, especially in remote districts. Like so much relating to Mexico's history of anticlerical legislation, such laws were largely symbolic. Officials, usually practicing Catholics themselves, typically avoided interfering with popular traditions. Bourguet's report, however, reveals that officials decided to enforce the law in 1947. He provides no explanation, but it could have stemmed from factional conflicts or tensions over authority surrounding the shrine.

In any case, Bourguet was on the verge of canceling the festival again in 1948 when permission came through. However, new health regulations prohibited the sale of livestock during the Virgin's festival, and this altered the trade-fair quality of the pilgrimage. In fact, Bourguet alleged that the new rules convinced coastal herders and ranchers to stay away, dampening participation. Nonetheless, the event went well, and he reported collecting a respectable 1,900 pesos.[16]

Was Juquila's pilgrimage truly in danger in the late 1940s? In the national context, it seems rather late for anticlerical radicalism and what some revolutionary officials labeled *desfanatización* (essentially, secularist reeducation). Attempts to substitute civic holidays for religious festivals were more typical of the 1920s and 1930s and mostly confined to regions with deeper radical traditions. It is also important to remember that sometimes regulatory enforcement functioned as a factional weapon. Thus, maybe a government official deployed these rules concerning religious gatherings to antagonize Juquila's pastor. In this context, the 1947 cancellation of the Virgin's festival may have been part of some local negotiations.

The livestock prohibitions in 1948 may have been related to heavy-handed federal attempts from 1947 to 1954 to eradicate foot-and-mouth disease in the Mexican countryside. This campaign led to the confiscating and euthanizing of cattle, which was met with considerable resistance in some regions, like Oaxaca's Mixteca.[17] Apparently, officials in other regions worried that religious pilgrims could spread the disease as they traveled.[18] Juquila's pastor does not mention this issue.

There is another way to look at the end of livestock trading during the Virgin's festival. In the decades following the Mexican Revolution, the nation's rapid and uneven economic modernization transformed the country. Many farmers and villagers moved to cities in other regions to escape rural poverty and benefit from state-supported industrialization, which largely omitted Oaxaca. Pockets of agricultural dynamism, however, emerged. Juquila and many nearby Chatino pueblos continued to develop as hubs of coffee production and saw considerable local violence linked to struggles over land.[19] As part of its modernization policies, federal authorities invested in road construction in hopes of stoking commercial development. Gradually, tourism became an increasing focus of state efforts in select parts of Oaxaca, mostly in the state capital, surrounding Indigenous towns, and archaeological sites in the Central Valleys. Efforts to draw visitors to Oaxaca's Pacific coast, and eventually Juquila, remained decades away.

In sum, economic trends and policy decisions were slowly integrating Oaxaca's Southern Sierra within the broader national economy. In this context, the seemingly intrusive regulations reshaped the festival as herders and cattlemen were becoming less dependent on trade fairs. The nature of the pilgrimage festival and Juquila's surrounding economy, it appears, was at a tipping point in the late 1940s. Government officials likely judged the Virgin's *feria* as less important to commerce than before and thought little of devotees as they implemented new regulations. What few observers probably understood was that a different kind of economy was beginning to take shape.

In the 1950s, the pilgrimage began to grow again, and Bourguet's promotional efforts and shrine remodeling probably helped. However, more auspicious conditions throughout the region were taking hold: renewed stability, regional growth, road building, newly established bus service, and improved communications (e.g., radio and telephone). Aside from some modest ups and downs, networks of cultural and economic exchange evolved alongside commercial expansion and infrastructural improvements that increasingly connected Oaxaca and the mountains surrounding Juquila to the rest of Mexico. In addition, goods and people flowed more efficiently between the interior and the Pacific coast, which had long been quite isolated. Beyond Oaxaca, particularly in surrounding states like Puebla and Veracruz, deepening commercial relationships likely carried news of Juquila's miraculous reputation to more Mexicans. Simultaneously many Oaxacans migrated to other parts of Mexico. Some of them almost certainly sustained, and shared, their devotion to Juquila.

Pondering Father Bourguet's reports from this period reveals that the 1950s inaugurated a sustained expansion that continued into the twenty-first century. Each year from 1951 to 1959, the funds he collected amid fees, sales, and donations ballooned, from 24,000 to 109,000 pesos.[20] In some of these years, Bourguet also provided a summary of festival costs, usually 3 to 4 percent of gross revenues. (In the early 1950s, they ranged from $1,700 to $2,500, and by 1959 they topped $3,000.) Sometimes Bourguet itemized festival outlays. Fireworks feature prominently: an array of rockets, explosives, and Catherine wheels as well as imposing structures called *castillos* (castles), upon which festive pyrotechnic displays take place. He also commissioned artisans to craft *marmotas* (giant doll-like figures to enliven processions as they whirl and dance), and he paid musicians and singers. Staffing included secretaries, altar boys, laborers, cooks, and vendors to sell devotional items and souvenirs. He also listed other expenses: sales tax payments, fuel for the basilica's generator, office supplies, and flower vases.[21]

Tracking the funds collected at Juquila's annual feast is an inexact measurement of attendance, but Bourguet provided figures for Mass intentions, fees collected dedicating the service toward a specific need or purpose. Of course, many pilgrims visit the shrine without paying for such extras. Still, these statistics give us a sense of shifts in the pilgrimage's popularity. In 1959, Father Bourguet itemized them in two different tiers, one costing twelve pesos and another (with additional liturgical embellishments) for fifteen pesos. All told, for 1959, the number of Masses reached 2,680.[22] When compared to the paltry thirty-eight recorded by Father Canseco in 1914, we have evidence of a seventyfold expansion. Admittedly, a very rough gauge, but it suggests a stunning revival.

We lack a clear accounting of how these funds were used. As revealed in his letters, Bourguet remitted various amounts to the archdiocese each year, but there doesn't appear to have been a standard amount or rate. For example, in 1960, just a few weeks after the impressive haul during the Virgin's 1959 festival, he described how he would send $60,000 in cash to the archdiocese, although he requested permission to keep $13,548 to spend on maintenance. Father Cornelio added that he would also be remitting $35,712 in additional Mass intentions and $6,416.98, which he had collected in tithes and archdiocesan mission contributions. Interestingly, he noted that he was also submitting five different account books for approval.[23] He requested their return for Juquila's archives, but their whereabouts is a mystery today. Considered more broadly, however, his correspondence provides a record of negotiations centered on how much could be designated for shrine expenditures and thus remain under his control.

The most frequently discussed topic in Bourguet's correspondence remained construction, remodeling, and maintenance expenses for the sanctuary and other buildings. We get a glimpse of the shrine's refurbishing in a long letter from September 1959 in which Father Bourguet describes an archbishop-approved budget of almost 60,000 pesos collected in 1958 and the first nine months of 1959. He notes extensive work on the main altar, the expense of flying in materials via air transport (by this time, Juquila had a small airstrip established by Guillermo Rosas, a coffee entrepreneur), and purchasing floor tiles from Puebla. He asserts that he needed an additional 30,000 pesos to avoid incurring debt.[24]

These kinds of expenditures represent a crucial facet of devotional promotion. As religious studies scholar Ian Reader asserts, building and maintaining shrine infrastructure anchor pilgrimage marketing globally—both historically and in the present day.[25] Devotees harbor aesthetic tastes and preferences regarding the sanctuary and other spaces at pilgrimage sites. Part of meeting "demand," from a manager's perspective, is satisfying pilgrims' expectations better than their devotional alternatives. Given Juquila's steady expansion after 1948, Father Cornelio's focus on the basilica appears quite insightful.

Sadly, the documentary record falters in the early 1960s. Bourguet's last two reports reveal that revenues declined slightly in 1961 and 1962 while expenditures ticked up to 5 and 6 percent of the shrine's income. Unfortunately for Bourguet, he faced public accusations of corruption, illegal political meddling, and a long-standing romantic attachment to a woman named Bernarda León. The ensuing scandal probably explains why reports for subsequent years no longer appear in the archdiocesan archive. In simplest terms, as the pilgrimage surged in popularity, Bourguet had become a regional powerbroker and factional figure allied with Ms. León's relatives against another family, the Zavaletas. These local clans competed in commerce, politics, and coffee production. Decedents of both families remain prominent, and hence this history is still grist for gossip. In fact, the León family had been allied with Father Canseco in the early 1900s, long before Bourguet arrived, and there are still whispers about the nature of these ties. Was the patriarch, Rafael León, Canseco's orphaned nephew, as he claimed? Local wags imply their ties were more direct. Their closeness was undeniable. In 2002, I interviewed a very elderly Don Rafael. He fondly recalled growing up in Juquila's rectory, and he credited Canseco—whom he called his uncle— with helping him secure coffee lands in the early 1930s.[26]

There is, of course, a history surrounding this kind of innuendo. In rural Mexico, parishioners historically tolerated clerics who abridged celibacy, if they remained committed to their ministry, kept up appearances, and did not evince predatory tendencies. In truth, gossip about priestly peccadillos is only important in terms of what it reveals about the stature of shrine pastors and the significance of pilgrimage devotion as a local economic motor. This is especially true when clerics remain in their posts for decades, like Canseco and Bourguet. Particularly in the

latter's case, managing thousands of pesos as Juquila's devotion flour-
ished, purchasing goods (often from the Zavaleta's store, according to
receipts), selling merchandise, and offering employment made Bourguet powerful. In this context it is hardly surprising that the shrine's
savvy pastor played a role in politics and represented a formidable rival.
Bourguet's political activities violated the Mexican constitution, but his
detractors' factional interests were probably more important than any
principled secularism.

Timing, nonetheless, matters. Most likely, Bourguet's relationship
with Ms. León and his stewardship of church funds would have been
of little interest, particularly in the state capital, if Juquila's devotion
had remained small. Bourguet's critics allege that he deployed the Virgin's money as investment capital for himself and his lover's relatives.[27]
As the scandal mounted in 1961, Ms. León's younger brother, Aurelio
León, a seminarian in Oaxaca City, even wrote to the archbishop wondering if it would scuttle his ordination, and he asked if he should return
home to defend his sister's honor.[28] Proclaiming ignorance of his parents' finances or how they felt about their daughter's relationship with
the priest, he indirectly corroborates the salacious news spilling out of
Juquila. He describes a history of close ties to Bourguet and notes his
father's disinterest in managing the family's coffee plantations and vague
duties as an employee of the parish. He also confirms that his sister spent
an inordinate amount of time at the rectory. Moreover, he reveals that
many locals assumed Father Cornelio funded the remodeling of the
León family home and Aurelio's educational expenses. He even recalls
gossip alleging that Bourguet had fathered children in Puebla and Mexico City. In the end, however, the young Mr. León's career progressed:
Bourguet announced his ordination to subdeacon in December 1962,
and in 1969 Aurelio León appeared on a circular of priests working in
the archdiocese.[29]

The pastor's support within the archdiocese and his influence in
Juquila must have been formidable. He remained in place, managing
the shrine until popular protests finally ousted him in 1980. Among the
new accusations were claims that he secretly intervened in party politics, attempting to control candidate selection.[30] This charge activated
nineteenth-century anticlerical narratives about the church, which characterized priests as self-dealing puppeteers, using money and social pressure to compromise government officials. In this case, it appears that
Bourguet provided critics plenty of material.

Disgraced and bitter, he gave an exclusive interview to the press in
which he blamed the Zavaleta family and preposterously alleged that
they were in league with distant, leftist guerrillas. He repudiated the

allegations of corruption, but he was evasive about Ms. León. Bourguet also complained about claims that millions of pesos had flowed through the shrine's coffers and into his pockets. The sums collected, he maintained, were never that great. Moreover, he argued that his collections and expenditures had been approved by the archbishop.[31] In his telling, his critics' motivations centered on their own attempts to access the funds generated at the shrine (a plausible accusation). He was duty bound, he claimed, to block such schemes and hence made many enemies.

Beyond this detour into shrine-town melodrama, how does Father Cornelio Bourguet help us understand Juquila's pilgrimage? First, the devotion's phenomenal growth and the subsequent controversy fueled both division and documentation. Conflict is the mother of archives. The saga also suggests that we should keep our minds on the wider context of devotionalism, lest we get lost in after-the-fact moral condemnations. Moreover, this case provides us with a cautionary reminder about sources. To what extent can we trust evidence produced by Father Bourguet? If he was corrupt, are his reports reliable? I believe they are, at least in a general sense. Although little beyond accusations emerged, it is possible that he skimmed shrine revenues without wholly fabricating data. In fact, Juquila's surging popularity likely provided the means of cloaking malfeasance; all Bourguet had to do was underreport his collections amid phenomenal growth.

Again, it pays to step back. Or, to take a different tack, we should connect the dots linking the pilgrimages described by Ruiz y Cervantes and Bourguet. Perhaps the first issue to reemphasize is the interwoven nature of pilgrimage and regional economies. For a variety of reasons, it remains difficult to convince observers of this central, commonsense fact. We cling to idealized divisions between spirituality and commerce. By extension, once we perceive the whiff of money, we tend to dismiss devotion as insincere. More broadly, we imagine religious culture as if it exists outside of economics, and vice versa. However, the inextricable nature of religion, markets, devotion, and exchange links ancient and modern-day pilgrimages. When thousands, or millions, of visitors converge on a sacred site with regularity, they create economies. Donations and fees are only part of the story. Economic structures develop around the spectrum of devotee demands, be it for decoration, souvenirs, and candles, or for food, entertainment, and rest.

In Juquila's case, our spotty data suggest that participation in the pilgrimage swelled amid periods of stability and commercial expansion. That does not mean that devotion evaporated amid unrest. Many devotees probably sustained their ties to the Virgin of Juquila but suspended

travel to the shrine. They may have quipped, like their present-day counterparts, "She understands." It was probably also true that intervals of
expanding development stimulated greater movement in general and
hence brought more potential devotees into contact with Juquila's followers and stories of her miraculous powers. It is during these periods
that texts promoting the devotion, like the different editions of Ruiz y
Cervantes's book, emerged from publishers and printers and circulated
thanks to devotee demand. In addition, during boom phases visitors
purchased more prints and devotional souvenirs, and these objects circulated as widely as the devout travelers involved. Bourguet's receipts
only mention the prints marketed by the shrine; there was almost certainly an array of votive merchandise produced and distributed by independent peddlers, and many of these items were perishable. Hence,
we simply can't gauge this realm of dissemination beyond plausible
speculation.

Indeed, Bourguet's complaints about exaggerated notions of shrine
riches and his rejection of corruption allegations should encourage us
to think more critically. He may have misappropriated shrine funds, but
he correctly pointed out that many people falsely envision extravagant
wealth surrounding reputedly miraculous images without any understanding of how shrines function. Echoes of these attitudes appear in
Ruiz y Cervantes's book from the 1700s, Archbishop Gillow's administrative reports from the late 1800s, and Ausencio Canseco's letters from
the early 1900s. They remain a standard assumption among casual observers, and even devotees, to this day. Ruiz y Cervantes invoked imagined "abusos" among the Chatino residents of Amialtepec, and he also
raised the specter of corrupt accounting practices at the shrine. Gillow,
the nineteenth-century prelate, believed local politicians were angling
for access to the Virgin's wealth, and hence he formalized Juquila's book-
keeping to preempt accusations that could justify intervention. Canseco,
as Juquila's pastor, worked with his allies to hide whatever wealth he
could from looters and nosy officials. Years later, when Bourguet took
over in 1941, he alerted his superiors that significant sums were missing.

In every era, individuals and groups look to Juquila's shrine as a
source of quick plunder or steady revenue. A kind of simplistic logic
endures. Noting the crush of devotees during the festival, pondering the
offerings left by devotees, and watching church employees take collections at Masses, observers conjure visions of bottomless affluence and
priestly embezzlement. Secular critics are among the quickest to vocal-
ize these assumptions, but pilgrims periodically suggest that the church
exploits humble devotees too. Religious authorities stoke these attitudes
with their secretive tendencies and their refusal to acknowledge their

financial interests. Of course, sometimes priests are corrupt. However, thoughtful juquileños concede that the entire town depends on the pilgrimage economy: "We don't need to immigrate to the United States. Here we have 'el norte chiquito' [the "little" United States—i.e., the land of opportunity]."[32] The COVID-19 pandemic reinforced this reality for locals. The temporary shutdown and greatly diminished flow of pilgrims in 2020 and 2021 forced some residents to try their luck in the United States like many other Oaxacan migrants.[33]

So, should we credit Father Cornelio, the man buried in the shrine's churchyard, as the architect of Juquila's remarkable resurgence and present-day popularity? Not without qualifications. The regional economy, political stability, and infrastructural improvements were at least as important as management decisions and marketing savvy. In other words, the polemical priest enjoyed a significant but only limited ability to revive Juquila's devotion. Pilgrimage, our evidence suggests, requires a synergy of conducive social conditions and energetic promotion. What remains mostly invisible, however, was the role of devotee initiative, a realm of history that usually escapes documentation.

CHAPTER 4

# Devotion and Market

Amid many trips to Juquila over the years it gradually dawned on me that the 1960s inaugurated the devotion's conquest of southern Mexico beyond Oaxaca. As I learned repeatedly it was about paying full attention to the evidence surrounding me. A key clue were the glossy banners strapped tightly to the sides of the trucks accompanying pilgrims: with rare exception, they list the group's inaugural year, the number of successive pilgrimages, and the participants' hometown. These banners represent devotee-generated documentation, an ephemeral archive—data on the move. Walking through the improvised encampments surrounding the shrine town, I've pondered throngs of vehicles broadcasting their respective histories. A tiny number began traveling to the shrine in the 1960s, a handful celebrate anniversaries in the 1970s, and dozens locate their origins in the 1980s and 1990s. The trucks, almost without exception, are work vehicles. When they are not in Juquila they are hauling fruit, livestock, or merchandise of some sort. Clustered around each vehicle pilgrimage groups relax in their temporary Juquila residences, sitting on plastic stools and crates, snoozing on blankets, cooking on smoky brasiers, and socializing. Each group has a story to tell, a story that begins around the dates printed on their banners.

To an extent, devotees underscored what archival evidence and the broader realm of scholarship had been telling me: pilgrimage and commerce evolve in tandem.[1] But working with oral histories is quite different. Distinct dynamics, shadings, and connections come to the fore when individuals recount their own past. Personal narratives bring out the intimate, complex nature of this intertwining.

My original contact with Juquila's devotees in Oaxaca's main public market (the Mercado de Abastos or Central de Abastos, usually just called Abastos or La Central) was Silvio. Some fifteen years before, I had heard about some vendors who organized an annual trek to Juquila. So, when I turned my attention to the pilgrimage in 2015, I simply went to Abastos and began querying those selling everything from cookware to workwear, and saddles to chocolate. Stall-keepers listened briefly and pointed me deeper into the labyrinthine market until a helpful stevedore walked me over to Silvio. After a brief conversation, he invited me to join Caminando Juntos (Walking Together), a pilgrimage group anchored by his extended family.

In the summer of 2016, I visited him again in hopes of solidifying my plans to join the group in November. Silvio stood well outside the bodegas (also known as *las naves*, because of the soaring white, arched roofs that shelter clusters of warehouses) on this occasion. He was manning an improvised stand in an area designed as a through street separating the bodegas from the rows of wholesalers selling bulk pet food and pharmaceuticals. The shops, with their clattering, roll-down metal gates (the ubiquitous security doors employed throughout Mexico), sit just beyond the vast, densely packed stalls of the main market. The bodegas reside still farther out. Thus, Silvio, like many of his fellow pilgrims, spends his waking hours in the bowels of Abastos.

Most likely, well-intentioned architects envisioned trucks easily servicing both the bodegas and the wholesale shops from this thoroughfare. Like so many things in Mexico—its public architecture, its shrines, and even the institutional church itself—the planners' vision and everyday function diverged. Or, perhaps, the designers knew that the spaces they sketched would receive much more intensive use than they acknowledged. Maybe politics required a conjured reality—a shared fiction—for the sake of selling the plan in the halls of budget allocation and favor-trading. In any case, vendors occupy most of the street and median between the storefronts and bodegas. They restrict vehicles to a single lane; a single, contested lane, constantly crisscrossed by loaders with hand trucks and large carts teetering with produce-laden crates. Complicating matters further, taxis, cars, and pickups wedge themselves into this tangle to pick up people and merchandise. And finally, although seemingly impossible, large, lumbering fruit trucks enter the disputed passageway. It is slow going, but eventually they get to their destination, one of the bodegas.

Silvio typically works amid mountains of pineapples at his own bodega, El Edén—hence his nickname, "Silvio Piñas." Other vendors, when asked about the pilgrimage, pointed deeper into the warren of day-to-day commerce saying, "Pregunta por Silvio, el de las piñas" (Ask for Silvio, the pineapple guy). Embracing his celebrity, Silvio sports a pineapple tattoo and dons guayaberas featuring embroidered cascades of his namesake. On this day, however, I found him manning a makeshift papaya and cantaloupe stand.

"I'm covering for a cousin," he explained. Male *bodegeros*—essentially, fruit-and-vegetable wholesalers—often conform to a physical type. Silvio fit the bill: squat, strong, barrel-chested, with muscular hands. (A few years later he began to lose weight for health reasons.) He is also charming, talkative, direct, and friendly, helpful traits for a life lived at the point of sale. As we talk, he constantly greets friends, aunts, cousins, clients, and colleagues as they hurry past, as if propelled by the currents of commerce. But Silvio, although an avid participant and recruiter of new devotees, couldn't tell me much about the Abastos pilgrimage.

He sent me to his cousin, Marta, in a nearby bodega, where she and her mother spoke enthusiastically, but briefly, about Our Lady of Juquila. They, in turn, stressed that I needed to speak to Marta's father, Don Valentín Robles, but they cautioned that I would have to find a slow moment, like a Sunday afternoon, when he'd be able to talk. In truth, speaking to Marta and her mother was quite informative. Between the two of them, they knew a great deal about the pilgrimage and its history within the family. However, as I would be reminded on other occasions, redirecting a prying male outsider to a patriarchal figure represents a standard reflex, particularly among women.

In Abastos, during daylight hours, talking for just fifteen minutes can be difficult, although devotees generally enjoy discussing the pilgrimage. Virtually all conversations take place in fits and starts, truncated by bursts of haggling, the cries of pitchmen, the grind and growl of trucks, the hawking of cure-all medications over loudspeakers, and wafts of *banda* and *cumbia* from overmatched car stereos. As I learned, conversations about faith, commitment, creativity, and generosity are simultaneously family histories. Among those organizing pilgrimages, deeper discussions reveal proud narratives framed as chronicles of service. A previous generation of anthropologists would probably assert that these activities, and the stories about them, center on the marking of social prestige and merit. Indeed, most Mexicans respect pilgrimage, even if they never take part. But they tend to caricature the practice from a distance as a demonstration of raw, pure, elemental faith—a good thing for *others* to do. Social standing is certainly in play, but mostly in the same way it operates among North Americans who volunteer to teach Sunday school, coach sports teams, lead church choirs, and marshal scouting troops. In sum, Mexicans generally see devotees and pilgrimage organizers as community oriented *buena gente* (good people).

Bodegero and bodegera livelihoods revolve around long hours and the flexible and extensive deployment of family labor. It isn't merely about buying low and selling high, as the cliché goes. The produce business hinges on selling for as many hours as possible. On busy days, the Robles family works eighteen hours, and slower days still mean manning (or wo-manning) the bodega for thirteen hours.[2] In other words, there is no way to learn about Juquila's devotion among vendors other than interviewing them amid the bustle of Abastos. The array of market-honed skills prove well-suited to pilgrimage; these merchants tend to be deft managers of people, perishables, vehicles, cash, and tarps. Vendors also share an unflappable, get-it-done culture that serves them well during the grinding walk to Juquila. The Abastos devotees essentially graft their livelihood's can-do ethos onto their pilgrimage.

In fact, broadly speaking, Mexico's culture of vibrant, local commerce and pilgrimage remain deeply entangled, but the inextricable nature of devotion and market should not surprise us. For scholars specializing in Roman or medieval Europe, for example, it represents an obvious truth: pilgrimage and trade shape each other, and the routes traveled by devotees and goods are one and the same.[3] In other words, stumbling upon pilgrimage devotees among fruit vendors and truckers is not a coincidence. Who is better placed to hear stories of miraculous images at faraway shrines? Who knows the roads and maintains personal contacts in far-flung communities along Mexico's highways? Who enjoys sufficient access to disposable income and vehicles? Thus, I learned, towns known as busy centers of domestic commerce tend to double as hotbeds of pilgrimage. This does not mean that an unchanging set of communities has sustained Juquila's pilgrimage over centuries, but experience and interviews reveal that the shrine's mid-twentieth-century resurgence and expansion blossomed in trading hubs along the highways connecting the cities of Puebla, Veracruz, and Oaxaca. Several agricultural communities near the city of Puebla offer an evocative case study. Today they represent fervent nodes of Juquila's devotion, and their histories suggest that twentieth-century roadway construction and the resultant expansion of interregional trade proved crucial to the pilgrimage's expansion.

In the 1920s and 1930s, the Mexican government began investing heavily in highway construction in hopes of spurring broader economic growth. The expansion of railroads in the nineteenth century had catalyzed Mexico's rapid modernization in select regions. Many areas, however, remained remote and underdeveloped. The revolutionary government, understandably, sought to remedy this through road building. By 1940, a network of highways finally connected almost all of Mexico's main cities. Rural Oaxaca, linked through Puebla, epitomizes a latecomer to integration efforts. In addition, a separate federal initiative added forty thousand kilometers of secondary, dirt roads between communities at about the same time. Paved arteries were still at least a generation away for most towns.[4]

Oaxaca, therefore, enjoyed only rudimentary rural infrastructure before 1940, and roads reaching mountain communities like Juquila remained primitive into the 1980s. Veteran pilgrims often speak with pride of their early journeys on rutted dirt roads and crow about their perseverance despite rudimentary equipment. For example, Lalo, the old-timer from Acatzingo, Puebla, laughed about conquering the crude roadways on "bicicletas de panadero" (i.e., heavy cargo bicycles) in the late 1970s.[5] Moreover, for riders of that era there were no support trucks to carry their luggage or provide return transportation, meaning these pilgrims rode or walked double the distance compared to those following in their footsteps in the present day. Cognizant of the distinctions, younger devotees often express great respect for their elders' dedication.

Outside observers often assume that the institutional church manages pilgrimage, but it grows and flourishes without much clerical oversight, particularly places like Mexico, where the Catholic priesthood remains stretched thin and overworked. Word of mouth and informal mentorship anchor the practice. In fact, it is difficult to find a priest who enthusiastically promotes these journeys, much less organizes them. This is true in both archival evidence and oral histories. Families, friends, neighbors, and business associates create their own groups, recruit participants, and sustain their "tradition" for decades. Sometimes their children inherit the mantle of leadership. There are exceptions. Cyclists from Tonameca, Oaxaca, acclaim Father Jaime Meneses as the 2002 founder of their pilgrimage.[6] Apparently, as part of his youth ministry, he mustered a large group of adolescent boys and a handful of men and drove a support vehicle before his transfer to a different parish. Meneses, nevertheless, represents an outlier. Priests, typically, only play a tangential role, blessing images, officiating farewell Masses, and celebrating thanksgiving services when devotees return home. Clergymen at the shrine in Juquila offer blessings, hear confessions, and celebrate Mass, but their engagement with pilgrims remains transitory.

In other words, local effort and ingenuity shaped the recent expansion of pilgrimage in Mexico, and it probably did so in previous eras as well. The lack of priestly involvement explains, in part, why archival records are scarce. If long-distance pilgrimage had been an integral facet of the parish ministry, it would appear in administrative documentation more often and in greater detail. Instead, given the testimony of present-day organizers, lay leaders mold their respective traditions to fit local economic rhythms and calendars, even if this means traveling to the shrine weeks or months removed from Juquila's traditional feast day on

December 8. For example, Los Reyes Juárez, a town in Puebla, sustains a large Juquila pilgrimage that takes place mid-January because many devotees work in distant Cancún during November and the Christmas holidays.[7] Since their livelihoods depend on working several hundred miles away from home during peak tourist season, they simply shift their trip to a later date.

Another pattern that holds among different organizers is that they initially tagged along with groups founded elsewhere and led by relatives, coworkers, or trading partners. Later, after learning routes and the complex of logistic tasks involved, they founded groups in their own communities. The cycle then continues as these individuals, in turn, mentor others and pass on expertise. In some instances, such as for devotees from Coscomatepec, Veracruz, benefactors from the original group sponsor the "daughter" pilgrimage, offering donations or a new image of Juquila to anchor an incipient tradition.[8] From the perspective of Juquila's followers, expanding devotion represents a worthy pious act, a concrete manifestation of gratitude. In thanks for Juquila's maternal protection and supportive interventions, devotees spread news of her miraculous grace and support novice travelers. In sum, it is common for pilgrimage groups to have historical ties to one another, particularly in the same geographic area. Or, as the Abastos pilgrims demonstrate, devotional traditions can emerge through extended family networks spanning regions.

Don Valentín, Marta's father, represents a remarkable source of information on these patterns even though he doesn't take part in the pilgrimage. He donates fuel and the use of his pickup truck when his children, grandchildren, and other relatives head to the shrine together. Valentín proclaims great respect for the pilgrims, but, by his own admission, he just isn't up to it.

Still, his testimony establishes the linkages between regional commerce, Juquila's surge in popularity during the mid-twentieth century, and evolving practices among devotees.[9] Luckily, I found a slow Sunday afternoon, and we were able to converse while Marta, and a couple of teenage granddaughters, attended clients. Simultaneously, a handful of smaller grandchildren played amid crates, chased each other around the fruit displays, and puzzled over my digital recording device.

Valentín, a robust sixty-five-year-old with thick salt-and-pepper hair and a short gray mustache, proudly recounts his family's long-standing commitment to Juquila's devotion and supporting her followers. On the day we spoke at his bodega, La Carmencita, he wore a tight black polo shirt and jeans, showing off his bodegero physique. In essence, he has done a lot of work-related weightlifting, moving boxes and crates around his fruit stand for decades, although lately he makes time for gym workouts too. According to Valentín, it began in his parents' and grandparents' hometown of Huixcolotla, Puebla, a town known as a center of artisanal *papel picado* (the cut paper decorations strung across streets and plazas during celebrations). According to government statistics, Huixcolotla boasted 16,790 residents in 2020, with seventy-eight of its inhabitants still speaking Nahuatl, the town's ancestral tongue.[10] Less understood is Huixcololotla's broader economic importance thanks to its location squarely in a fertile and relatively prosperous valley south of the nation's capital and the city of Puebla. Although the pueblo's steady expansion swallows more farmland every year, and many towns have grown steadily toward the nearby main highway, Route 150, the area remains largely covered by truck farms. It is a Mexican version of strip-mall sprawl. Most towns in the region have a colonial plaza surrounded by municipal buildings, parish offices, and mission churches and a grid-patterned center built on top of a pre-Columbian urban core. Over the last two generations, however, new storefronts, workshops, and warehouses sought proximity to the nation's transportation arteries, decentering these historic pueblos.

In truth, although the Robles family's historical roots reside in Huixcolotla, a town known in the present day for its intense commitment to pilgrimage, the practice represents a regional phenomenon. It spans the entire Tepeaca Valley, comprised of ancient Nahua communities like Acatzingo, Tepeaca, and Actipan, and links up with towns in the wider region, like Tecamachalco. But residents of the valley and Juquila alike single out Huixcolotla's devotion as the largest, most lavish of all active communal pilgrimage traditions. The Huixcolotla pilgrims have long scheduled their trip for mid-November, sending a large semitrailer full of fresh flowers and florists to decorate the shrine lavishly every year in advance of their arrival. Several hundred cyclists, walking pilgrims, a large convoy of support vehicles, and many hundreds of others in vehicles converge on the shrine town almost simultaneously, approaching together in a large procession for a special Mass. Like other towns in Puebla, they also hire well-known dance bands to enliven their celebrations at their vast encampment on the outskirts of Juquila (see plate 14).[11]

The Tepeaca Valley was an important zone of pre-Columbian urban civilization before the arrival of the Spanish, with several Nahuatl-speaking city-states, hereditary nobilities, complex economies, skilled craft specialists, and dense populations. Then, as now, it was an important agricultural region. During the colonial period and into the nineteenth century, large agricultural estates and peasant subsistence farming dominated the region.[12] In the 1930s, several agricultural collectives (*ejidos*) emerged from the postrevolutionary land reform and focused on growing corn and beans, the perennial Mexican staples. However, in the 1950s farmers began to shift to an array of cash crops—among them tomatoes, carrots, broccoli, and cabbage—and the main market in Huixcolotla became one of the most important centers of agricultural trade. At the same time, logically, some farmers abandoned the fields to become middlemen and truckers amid Mexico's rapid urbanization. By 2005, the area was responsible for 18 percent of the nation's agricultural production. This region mostly supplies produce for domestic consumption, in contrast to states like Sonora and Sinaloa that focus predominantly on the US market.[13]

In short, this archipelago of pre-conquest towns represents a key trade corridor that has depended on the production and transport of agricultural produce for centuries. In addition, over time local traders expanded and began buying fruit from tropical elevations, particularly in Veracruz, and distributing these sought-after products to highland cities. Not surprisingly, alongside farmers, exporters, and merchants, many truck drivers call the region home. Some towns like Acatzingo are also known for the ancillary businesses linked to agricultural commerce; for example, some local entrepreneurs specialize in building custom cargo holds for produce trucks (*carrocerías*). The impressive growth in domestic commerce from the 1960s to the present, precisely at the time when this part of Mexico embraced pilgrimage to Juquila, undoubtedly influenced the expansion of the devotion.

Of course, there is a dark side to the region's strategic location and trading culture. One of Mexico's most important oil pipelines traverses the area as it connects refineries along the Gulf Coast to Mexico City. As infamous drug cartels branch out into new ventures, they have seized upon contraband petroleum products—gasoline and diesel taken from illegally tapped pipelines.[14] The fuel is then sold surreptitiously or, with the help of corrupt managers and employees, funneled back into the legal supply chain available at gas stations. These developments have caused massive losses for the national oil company, Pemex, and a national political scandal. The brazen nature of this illegal trade in Puebla's Tepeaca Valley has become so notorious that the area became known as the "Red Triangle" of fuel theft for a time. In sum, organized crime siphons away millions of liters of fuel each year in this clutch of communities renowned for their devotion to Our Lady of Juquila.[15]

Particularly after 2013, Puebla outstripped all other states in this illegal bonanza. Not surprisingly, the new illicit wealth stokes violence as criminal groups battle for control of the lucrative trade. A subsidiary illegal activity also characterizes the area: the rampant theft of vans, pickups, buses, and trucks for use in distributing contraband. Likewise, it is possible that proceeds from these illicit fuel sales flow into pilgrimage, in the form of less expensive but illegal diesel purchased to lower travel costs, and smugglers or their family members may also be among Juquila's followers. If nothing else, pilgrims engage these markets at the point of consumption.

Whatever the connections, Huixcolotla and the surrounding towns find themselves anchored amid the brisk commercial currents—both legal and illegal—coursing back and forth between Mexico City, Puebla, and Veracruz and flowing further south to Oaxaca as well. They form a chain along one of Mexico's most important arteries, the route where the Gulf Coast state of Veracruz and the states of southern Mexico historically connected to the nation's capital: first by mule trains and oxcart roads, then railroad, and, eventually, highway. Remarkably, the Robles family's ties to Huixcolotla remain strong two generations after their ancestors moved away; such bonds proved crucial to the expansion of Juquila's devotion beyond Oaxaca.

Valentín's paternal grandfather, a Huixcolotla native, was a particularly energetic and shrewd entrepreneur in the early twentieth century. Propitiously, he married a woman whose father owned and rented mule trains. First as a paying customer, later as a son-in-law, he used these beasts of burden to transport fruit, especially bananas and oranges, from warmer climes to towns in Puebla. Gradually, Don Valentín's grandfather shifted his focus to the fruit trade between Córdoba in Veracruz and Tehuacán at the southern edge of the state. The city, some sixty miles removed from Huixcolotla, not only connects the farmers and traders in the Tepeaca Valley to the Gulf Coast, but it also serves as the gateway to states further south. From there Valentín's predecessor began sending merchandise to Oaxaca via railroad. In 1948, he moved permanently to Oaxaca and opened a fruit stand at the venerable Juárez Market, mere blocks from the city's central plaza (Abastos did not open until 1978). When they moved to Oaxaca in the late 1940s, however, the Robles family had no prior history of devotion to Our Lady of Juquila.

According to Don Valentín, maintaining close ties to relatives in Huixcolotla remained crucial for his grandparents. He speaks of this connection in terms of a cherished family ethos, revealing its cultural, social, and economic dimensions. Not surprisingly, the Robles family continues to reinforce these bonds; for generations, these transplants have returned to Huixcolotla annually for the festival celebrating the town's patron saint each August and for important family events. Marriages in the subsequent generations have further fortified these ties. For example, although Valentín's father, Rubén Robles, moved to Oaxaca with his parents in 1948, he married a woman he met in Huixcolotla some years later.

This couple, Valentín's parents, gradually embraced devotion to the Virgin of Juquila. In his telling, during the 1960s (when he was a teenager), perhaps a dozen individuals from Huixcolotla decided to visit Juquila's shrine. They asked his parents if they could spend a night at their centrally located home a handful of blocks south of Oaxaca's historic central plaza. Thus, somewhat counterintuitively, their ties to the famed image evolved as an outgrowth of their Puebla roots rather than assimilation in Oaxaca. In other words, alongside deep cultural ties and familial bonds to the Tepeaca Valley, devotion to Juquila and the emergence of robust poblano participation in the pilgrimage reinforced the interweaving of previously established devotional and commercial bonds. Moreover, the individuals enmeshed in these relationships increasingly found collective purpose and meaning in visiting Juquila and facilitating the journeys of others.

This first group of Huixcolotla pilgrims took the train to Oaxaca and then completed the trip to Juquila in trucks. Shortly afterward, Cepillín Reynoso (an individual nicknamed in honor of a clown on Mexican television) started walking to Juquila with four other devotees. According to Valentín, Reynoso represents the true forerunner of the scores of pilgrimage groups that set out from the state of Puebla in the present day. He spent years establishing the safest and most efficient path to the shrine. Soon the Juquila pilgrimages diversified and multiplied. Within a few years, several distinct Huixcolotla pilgrimage groups numbered eighty to one hundred devotees apiece. Their cycling pilgrimage gained fame as a devotional behemoth surpassing six hundred riders and involving scores of support personnel and vehicles. Their Facebook page celebrated their founding in 1963 as they planned their fifty-ninth pilgrimage in 2022.[16] According to Valentín, all the pilgrimage organizers from towns like Tepeaca, Actazingo, and Tecamachalco initially traveled with Huixcolotla before starting their own groups.

In 2018, I spoke on the phone to Agustín, the president of Huixcolotla's *Comisión*, immediately after the group's return from Juquila. He informed me that he and his colleagues raised and spent approximately one million pesos (about fifty thousand dollars at the time) to fund the year's trip. Agustín proudly claimed that 630 riders participated. Part of their tradition, he told me, was sending trucks out to different communities to pick up additional pilgrims each year. In a sense, this kind of outreach seeds the Juquila devotion in nearby towns. Agustín claimed that the first cyclist from Huixcolotla traveled to Juquila in the early

1960s alone, and in subsequent years others joined him.[17] The group's Facebook page honors these pathbreaking figures in short, filmed ceremonies during which they bestow certificates and medals on the now elderly men.[18]

This pattern suggests both a person-to-person and a community-to-community process of expansion and dissemination of pilgrimage practices linked to Our Lady of Juquila. It is easy to understand how this takes place between neighboring towns or clusters of socially and economically interconnected towns, as we find in Puebla's Tepeaca Valley.

It is a mistake, however, to imagine shrine visitation as a new phenomenon in Puebla and Veracruz; in fact, it has centuries-deep roots in this region. Pilgrimage didn't begin with Our Lady of Juquila for these communities. Residents of towns like Huixcolotla often state, "somos un pueblo fiestero" (meaning, we're a people who love festivals, hosting them and visiting them). Young and old pilgrims alike reveal that embracing the Juquila pilgrimage represents an extension of long-standing social and devotional customs rather than a complete innovation. Many devotees in Puebla and Veracruz report first taking part in pilgrimages to the Virgin of Guadalupe's shrine. A sense for this wider tradition comes through in the foundation dates celebrated by different pilgrimages: in Huixcolotla, for example, a walking group dedicated to Guadalupe originated in 1950, whereas a cycling group to Juquila dates its foundation to 1961.[19] I know of no ongoing Juquila pilgrimage in Puebla that celebrates an earlier foundation.

Long personal histories of shrine visitation emerge when pilgrims from Coscomatepec, Veracruz, search their memories—such as childhood van rides to Tepeaca's feast of the Santo Niño Doctor (a reputedly miraculous Christ child attired as a physician), adult participation in two-day walks from Coscomatepec to the Christ of Tlacotepec every July, or three-day bike rides to the Basilica of Guadalupe.[20] These journeys, we could say, function as practice for the longer sojourn to Juquila, but it isn't simply the journey, the reputation of the images, or the convivial nature of these gatherings that matters. Personal devotional histories represent the outward manifestation of a particular kind of Catholic practice centered on images, shrines, and fiestas. In all of them the dynamics of travel, visitation, penitential offerings, requests for intercession, and promises of humble gratitude appear center stage. As historian Jennifer Scheper Hughes argues, moreover, popular devotions like the Santo Niño Doctor offer a space for religious innovation.[21] These are also large, profoundly social gatherings, the Mexican analog to county fairs in the United States. For some devotees, this kinetic, alternative realm of religious expression speaks to their cultural preferences: for some, it supersedes attending Mass on Sundays. In sum, this approach to Catholicism revolves around a loose, personalized cycle of festivals and shrine visits rather than the Vatican's norms of religious observance. It features deep historical roots in cultural and social practices that extend beyond what many outsiders might understand as "religion." This approach to religiosity likely also has roots in Indigenous adaptations of Catholicism to native sensibilities.[22]

From a certain perspective, it is as if Mexico's boisterous baroque religious culture of the seventeenth and eighteenth centuries endures among present-day pilgrims. Their focus remains on group actions connected to images and festivals instead of strictly contemplative piety and the sacraments. The context, however, is profoundly different, and the modern adaptations are many. Today's devotees carry cell phones, connect on social media, use walkie-talkies, and coordinate fleets of support vehicles, yet the expressive, public, and collective quality of baroque piety endures in these spaces.

For the Juquila pilgrimage, then, what we have witnessed over the last fifty to seventy years is the addition of a distant shrine devotion to a preexisting religious culture thanks to the commercial relationships anchoring social networks and catalyzing the spread of Juquilita's devotion. For example, Don Carlos, the founder of a walking pilgrimage in Coscomatapec, Veracruz, began visiting Oaxaca's Chatina Virgin at the invitation of steady customers from Huixcolotla, a town approximately eighty miles (130 km) from his home.[23] He met these customers while selling (reselling, in fact) *chayote*, a mild-flavored squash popular in Mexican cuisine that grows well in Coscomatepec. This municipality represents the greatest producer of chayote in Mexico, most of which is exported to the United States via middlemen in Puebla, who, unsurprisingly, also take home the lion's share of the profits.[24] Thus, we again find Juquila's devotional expansion interconnected with commerce.

Don Carlos, a man of modest means, patches together a living as a small-time trader and go-between. He buys and resells farm produce as best he can, and he looks up to his patrons from Puebla as models of merchant success, leadership, and religious dedication. After getting to know Huixcolotla devotees through the chayote trade, he joined their walking pilgrimage. Schooled on the trail for over five years, he absorbed the nuances of planning, coordination, and management required to shepherd devotees and supplies over long distances before marshaling a group of neighbors and fellow believers from several pueblos near his hometown in Veracruz. The strong connection to his previous colleagues and business associates in Puebla endured and bolstered his efforts. For several years, Don Carlos and his group linked up with the larger Huixcolotla pilgrimage en route to Juquila. They hiked the first three or four days skirting the eighteen-thousand-foot Orizaba Volcano and winding their way down to the Tehuacán Valley before merging with the larger company of devotees from Puebla. Eventually, they separated definitively, but benefactors from Tecamachalco, a married couple who had walked alongside Don Carlos in the Huixcolotla pilgrimage, bought the *veracruzanos* a copy of the Virgin of Juquila to anchor their embryonic "daughter" tradition.[25]

Today this likeness spends most of the year moving between devotees' homes in and around Coscomatepec. Individuals *cuidando* (caring for) the image consider it a solemn honor, and they host recitations of the Rosary and modest rituals when their Juquilita arrives and departs. Then, each November, Don Carlos and other devotees reverently place the image in a bulky, custom-made, mahogany-hued wood vitrina and secure her in the pickup-truck altar that accompanies the pilgrims on their fourteen-day trek to Juquila. At each stopover, they carefully set up the vitrina in a prominent location, with the Virgencita safely ensconced within. She presides, as it were, as they take their meals, socialize, and bed down at each stopover.

Conversely, in the 1970s, the Oaxacan branch of the Robles family had still not become involved in organizing pilgrimages, remaining focused instead on hosting devotees as they passed through. Every November and December, different pilgrimage groups stopped at the house near the city center on their way to Juquila. The family greeted them with coffee and a simple meal, and some would spend a night. As the groups grew in number, Don Ángel and his wife (Valentín's parents) began collecting donations of food and other items to support the travelers. By the 1990s, Valentín recalled, many referred to his house as *La Casa del Peregrino* (The Pilgrim's House). Perhaps three thousand devotees visited the Robles family each year.

Eventually the impromptu throngs drew the ire of authorities. The local Red Cross complained that pilgrims were using storm drains as latrines, and, finally, Oaxaca's transit police, pointing to traffic congestion, prohibited pilgrim stopovers at the Robles home in 2000. Nonetheless, the legacy of devotional hospitality remains a point of pride in the family, and it endures in a slightly diminished fashion. Many pilgrimage groups from Puebla, Tlaxcala, the state of Mexico, Veracruz, and Morelos still spend nights at Abastos, bedding down behind the bodegas along the river.[26]

These processes, obviously, work in concert—travel, devotion, leisure, visitation, and celebration establish and maintain social ties across distance and decades. They take place and evolve simultaneously alongside work, consumption, and trade, over hundreds of kilometers, and amid large fiestas and intimate religious experiences. Interestingly, the Robles family's involvement as organizers of their own pilgrimage group emerged only with Silvio and Marta—three generations after their ancestors moved to Oaxaca in 1948. Naturally, there were precedents. According to Valentín, his parents visited the shrine together first, and eventually they included their children. He vaguely remembers a childhood trip in the late 1950s. The family rode in a car to Sola de Vega—approximately halfway—and then traveled on foot to the shrine with rented mules carrying their baggage.

In the mid-1990s, individual bodegeros from Abastos began traveling to the shrine with groups from nearby communities. Gradually more vendors and laborers joined them. Marta proved to be among the most avid, frequent participants, beginning as a teenager.[27] Then, in the early 2000s, Silvio and Marta teamed up and began organizing friends and coworkers in a loose, slightly unstable collective. For a time, they numbered perhaps sixty fellow walkers, but then the group split because some individuals wanted to sustain a more demanding pace. Silvio and Marta, however, prefer to adapt the group's progress to the speed of the slowest participants. This fissioning of groups, as the Huixcolotla story confirms, is normal. For the last few years, however, there has been talk of merging the two Abastos groups again.

Valentín remains in same house near Oaxaca City's main plaza, and pilgrims still seek him out at Abastos. Sometimes, as an expression of gratitude, they slowly walk their traveling images and standards through his home. For the devotees, these likenesses represent more than mere copies of the famed sacred figures or emblems of affiliation. The images are usually copies of the Juquila statue within a small vitrina, but some groups travel with framed paintings or photographs of the Virgin or depictions of Christ. Typically, standards are embroidered cloth banners, perhaps five feet long, attached to cross-like frames so that walking pilgrims can carry them. They may represent the pilgrims' hometown patron saint or a popular local Marian image, in addition to the Virgin of Juquila. Standards, like the vinyl banners on trucks, list the group's name, place of origin, and the date of their founding. They identify the travelers to other pilgrims and observers, yet they are also symbolic representations of the ties between the individuals and families involved. Valentín speaks with reverence about the images and standards potentially visiting his bodega—his unique space in the public arena of Abastos, the commercial hub around which pilgrimage devotion has coalesced. If his friends and relatives from Huixcolotla honor his workplace with their images, "Well, that would be like a fiesta for the family."

# CHAPTER 5

# *Póngalo en Fais*—Put It on Facebook

On December 21, 2012, Candy C. posted "Mañanitas a la Virgen de Juquila" on YouTube.[1] On the surface it is simply another *ranchera* arrangement of the classic standard, the musical homage sung at anniversaries, birthdays, and Marian shrines. Just as hopeful suitors sing it at boozy *serenatas*, fervent devotees entering the shrine intone the lyrics every Mexican knows by heart, "Qué linda está la mañana en que vengo a saludarte . . ." (The morning is so beautiful as I come to greet you . . .).

In this case, Edelmira del Castillo of Alto Lucero, Veracruz, rewrote the words and sings, pairing a personalized musical tribute with low-resolution photographs. The result is a seven-minute-sixteen-second intimate testimonial emphasizing gratitude and fervor, while documenting a bus pilgrimage. As Doña Edelmira sings, she proclaims her heart is bursting with metaphorical floral offerings and conveys her elation upon reaching the shrine. The images accompanying her tribute include pictures of the Virgin of Juquila and a blurry photograph of a Juquila-shaped marking on a wall in her hometown, implying that the Virgencita's miraculous presence has been felt in Veracruz as well.

A YouTube video may not seem like traditional devotion, but the earnest Doña Edelmira offers a digital version of the venerable *ex-voto*: a narrative, votive offering, testifying to a miracle and proclaiming gratitude. In short, this is a traditional act, although the medium is new.

Portions of chapter 5 were previously published in Edward Wright-Ríos and Carlota Guadalupe Martínez-Don, "Posting the Journey to Juquila: Pilgrimage, Digital Devotion, and Social Media in Mexico," *Latin American Research Review*. Published online 2024: 1–20. doi: 10.1017/lar/2024.8. Copyright © 2024, Cambridge University Press. CC BY, https://creativecommons.org/licenses/by/4.0.

But this offering will never end up on a trash heap, like so many other offerings deposited at the shrine. In addition, her voice, her story, her *Mañanitas* could remain in cyberspace for decades, maybe centuries, and reach far more fellow devotees. By May 2021, Doña Edelmira's on-line offering had tallied 162,000 views and had inspired forty-five supportive comments.

This pious *veracruzana* is not alone. YouTube hosts scores of videos documenting pilgrimages to Juquila, ranging from huge groups of cyclists, walkers, and runners to chartered bus trips, taxi caravans, and family road trips. Many feature slide shows and overdubbed music, including ballads, praise pop, regional dance genres, hip-hop, and "Indigenous" flutes. Some are primitive, but others reveal careful editing, voice-over narration, and even drone footage. A handful appear patterned on cinematic documentaries, and a few are presented as multipart series. Others borrow the stylings of music videos, travel shows, and social media campaigns.[2]

When I began researching Juquila's pilgrimage, I had no plan to examine "digital religion," but I quickly realized that, just as devotion

Figure 6. Digital devotion. Many devotees take pictures and videos during the pilgrimage, which they share on various platforms. Social media allows pilgrimage organizers to communicate and recruit more effectively. Some pilgrims carefully craft and post music videos, ballads, and documentaries. Moreover, the tradition of the leaving of symbolic objects and texts at shrines has colonized virtual spaces. Photograph by Mike DuBose.

became intertwined with social networks and domestic commerce in twentieth-century Mexico, it now also depends on twenty-first-century social media, especially Facebook and YouTube. Pondered from a distance, these platforms offer us a stunning evidentiary trove that grows daily. In many ways, social media offers the rich archive of grass-roots religious expression that historians have always wished they could consult. For the first time, we have reems (well, virtual reems) of evidence produced by common people. Eventually, we will be able to analyze religious change over time in previously unimaginable detail. It is still too soon to tell if social media will drastically reshape the nature of pilgrimage, but it is indeed already influencing practices, facilitating communication, and expanding the reach of devotee expression. It pays, however, to remember that pilgrimage's loose, flexible nature has remained central to both its endurance and its recent surge in popularity.

## Facebook

If the Juquila data is representative, Facebook is the most popular digital space for pilgrim expression.[3] Four kinds of Juquila-related pages are found on the platform: official church pages, prayer groups, virtual votive spaces, and pilgrimage group pages. An examination of these reveals considerable overlap, but their main functions remain distinct. The emergence of new virtual spaces may fade as the pandemic recedes, but in considering organized pilgrimage groups, Facebook is unquestionably central to Juquila's devotion. Organizers typically create an online "group" on the platform to facilitate communication, recruit participants, celebrate trips to the shrine, share news, and coordinate tasks. In sum, announcements, photographs and videos, and comments offer a window on thriving devotion. Simultaneously, Juquila-related pages often function as support networks. Alongside virtual devotion and information sharing, they offer individuals a place where they can voice personal concerns and receive encouragement from fellow devotees. In addition, within group pages, virtual votive spaces, and Juquila prayer groups, we see members sharing content from other social media sites and Facebook also hosts Juquila promotional material generated by tourism promoters, share-bait, and a variety of religious content. In other words, Facebook acts as a hub, which distinguishes it from other platforms.

From a different perspective, Juquila-related material also demonstrates the "networked" nature of devotion in the present day.[4] Devotees can scroll and click from one digital space to another at home, during the workday, and while traveling to Juquila. As they do, they may offer comments, prayers, emoji, and encouragement. They can share and up-vote posts, follow links to religious music videos, ponder devotional im-ages, watch clips from other pilgrimages, and upload their own content. There is also a performative aspect at work. On Facebook, individuals can curate a representation of themselves as a devout follower of Our Lady of Juquila.

The most strictly devotional, and sometimes heartrending, are the Juquila prayer groups. With evocative names like "Comunidad Virgen de Juquila en Facebook" (Virgin of Juquila Community on Facebook), "Virgen de Juquila en Ti Confío" (Virgin of Juquila in You I Trust), and "Pedido de Oraciones en comunidad a la 'Virgen de Juquila'" (Request for Communal Prayer to the Virgin of Juquila), they attract individuals hoping to magnify appeals for miraculous intercession, pleas for prayers, and grateful testimonials.[5] The idea is not only to communicate with Juquila but also to increase the efficacy and power of petitions by in-spiring the pious pleading of fellow devotees as well. In general, these groups have taken shape in the last five years and enjoy moderate success in attracting members (516, 5,554, and 28,431 followers, respectively, as of January 2022). They also usually address offensive speech and fraud directly. Thus, in hopes of protecting their spiritual goals and policing off-topic tirades, profiteering, and online bullying, they provide firm guidelines and promise to block violators.

It is important to acknowledge, though, that Facebook pages ded-icated to fomenting religious tourism can also function like prayer groups or even news bulletins. For example, the site called "Virgen de Juquila," which is linked to the promotional website "Oaxaca Mio," often features news articles about missing children and announcements of AMBER alerts, in addition to a constant stream of devout postings and commentary.[6]

In terms of content, posts on group pages essentially mimic shrine practices. Online, however, sustained interaction remains possible. Many ask others to pray for family members. Some individuals repost videos of Masses and novenas originating on the shrine's official Facebook page.[7] Alongside this kind of content, devotees also share devotional music videos.[8] Many posts attest to Juquilita's support (for example, in raising children) or attribute a healthy pregnancy to her miraculous protection.[9] Comments are almost invariably positive, praising the poster's faith, en-couraging Juquila to bless the poster, deploying the praying hands emoji, or simply typing the word "Amen." Given the coronavirus pandemic context, the comments sections also include requests for information about shrine accessibility and the Mass schedule.

Virtual prayer groups also serve as online grief forums. For example, in August 2021, a devotee from Tlapa, Guerrero, posted a photograph of the well-known stone image of the Virgin of Juquila at the Pedimento (the main votive chapel near the shrine) and requested that the Virgin halt her aunt's cancer. In doing so, she borrowed imagery from the space where devotees frame in-person requests to Juquila, testify to their fervent devotion, and leave offerings. In short, she conjured a digital Pedimento. In the fifty-one comments that followed, she received an outpouring of support and prayers for her aunt. A handful of days later, however, she announced her aunt's death.[10] The subsequent comments, naturally, shifted to condolences.

Not surprisingly, during the same year a cyber votive chapel appeared on Facebook, called "El Pedimento Virtual de la Virgen de Juquila (oficial)." Citing the pilgrim tradition of making clay models of votive requests and leaving these items at the chapel, the group stresses that the pandemic-inspired closure of the Pedimento necessitated the establishment of a virtual chapel. It invites devotees to make offerings at home and then share pictures of them. The page assures visitors, "With the faith of all of us, very soon the Virgin will grant your plea."[11]

In sum, devotees are making use of the opportunities social media offers—virtual space, networked communication, content sharing, opportunities for creative expression, and a cyber social group. The virtual Pedimento, however, remains public and lacks content rules. As a result, pious requests and shared prayers appear alongside posts unrelated to Juquila's devotion. These range from pages promoting obscure folk saints, new age counselors, and disc jockeys to homemade videos of alleged occult happenings and live-streamed raffles. Without regulation, Facebook groups attract individuals seeking to profit from devotees.

Among prayer groups there are also pages dedicated to organizing and promoting Juquila's devotion in the United States: for example, "Virgen de Juquila en Greensboro."[12] Although some immigrant devotees return to Oaxaca for pilgrimages, the journey remains a dangerous and expensive proposition for undocumented migrants. Thus, this Facebook group represents an effort to establish a Juquila tradition in North Carolina. With nearly eight hundred followers, it announces group Rosaries every few weeks in private homes and reports on the construction of a Juquila chapel in Greensboro. Members also share posts narrating the legendary history of the Oaxacan image. Finally, this page promotes rituals in members' homes and a large celebration on the eve of Juquila's feast (December 8). In other words, as pilgrims converge on the shrine in Oaxaca, devotees also come together in the United States.

Facebook pages maintained by pilgrimage groups are a distinct genre. Some elect to set their page up as a "public group" with members, while others create a profile as if their pilgrimage page were an individual with "Facebook friends." They can vary greatly in size. For example, market vendors in Oaxaca City maintain a group with only sixty-six members.[13] In contrast, large groups located in the state of Puebla employ personal profiles and list nearly five thousand friends.[14] In contrast to prayer groups, many of these people know each other personally.

On the surface, these pages have three functions: communication and coordination among organizers, information dissemination to participants and supporters, and the celebration of the group's annual journey. In this third aspect, the advent of social media offers an extraordinary advance in organizing capabilities. Most pilgrimage groups travel to the shrine between mid-November and early January, and thus a few months prior their leaders announce planning meetings and invite new pilgrims to join. Often these posts include selfies of happy devotees, images of the group in transit, and pictures taken at the shrine. Comments added to these posts often speak to individuals' eagerness to make the journey as well as their praise for the Virgin.[15] Additional posts discuss task delegation: for example, making posters/flyers, ordering T-shirts, and planning meals. Among larger groups, organizers often produce brightly colored posters in both hard copy and digital formats announcing the itinerary and naming sponsors. Rendered in the same style as announcements for village festivals, they appear plastered on the walls in towns and neighborhoods where members live. Some of them essentially convey a sociological sketch of the pilgrimage group, listing leaders, donors, drivers, and sponsors in order of importance. A digital version usually appears on the group's Facebook page too.[16] In addition, organizers often acknowledge donors with separate posts, including photographs and a celebratory caption. By design, these shout-outs appear in the members' feeds and presumably sometimes inspire other donors.[17] Groups also show off their custom hats and T-shirts and sometimes announce the following year's organizing committee.[18]

Local entrepreneurs also create advertisements and share them with the membership of pilgrimage groups. For example, in the fall of 2022, Mary Mauricio Méndez announced a parallel tour-bus pilgrimage and shared it on the Facebook page of Puebla's Juquila walking group from Tecamachalco.[19] Subsequently, another organized pilgrimage, the large cycling group from Huixcolotla, promoted the post on their page as well. Méndez structured the post as a burst of short phrases and punctuating emoji, pitching a carefully crafted three-day bus trip to Juquila designed to coincide with the arrival of cyclists and walkers from Huixcolotla on

November 17, 2022. This timing was a crucial facet: as planned, the bus pilgrimage would allow clients to approach the famed image alongside hundreds of other devotees from home, celebrate Mass at the shrine in community, and then join the celebrations at Huixcolotla's encampment afterward. To entice potential customers, Méndez also listed recreational stops and activities, including a side trip to Huatulco's beaches and an opportunity to eat breakfast and buy bread, chocolate, chili-marinated pork, and mescal in Oaxaca City's Mercado de Abastos.

Over the last two decades, it has become common to meet devotees on similar bus tours. During peak pilgrimage season, many are visible on the road, and they fill temporary parking lots in Juquila. In addition, these buses are readily identifiable in nearby beach towns thanks to banners and pilgrimage decorations. Some tours are quite elaborate. For example, bus pilgrims from Morelos (a state near Mexico City), described an extensive itinerary to me as they relaxed at a food stand near the basilica: Juquila, different beaches, natural marvels, Oaxacan market towns, archaeological sites, and, finally, the historic city of Oaxaca. One participant confided that it was her ninth Juquila bus trip, suggesting a much deeper connection than mere sightseeing.[20]

Is this tourism or devotion? Arguably it is both. Moreover, we should resist the temptation to see these practices as contradictory. Anthropologists specializing in pilgrimage, like Willy Jansen, suggest that the pervasive overlap and interaction of cultural practices at shrine sites renders distinctions unproductive and untenable.[21] Although chartered bus trips are easy to dismiss or overlook, devotees (like Doña Fina; see chapter 1) describe them as deeply meaningful social and religious experiences. Essentially, niche-marketing strategies have emerged among promoters of Juquila's devotion aimed at a broad spectrum of devotees, men and women, young and old. There is a way for everyone to visit Juquila.

It also makes sense that the local promoters of bus pilgrimages nestle their advertisements on the Facebook pages of cycling and walking groups. Typically, these groups have many online followers who do not ride or walk, such as the parents, friends, sisters, and supporters of the organizers and devotees. A bus trip synchronized with another pilgrimage from the community broadens the circle of communal participation and celebration at the shrine.

Finally, beyond promoting different modes of transit to Juquila, pilgrimage-related Facebook pages also serve as simple sharing platforms. Individual members and organizers upload photographs and video clips during and after the pilgrimage, documenting progress in the first instance, summarizing the journey at the end.[22] Group pages also serve as message boards. At the most basic level, members and administrators post greetings and blessings on religious holidays, but it is also relatively common to see birthday greetings, invitations to in-person events, and posts announcing members' important life events. Individuals also sometimes share posts from prayer-group pages and recitations of the Rosary on Facebook live.[23]

In this capacity pilgrimage groups are especially attentive when group members die. Posts often show the departed during past trips to the shrine, typically superimposing their images over dramatic landscapes alongside pictures of the Virgin of Juquila.[24] Digital memorials generate considerable activity; often, many members of the group are also rela-tives of the deceased. Individuals offer their sympathies in the comment section, testify to years of friendship, and post images and GIFs of graves and angels, black mourning ribbons, and crying emoji.[25]

In sum, Facebook pages run by pilgrimage groups are integrated into the dynamics of workplaces, neighborhoods, families, and towns. Ostensibly, they serve as mere bulletin boards for devotees and orga-nizers planning trips to the famous Oaxacan Virgin, but they also reveal deeper connections to daily life and both in-person and virtual social networks.

## YouTube

Sampling YouTube clips posted by Juquila's followers becomes a kind of archaeology of cultural expression and a testament to social media's rapid global dissemination in the last dozen years. On one level, the videos simply revisit a venerable tradition, the narration of pious travel. As such, they document the recent evolution of a long-standing genre, which in the digital realm mixes text, video, and music. Likewise, You-Tube provides us with an opportunity to develop a deeper understand-ing for devotee motivations and perspectives.

It is important to acknowledge the wider matrix of material on the platform because Juquila's followers consume and share this content, too, and the transfer of audio-visual techniques and tropes appears con-stant. For example, comments reveal that many pilgrims enjoy tourism videos in which Our Lady of Juquila presides over an enchanted land-scape, salt-of-the-earth people, vibrant folklore, centering calm, primor-dial fervor, and sublime grace. This material emerges from established marketing conventions: promoters have long sold Oaxaca as a quintes-sential, authentic space—*México ancestral*. Stereotypes pervade these advertisements, but it is an idealizing romanticism that many Mexicans applaud. Peregrinos, like the blanket weavers, Indigenous dancers, and makers of traditional *moles* (sauces), enact and represent primordial traditions. However, for the moment, religious Mexicans, not foreign tourists, remain the target audience.

Clearly, various realms of content creation are in conversation, and Juquila's devotees appear "connected" and on-trend. As new tools emerge, their videos appear more ambitious and exhibit higher production values. In truth, this is the logical extension of deeper patterns evident in the global history of pilgrimage. Just as devotees and promoters embraced advancements in previous eras—trains, photography, highways, print media, and bus tours—they now adopt new technologies and media that allow them to communicate better and, crucially, travel cheaper and safer.[26]

The earliest pilgrimage videos on YouTube date from about 2008, only a few years after the site's launch. Unsurprisingly, they are unsophisticated, often featuring brief montages of grainy photographs, rudimentary transitions, and minimalist captioning. Typically, these early do-it-yourself filmmakers merely added music to images, essentially producing devotional music videos.[27] Nonetheless, epic narrative peeks through.

A 2009 pilgrimage clip of the small Zapotec town of Guelavía, Oaxaca, offers a good example.[28] It begins with a title shot noting the year and celebrating the town's twenty-fourth annual trip to the shrine. Paired with a soaring 1980s English-language love ballad ("Right Here Waiting" by Richard Marx), images showing the group ambling through the mountains are interspersed with snapshots of resting friends and shared meals. The English lyrics make little sense, but the melody and gushy vocal performance suffuses the video with dramatic longing. Close to the end, group pictures tacitly announce, "We made it . . . together," and the final frame features the statement, "Saludos a los radicados en USA" (Greetings to those living in the USA), implying that beyond its local function, this video keeps emigrant *paisanos* connected. A wider sampling of videos reveals cultural variations. For example, Indigenous communities often include ritual dance and village bands. Thus, a video from the Mixe community of Tlahuitoltepec focuses on their famed brass ensemble, the Banda Filarmónica Rey Condoy Mixe, and dancers in typical outfits performing at the Juquila basilica.[29]

Between 2013 and 2015, longer, more elaborate videos became common. By this time, some veteran pilgrimage groups were posting videos to YouTube annually. Many of them reveal the hallmarks of novice filmmaking, with runtimes of one or two hours and haphazard transitions. Others hired tech support, which is readily available in Mexico, to produce more polished videos. In fact, it is relatively common to find

YouTube channels on which digital entrepreneurs posts pilgrimage videos alongside clips of local festivals, *quinceañeras,* and sporting events.[30]

Most clips, however, simply document the journey, showcasing camaraderie and struggle. Visual style, plotting, composition, and musical accompaniment reflect a vernacular marketing tool kit that draws on news media, documentary film, advertising, reality television, social media, and music videos for inspiration. There is no revolution in storytelling or filmmaking here. Innovation isn't the point. As Antonio Rubial García, a historian of colonial Catholicism, argues, pious genres typically foreground "the exemplary," embrace formulas, and stick to conventions.[31] Thus, pilgrimage films conform to long-standing expectations for how devout narratives should unfold, as well as how they should look and sound. The structure and ethos remain traditional, charting the episodic progress through a symbolic landscape: daily advancement, humble perseverance, good-natured fellowship, solidarity amid struggle, personal piety at emblematic locations, and a festive, votive spirit. As has long been true of pious display, competition between groups emerges in the attention lavished on meals, the celebration of pilgrimage anniversaries, decorative practices, and the musical groups hired to enliven the experience. Innovation appears in subtle but important decisions, like selecting music from Protestant artists, or centering female experience.

The cycling group from Candelaria Purificación, a town near Tepeaca, Puebla, offers a good example in its one-hour and twenty-four-minute video chronicling their 2014 trip to Juquila.[32] Featuring an all-male cast of riders, the video captures the mobile-fiesta character typical of large groups by using a music-video-montage framework. Tapping different genres—like corrido, praise pop, and norteño—they graft a series of songs to clips featuring devout riders. Most selections include Juquila-related lyrics proclaiming filial love, humility, and gratitude, and one of them narrates the official legend of the Virgin of Juquila's history.[33] Amid the climactic final climb, riders are shown battling fatigue to the sounds of Protestant power pop artists Miel San Marcos and Christine D'Clario performing their hit "No hay lugar más alto." The chorus repeats the song title's sermon-like "hook" wrapped in paradox: "There is no higher place . . . than being at your feet," echoing the common votive promise among pilgrims to "arrive at the soles of your feet." The video then moves deeper into ecumenical territory, ending with an evangelical Protestant folk hymn in Tzeltal Maya (a language that is not spoken in Puebla) by Fuente de Agua Viva. It is a curious choice and may represent an attempt to add a sheen of primordial authenticity, or it is perhaps an appropriation of something deemed elementally sacred if only vaguely understood.

Taking a different tack, a large walking group from Tlaxiaco, Oaxaca, posts carefully crafted documentaries. Calling their event "Caminata de Fe" (Walk of Faith) and presenting themselves as a production company called "Peregrino Films," the filmmakers upload polished pilgrimage videos on their own YouTube channel specializing in local events. Their ambitious goals first appear in the self-consciously titled "Anthropological Documentary" from 2014—a ten-part series of short videos featuring the stately, masculine voice-over common in radio advertising.[34] The series begins by placing Juquila in the context of pilgrimages worldwide and then offers a melodramatic chronicle of daily progress. In addition, the narrator explains devotional practices (which is rare), thus producing a social-science-style series.[35]

Caminata de la Fe, however, chose a different strategy for showcasing the following year's pilgrimage (2015), posting a single, fifty-two-minute documentary.[36] After a brief introduction, they jettison the male narrator and opt instead for a first-person female narration based on the testimonies of five different women. The text remains scripted, but a young woman voices these testimonials as a single account, airing feelings of self-doubt, charting struggle and resolve, chronicling an evolving appreciation for collective solidarity, voicing a sense of divine companionship, and celebrating spiritual joy and personal fulfillment. As with other videos, each day's challenges provide structure and rhythm. This distinct format, however, amplifies the self-discovery theme. Music establishes mood: soft orchestral pieces accompany introspective moments, ominous strings coincide with cold rain at twilight, and languid mariachi instrumentals complement sunny mountain traverses. If the group was hoping to attract a wider audience, it worked. The documentary is one of the most viewed Juquila videos on YouTube, with over 240,000 views as of July 2023.

The YouTube comments section provides space for praise and critique. Some refer to their own pilgrimages or laud "la Virgencita." In other instances, individuals claim to be recipients of miraculous intercession or personally call out to Our Lady of Juquila, asking for help.[37] Every so often, Protestant commenters criticize image devotion. Some assert that Satan is likely behind any miracles. Others seem to relish mocking pilgrims. For example, one troll scoffs at devotees and slanders Juquila as a "MUÑECA BARBIE . . . COLOR DE POPO" (Shit-colored Barbie).[38] Another refers to her as a disgusting doll, abhorrent and abominable.[39] Devotees respond, suggesting these critics mind their own business.

The videos posted by pilgrimage groups do not provide the full picture. Alongside them, we find videos produced for commercial and

promotional purposes. Some of these clips mix advertising and devotion. At the upper end of production values are the videos produced by
the tourism industry, which often reside on YouTube channels such as
Vive Oaxaca, Sobre Tierra Oaxaqueña, and Oaxaca Bonito. They employ drones and slow-motion, time-lapse sequences. They, too, often
utilize the music-video style, although they almost always choose up-
beat generic electronic music of the kind that accompanies dramatic TV
series and romantic comedies. They are also fond of the loosely repurposed variation of the quick-cut, falling-in-love montage typical of the
latter.[40] In some instances, these clips copy the episodic narrative style
of many devotee-made videos. For example, an advertisement produced
by Oaxaca's state government builds their sales pitch around an attractive, wide-eyed bourgeois couple enjoying the rustic marvels of Oaxaca,
guided by the soothing, baritone-voiced narrator extolling "millenarian
traditions," natural wonders, and the region's mystical, life-changing
powers. Deploying personal-discovery tropes, the narrator implores,
"Take a pilgrimage to yourself."

The video pedals a dreamy, vaguely devout cultural nationalism,
which frames pilgrimage in a warm, golden glow. We never hear devotees' voices, and we contemplate the actors portraying them from a
distance. In addition, the locals they encounter share their traditions
and serve them local delicacies. At the end, we see the adorable duo
approaching Juquila's altar, heads reverently bowed, floral offerings cra-
dled in their arms, as the narrator entices: "Oaxaca is a journey. Choose
your route. The Route of Faith, Juquila."[41] Remarkably, this advertisement idealizes the locations along the route to an extent that makes
them nearly unrecognizable, sanitizing the loud, gritty realities of the
road to Juquila. Nonetheless, a core commonality links tourism videos
and devotee clips: in both cases, the message is that Juquila will transform you.

More humble promoters also contribute content—for example, a
handful of "influencers" offer Juquila featurettes, which tend to be niche
marketed: vlogs from young couples, a motorcycle enthusiast's road-
trip video, bus companies promoting tours, and a DIY children's travel
channel.[42] In a different vein, a local Oaxacan band, Los Borja, offers a
music video in which they sing about and dramatize a visit to Juquila,
complete with performing traditional votive practices.[43] At the end, they
include a phone number for bookings. This set of examples may seem
transparently commercial, but the intertwining of devotion and commerce is both common and traditional.[44] Requesting "help in business,"
increasing sales, and attracting clients were part of votive petitioning
long before the advent of the internet.

Official Catholic Church postings, on the other hand, are typically staid and unimaginative. For example, they offer overlong videos of low-resolution, live-streamed Masses on Juquila's feast day or short benedictions from the shrine.[45] Personal concerns and requests for miraculous intervention are absent. In truth, the authorities are trying to catch up with an autonomous online practice sustained by devotees, inserting themselves within a wider network of online, Juquila-related communication. There is no need to exhort this population to embrace Marian devotion, however. The church's message via rituals and sermons is simple: it exhorts devotees to focus their energies on becoming better Catholics by taking part in priest-mediated services and sacraments and fully embracing its moral teachings. Individual devotional practice barely earns any mention at all. Given the modest number of views documented on YouTube, Juquila's followers are not very interested in these messages. Devotees participate in standard liturgies as they fit within pilgrimage and shrine activities, but they cling to individual practices centered on personal bonds of love and miraculous support connected to Juquilita.

The Catholic clergy rarely plays a prominent role in group pilgrimages. I know of only one parish where a priest founded the town's annual pilgrimage.[46] Sometimes an individual priest accompanies parishioners to Juquila. For example, Padre Martín Rodríguez, a priest with his own YouTube channel, traveled to Juquila with his parish's cycling group in 2019 and posted videos of his interviews with pilgrims. He attempts to convey doctrine through lighthearted dialogues with children include marking doctrinal errors with a baffled Jesus emoji.[47]

Mostly, however, Catholic authorities remain at a distance from pilgrimage on YouTube. The notable exception remains the promotional campaign for Juquila's pontifical coronation on October 8, 2014. Online video promotion was only part of this effort. The image received an elaborate, heavy-handed makeover, and the archdiocese sent out press releases and posted explanatory guides to Juquila's revamped look and more complicated iconography. Posters appeared online and on city walls, extolling the Virgin's crowning. Banners also festooned churches in the state capital.[48] Many clips of the event featuring the archbishop and a dozen additional prelates remain on YouTube.[49] Some offer the exhaustive, nearly four-hour spectacle.[50] The most viewed videos of the coronation, however, are highlight videos from tourism promoters.[51]

It bears mentioning that devotees who routinely visit the shrine rarely mention the coronation. Pilgrims do not need the Vatican's seal of approval; their commitment remains rooted in collective and personal traditions. In addition, coronation videos are dull. They lack the rhythm and intimacy of many pilgrim clips. YouTube's statistics underscore the contrast: Peregrino Films' women-centered documentary garnered 191,000 views and 902 likes; meanwhile, the most popular coronation video on YouTube boasts only 21,000 views and 173 likes.[52]

Individuals within the church do, however, show impressive results when they take the initiative. For example, a YouTuber priest from Mexico City, Padre José de Jesús Aguilar Valdés, cultivates an audience like a secular podcast host or influencer. He posts shorts centered on Catholic trivia, live-streamed Masses, and simple, brief answers to doctrinal questions alongside church-related travel clips. On camera he communicates like a friendly, learned uncle. In his Juquila video, he recounts the official history of the image rooted in Ruiz y Cervantes's *Memorias*, describes devotional traditions, and takes the viewer to key landmarks along the route. His video had amassed an impressive 645,000 views by August 2021, a mere two months after its initial posting.[53]

## Networked Devotion and the New Promotional Landscape

Almost at the internet's inception, scholars began to debate the web's impact on religion. Predictions that it would render churches obsolete and neutralize the power of religious hierarchies never materialized. In fact, many denominations quickly became quite effective at using new technologies for outreach, internal communication, and recruitment, while user-produced content and sharing practices often extended institutional messaging. Heidi Campbell, one of the most prominent researchers analyzing "digital religion," refers to the increasing prevalence of "networked religion."[54] By this she means that many individuals seamlessly sustain traditional in-person, collective religious identities while also embracing new online practices and virtual religious community. In her view, it isn't a question of separate spheres: social media facilitates participants' increasing disregard for imagined borders between spirituality, mundane activities, and traditional, in-person religious experiences. Information, practices, and expressive forms flow freely among these realms, and users often consume content from a variety of sources simultaneously.

Simple continuity, however, is not what Campbell emphasizes. She underscores networked religion's complexities: its facilitation of serialized individual self-fashioning, ongoing hybridity of practices, and multisite lived realities. Campbell does not engage pilgrimage or Catholicism directly, but the Juquila-related evidence on Facebook and YouTube echoes her insights. Devotees using these platforms to access information about Our Lady of Juquila and her devotion make wider

personal connections and post promotional material of their own making. This content then circulates in conversation with commercial and
government-funded religious tourism promotion, as well as archdiocesan official, and semiofficial, publicity efforts.

Another circle of discussion anchored in anthropological scholarship
on Catholicism employs the concept of "mediatization" to describe the
ubiquity of media technologies and logics in nearly all social spheres,
including religion, and their ability to shape cultural interactions.[55]
From this perspective, the older concept of "mediation," which refers
to institutions and actors who served as conduits of ideas and nodes of
information transfer, no longer suffices. But Catholicism, these scholars suggest, seems designed for our era. Venerable teachings on priestly
mediation and saintly intercession alongside the sensory, performative
practices, and the enduring emphasis on images and objects as transmitters of grace, have deep roots. Simultaneously, the modernizing Catholic Church of the late nineteenth and twentieth centuries tended to
embrace new communication technologies. The current level of media
saturation, however, is unique. For many devout individuals, there is
nothing remarkable about engaging a steady stream of religious messaging from Catholic institutions and individual content creators.

Pilgrimage-related material online offers us a glimpse into a particular
corner of the digital religion phenomenon where social media provides
a powerful new tool for devotee communication. In this space, participants consume and deploy storylines, metaphors, and settings drawn
from Catholic teaching, tradition, and legend, but they also tap film,
fiction, popular music genres, and advertising. Present-day pilgrimage
is also awash in ideas and contemporary discourses of wellness and personal improvement. Given this complex set of connections and inter-
sections, social media, it would appear, is a natural fit for pilgrimage
devotion.

In this sense, the insights of anthropologist Simon Coleman pair well
with the interventions of digital religion scholars.[56] He stresses that pilgrimage has proven itself a "great cultural success story" because of its
boundary-blurring nature. It isn't, in his view, simply religious. Pilgrimage thrives in flexible "articulation" between realms labeled "religious"
and others presumed "rational" or "secular," such as politics and economics. Furthermore, devotees commonly slip in and out of devotional,
work-related, and leisure-centered mentalities and emotional states
while traveling to shrines, and even after they've arrived at the ostensibly
sacred destination. To put this in the argot of the internet, the braiding
of secular connections within a loose religious repertoire is "a feature,
not a bug" of pilgrimage.

It is still too early to tell if social media will fundamentally change pilgrimage. Many traditional practices and expressive customs work quite well in online spaces. Access to various platforms, computers, smart phones, and software appear to be fueling pilgrimage devotion by making it easier for devotees to communicate with each other, express feelings, fashion online identities, and promote their devotion. In other words, Facebook and YouTube appear to be expanding and enlivening Juquila's pilgrimage. Are these online media dynamics also shaping the way devotees make sense of devotion? If that is the case, perhaps they are setting the stage for profound transformation.

# CHAPTER 6

# A Contingent Alchemy

In a sense, every organized pilgrimage is a play, a play featuring a loose script reinterpreted by a changing cast of characters every year. Caminando Juntos, a group of devotees of varying age, experience, ability, and commitment taught me this over several years of conversations, observation, and friendship. As with almost any collective endeavor, particularly one that entails several days in close contact, nuanced social dynamics emerge if you spend time with the participants and observe their varied roles. But such things are not obvious if you ponder pilgrims from afar or while peering out the car window as they walk past in matching shirts and safety vests. You must get closer. Although this should have been obvious from the start, it hadn't crossed my mind when I joined Caminando Juntos in 2016. I imagined traversing about 120 miles in six days from Oaxaca City to Juquila as a habitual kinetic rite—cherished, cultivated, and sustained year after year by a standing company of devout sojourners. What I learned, however, is that for most devotees, life is too complicated for inflexible commitments.

Caminando Juntos is the shorthand version of their name. No one can offer an actual inauguration date for the group. They don't mark an anniversary, carry traditional standards, or announce a tally of shrine visits, like many other groups. The Abastos pilgrims coalesced gradually, as relatives, friends, and coworkers in the fruit stalls of the sprawling public market joined streams of devotees from various communities heading to the shrine each November and December. Some members began traveling to Juquila with other groups and then, without much forethought, banded together. At times, they have used longer names, like Grupo de Amigos Caminando Juntos Bajo una Misma Fe (Group of Friends Walking Together of the Same Singular Faith) or Caminando Juntos con una Misma Fe (Walking Together of the Same

Singular Faith). In 2021 they added *sin fronteras* (without borders), after Santiago recruited additional devotees from Texas. These longer variants fit on the vinyl banners commissioned from a shop near the market, which pilgrims stretch across the sides of their support trucks, but long names don't work well on hats and T-shirts. Somebody opted for the simple, evocative Caminando Juntos—Walking Together—when creating their Facebook group. It also fits nicely below the machine-embroidered representation of Juquila stitched on matching caps: bold primary red for 2016 and commanding navy blue in 2018. As is often the case, Juquila appears delta-shaped and logo-like thanks to the stylized drape of her vestments. Best of all, Caminando Juntos has a poetic simplicity. This group is truly and simply "walking together," literally and figuratively.

Appellations aside, pilgrimages are subject to a contingent social alchemy. Groups feature nurturing stalwarts, meticulous planners, charismatic recruiters, and savvy fundraisers, but they can also include slackers and malcontents.

Essentially, there is something extraordinary about walking one hundred or two hundred miles with a group. The shared struggle over seemingly endless terrain and the sheer number of hours of companionship provide the time to share hopes, worries, histories, and trifles. The experience offers a cocktail of time, pace, rhythm, exertion, and vision. En route to Juquila, plodding and exhausted, I often found myself looking ahead, mostly due south, contemplating the mountainous folds of the Sierra Sur, like successive waves, scanning the horizon where Juquila resides. It defies belief that the journey will require hiking up and down those looming ridges, but a glance back to the northeast reveals the knotted ranges already traversed and sparks a realization, "I've already crossed all that?" A bit of figuring suggests that perhaps a dozen miles remain before nightfall, and some days have surpassed thirty miles of hiking. Mulling miles conquered and ridges crested makes the remaining trek less daunting.

The periods of rest and repast are also crucial. Pilgrimage entails taking meals with your colleagues, over and over. At times you're mixed in with other groups, some hailing from distant towns in neighboring states, some easily double what Caminando Juntos attempts in both distance and time. A few individuals live in the United States, although they are originally from Mexico. In other words, people and entire families return to the shrine and their homeland from cities as distant and disparate as Toppenish, Trenton, Tecamachalco, and Tlaxiaco. But the pilgrimage's bedrock spirit isn't in the casual meetups on the trail. The social magic resides in serial communion of a mundane, rather than sacramental, sort: the pan dulce and sweet coffee before dawn, the *memelas* (thick, toasted corn tortillas slathered with beans and crumbled cheese) and Fanta at mid-morning, the *barbacoa* and beer midafternoon, and, maybe best of all, the grilled *tasajo* (steak), handmade tortillas, and *frijolitos* (beans) after sunset.

This dynamic explains why veteran pilgrims often speak in terms of "getting hooked" on pilgrimage. Javier, a construction worker who is part of a group from Coscomatepec, Veracruz, describes joining as merely one of the *muchachos* (boys) and promising to visit Juquila three times: a commonplace vow (*manda*), a trinity of treks. In 2016, he was taking his seventh successive trip to the shrine, but now he manned *la punta* (the point), walking alongside his group's Virgin of Juquila standard. He had become the route finder on the tricky slopes of the Orizaba Volcano and the twisting shortcuts between Coscomatepec and Oaxaca's Sierra Sur.[1]

There seems to be something special about the bonds cultivated among walking pilgrimages. For example, divergent levels of cohesion and enthusiasm are readily apparent between the walking pilgrims and the cycling pilgrims of Acatzingo. After grinding out over two hundred miles in fourteen days, the town's walkers flash a trail-hardened solidarity and devout swagger. In 2018, at least, they seemed to dwarf the far more numerous cyclists by pure dint of zeal.

Other variations are apparent as well. Some groups are highly regimented, whereas others, like Caminando Juntos, are almost improvisational. Large groups embrace discipline and planning. They have no choice. Thus, in late June, five months before their pilgrimage, organizers travel the entire length of the route, from their hometowns to Juquila, securing campsites and making agreements with friendly merchants who donate meals at stopovers.[2]

At the opposite end of the spectrum, some devotees head to Juquila without any planning or provisions, counting on Juquila's miraculous support during their journey. For example, Camila, a woman from Oaxaca, described her mother's desperate *peregrinación de limosna* (alms pilgrimage): Camila's older brother suffered from frequent seizures as a child, which her mother feared would result in permanent dependency. Impulsively, this woman set out for the shrine with the boy in tow and a small amount of money sewn into her clothes, intending to cure him or bury him in Juquila. She soon found, however, that any attempt to buy food resulted in her money's inexplicable disappearance. She concluded that she must embrace a deliberate, radical dependence on serendipity and charity. She had to demonstrate extraordinary faith and resignation, trusting the Virgin of Juquila to provide protection, food, and shelter. According to family lore, Juquilita came through. Mother and son made it to the shrine, and the boy (now a man) never suffered another seizure.[3]

Regardless of preparation or faith, waxing and waning participation is a reality. Tensions exist in every group. Some are deeply rooted in shared histories and lasting conflicts; others erupt as tempers flare amid the stress and fatigue of the pilgrimage. Kino, for example, describes growing up with many of the other men in Caminando Juntos and taking part in several pilgrimages before quitting due to unspecified disagreements. Then, he simply set aside his frustrations and rejoined in 2016.[4] A few years earlier, a larger market-vendor pilgrimage split in two. According to Silvio and Santiago, the rift centered on whether to accommodate unfit participants and slow the group's progress to support stragglers. Those who remain in Caminando Juntos agreed to sacrifice speed and efficiency to sustain a leave-no-one-behind ethos. They maintain good relations with their former colleagues, though, and reunification remains a perennial topic.[5]

Of course, groups sometimes naturally cease to exist, most likely when pivotal leaders retire or step down. Typically, pilgrimage organizers describe feeling overwhelmed by responsibilities, the year-round time commitment required to fundraise and plan, and the sleepless nights during the journey as they manage the logistic tasks and keep everyone safe.

In sum, each pilgrimage group remains somewhat ephemeral, even vulnerable. It is hardly surprising that most groups are not very old. Many are fifteen to twenty-five years old, but only a few can claim 1960s foundations, like Huixcolotla's cyclists. Even among institutionalized pilgrimages—those with elected officers, hometown chapels, and formalized fundraising mechanisms—each year's journey is distinct. In other words, there is a lightning-in-a-bottle quality to each shrine sortie, and perhaps therein lies its attraction. The collective sentiment that accompanies communion on the road can be quite inspiring, and feel fresh, year after year.

Still, for myself, grasping the unstable nature of each group brought on a sense of disappointment. The full cast of pilgrims I grew fond of in 2016 was no longer together in 2018. In fact, approximately 50 percent of the fellowship no longer participated. By 2022, only Santiago, Silvio, Marta, Francisco, and Manuel remained, alongside several new additions.

And yet . . . Caminando Juntos endures—*sigue caminando.*

# Leadership

During the summer months, Santiago begins thinking about the pilgrimage to Juquila. He often sends out a query through Facebook: a who's-in, who's-out, we-need-to-start-planning post.[6] Santiago lives in Texas, but he was born in a village near Ocotlán, an important Zapotec municipality in the southernmost of Oaxaca's Central Valleys. Bustling towns like Ocotlán are a big part of the state's enthusiastically marketed reputation as a locus of traditional culture thanks to its vibrant Day of the Dead celebrations, folk art, impoverished but assertive Indigenous peoples, and unique cuisine. Witness Walt Disney's blockbuster *Coco*, set in a fictional community partially modeled on San Martín Tilcajete, a town close to Ocotlán.

Santiago would have remained in Oaxaca if circumstances hadn't forced him to make hard choices. He prefers the rhythms and customs of Mexico. Like so many others in the region, when his prospects seemed dim at home, he sought opportunity in the United States. Santiago, however, doesn't fret over the past.[7] In his late forties, an amiable figure, he feels a special connection to the Virgin of Juquila. His wife's chronic hip problem keeps her from joining the pilgrimage, but she is healthy otherwise. His two children are US citizens, earning good grades in North American public schools and making their parents proud. It isn't clear if they want to do the pilgrimage, but they can't get away in late November anyway due to the school calendar. Santiago brings the whole family to Oaxaca when he can: typically, on marathon road trips. Taking part in the walking pilgrimage, therefore, represents an individual commitment for Santiago. This is a surprisingly common phenomenon. Many men who embrace walking pilgrimage describe similar situations: their families support their devotion but don't join them.

Santiago's life story offers a classic example of peripatetic, immigrant perseverance, which is partly rooted in his faith. He left Oaxaca as a young man and worked for several years as the soundman and roadie for a *cumbia* band touring the Mexican dancehall circuit in the North American Southwest. Then he returned home, trying his hand as a cab driver and tour guide until a violent, intractable teachers' strike upended the Oaxacan economy in 2006. For many locals, the lasting turmoil felt like a debilitating economic siege as they tried to survive with little or no income. Pragmatic about disorder in Oaxaca, he returned to Texas, embracing life as a technician for various heating and cooling companies, before starting his own business. Santiago credits the Virgin of Juquila with his success. In fact, he named his company in her honor.

On the trail, Santiago serves as medic and philosopher. He hands out the equivalent of acetaminophen and ibuprofen, as needed, provides occasional shots of mescal before difficult climbs, and massages sore muscles. He is thoughtful about life in general, and he is convinced that Juquilita's advocacy has helped him. At the same time, he is somewhat ambivalent about the institutional church, although proud to be Catholic. Santiago unabashedly defends his beliefs in the face of Protestant critics, detailing the difference between veneration and adoration in Catholic thought. Moreover, he sees the Juquila devotion as his tradition, his inheritance. He doesn't cede the image to priests: "Religions, Catholic or Protestant, once you get past people's beliefs and customs," he claims, "son negocio" (they are businesses).[8]

Marta, an important, somewhat reserved member of Caminando Juntos, the daughter of Don Valentín (see chapter 4), and a fourth-generation vendor, spends her days managing the family bodega, often wearing a black apron featuring the enlarged, blue likeness of Eeyore, the gloomy-cute donkey of Winnie-the-Pooh fame. Gradually, as her parents age, Marta is taking control of the family business, and like so many bodega owners, she seems to live in the market. Serious and efficient, she constantly moves between the handsome, colorful piles of fruit and a display case of homemade sweets, attending to customers.

Marta has been walking to Juquila longer than anyone else in Caminando Juntos, starting perhaps twenty-five years ago. She and her family enjoy a public reputation as devotees, pilgrims, and patrons of Juquilita's devotion. They, too, believe Juquila's favor and protection has been a crucial factor in their economic success. Her leadership approach is subtle. A behind-the-scenes, steady figure, Marta excels at arranging for supplies, hence discussions of logistics and organization flow through La Carmencita. She is also the conduit of important resources. Her father, Don Valentín, lets Caminando Juntos use his pickup truck, and he donates fuel and pays a driver to ferry their supplies.

Silvio, Marta's cousin and the owner of another bodega perhaps one hundred yards away, plays a distinct role. In a sense, he functions as the social glue of Caminando Juntos. Many mention him in describing their initial connection to the pilgrimage: growing up with him in the frenetic warren of Abastos, playing soccer alongside him as adolescents, going to school with his son, or, as in Marta's case, being his cousin. Stocky and jovial, Silvio is almost always warm and chatty. His open, friendly persona has much do with the group's existence and endurance. He is a more-is-better character, inviting friends and associates to come along.

Silvio isn't, however, a methodical planner like some other pilgrimage organizers. He is a figure-it-out-as-we-go *simpático* who doesn't see

himself as *el responsable* (the boss). Instead, he plays the role of the affable big brother. In fact, some more detail-oriented members of the
group privately grumble about his occasional failure to follow through
on tasks. Nonetheless, his bodega serves as the meeting point and staging area. The group's copy of Our Lady of Juquila resides on an altar in
his shop. There she remains most days of the year, adorned and arrayed
for the pilgrimage amid family photographs, clutter, and fruit crates. Sig-
nificantly, several devotees point to Silvio's generous spirit on the trail
as a key reason for their participation in Caminando Juntos. He makes
a point of accompanying the most out-of-shape pilgrims at the back of
the pack and helping them persevere.

Alicia (see chapter 1) represents a different kind of pilgrim. She is a
young accountant who credits Silvio's attention to safety as the funda-
mental reason for her presence in Caminando Juntos. In 2016, at the age
of twenty-eight, she took part in her third pilgrimage and convinced
Francisco, her fiancé (as of 2018, husband), to join the group too. The
two of them are professionals with advanced degrees, and they are aware
that this sets them apart. Alicia chafes at class prejudices caricaturing
pilgrims as ignorant fanatics. She rejects any notion of incongruence in
her identity as both an educated woman and an ardent pilgrim.

Alicia also exemplifies a particular approach to image devotion. She
joined the group in 2014, seeking Juquila's help for her diabetic mother's
precarious health. She desperately wanted her mother to improve and
enjoy her remaining years, not simply endure them. She made her first
trip, plead her case at the shrine, and credited Juquila with her mother's
subsequent improvement. In addition, she spoke hopefully about eventually convincing her siblings to join the group.

In essence, Alicia takes personal and spiritual responsibility for the
well-being of her loved ones, views Juquila as a close ally, and wants to
share her devotion with others. Not surprisingly, she leads prayers on
the trail and penitential acts at the shrine. In 2017, she walked alongside her now-husband Francisco again, and she gave birth to a healthy
daughter several months later. Few match her enthusiasm: she loves the
camaraderie and claims pilgrimage facilitated greater self-awareness and
a deeper understanding of her faith. She and Francisco sometimes host
group gatherings at their home as well.[9]

Only Juan articulates a similar zeal. Warm-hearted and friendly, he
is driven to organize fellow Catholics for holidays, prayer, courses, pilgrimage, and personal transformation. In many ways, he represents the
voice of contemporary church teachings within the group. His views,
sketched here, may make him seem like a stickler for reserved personal
piety, but he shared these thoughts with me privately, months after the

2016 pilgrimage. On the trail, Juan is a thoughtful and generous comrade. He doesn't lecture other devotees. He attempts to lead by example.

Juan has been drawn to church activism since he was quite young in his native Coscomatepec, Veracruz, where a pastor made him a catechism coordinator at age thirteen. But in 1994, he moved to Oaxaca when his parents' marriage collapsed in dysfunction and discord. In key ways, however, he remained an outsider. He didn't grow up in the market's tangle of fruit stands, and he has no family ties to the other devotees. Juan became acquainted with the group as Raúl's employee. He works long hours, officiates weekend soccer games, and teaches marriage and catechism classes at his parish outside the city limits. Likewise, from 2009 to 2017, he organized preparations for Caminando Juntos, calling meetings and then creating and administering the group's Facebook page. In 2018, he quit working for Raúl, began driving a taxi, and joined a different pilgrimage group closer to home.

In many ways he was the group's scholar, having eagerly completed a spectrum of lay trainings offered by the parishes he has attended over the years. He laments abandoning school to work while still young, but Catholic activism gives him a sense of purpose. His "mania" for organizing, he jokes, is a personal defect: "Almost all year round I'm busy bringing people together."[10]

For some, Juan suspects, he takes his faith too seriously. Neither his wife nor his daughters embrace his zeal for parish activities or pilgrimage. Their reticence, he feels, stems from an unwillingness to give time and effort or to weather discomforts. His daughters, he fears, are distancing themselves from the faith as their education advances. Undaunted, Juan represents a Catholicism centered on individual accountability, firm moral commitments, and reasoned consistency.

Pilgrimage, in Juan's view, shouldn't be centered on miracles, effusive gratitude, and short-term *juramentos* (oaths). It is relatively common for men who go to Juquila to swear off alcohol for a stipulated period, which he finds superficial. He also doesn't support initiatory pilgrimage god parentage traditions (*padrino/a de levantada* or *padrino/a de velación*). These practices may feel good momentarily, he asserts, but often they represent little more than reenacting an old script. Juan has even turned down requests to serve as a *padrino* for other members of the group.[11] His stance, however, suggests he has missed the important social function of this practice. When I've witnessed veteran pilgrims *levantar* (initiate) new participants at the shrine, it seems clear that the main purpose is conveying belonging to the group and an emergent bond between veteran and novice devotees. The ritual aspect is simple and unscripted: a sign of the cross on the new pilgrims' foreheads and the placement of a modest scapular and image of Juquila around their necks, followed by a few words about devotion. Immediately afterward, the participants begin calling each other *compadre* or *comadre*. It may not fundamentally alter their behavior, but the resultant bond may prove important.

In a sense, Juan channels post–Vatican II teachings. He believes pilgrimage should inspire contemplative self-examination and moral transformation. Ideally, devotees return from Juquila ready to sustain their personal obligations, amend ethical shortcomings, and plow their energies into pastoral work. They shouldn't seek miracles; they should be firm in their faith without them. Juan acknowledges wayward periods in his own past, but he claims that most people, although good-hearted, remain lazy, unreliable, and ignorant. As he notes, "We don't want to be bothered. . . . We don't like to serve. We don't want to abandon our immoral habits."[12] Most of us, Juan tells me—including pilgrims tearfully approaching the four-hundred-year-old image in Juquila—do not intend to change.

## Preparation and Departure

Pilgrimage groups need figures like Santiago, Marta, Silvio, Alicia, and Juan. Other participants make significant contributions, but for Caminando Juntos this quintet took on the most important tasks in 2016. In talking to an array of pilgrimage organizers, I have found that certain debates reoccur repeatedly: for example, should the group bring a cook and food for the whole pilgrimage? It is the most economical choice, but it requires greater logistic effort. Also, planned meals sometimes inspire complaints because of differing tastes. Many groups, however, must bring their own food to save money. Such meals are often quite good.

Don Carlos, the leader of Coscomatepec's walking pilgrimage, emphasizes the importance of sustaining the devotees' strength and boosting morale with hearty meals. Just as he preplans every stopover during his group's fourteen-day trek to the shrine, he crafts menus for the group. He even reprises particularly popular dishes year after year in the same locations. Such was the case with the hearty seafood stew they shared with me when they paused mid-morning in the city of Oaxaca on day seven of their trek. Not surprisingly, devotees look forward to these feasts, as well as their annual stop at an artisan ice cream maker's stand in Zimatlán. The owner, a friend of Don Carlos, gives every pilgrim a complimentary bowl or cone of their choice.

Another common challenge revolves around securing support vehicles, and organizers do this ahead of time. Among the other arrangements requiring attention are collecting cash contributions, commissioning

T-shirts, hats, and safety vests, arranging snacks and sandwiches for the first night's trek, rounding up first aid supplies, scheduling and paying for Masses—one to bless the beginning of the pilgrimage, one to mark their arrival in Juquila, and another when pilgrims return home. Additionally, a member of the group must secure banners and purchase flowers and streamers to decorate the support vehicles. The Abastos pilgrims organize meetings in the weeks preceding their departure and divvy up the various tasks. However, despite their best efforts, in many ways Caminando Juntos comes together in the frenetic handful of days preceding departure.

There is a commonsense reason for what can seem like an unwillingness to plan. For many working-class Mexicans, taking part in pilgrimage is, by necessity, a last-minute decision. They cannot be sure they can afford the minimum contribution, expenses along the way, or the time away from work. Thus, in many groups, there is a flurry of activity before departure, as undecided individuals finally commit. Often organizers don't know their group's full size until moments before they set off. In some instances, even leaders within the group withdraw from participation at the last minute because of other obligations. In sum, pilgrimage groups must accommodate uncertainty.

The departure Mass, scheduled for 4 p.m., is really when Caminando Juntos begins. By 4:30 the impatient priest who officiates at the chapel near the market is reprimanding arriving devotees because of their tardiness. By 4:40 p.m., with the gathering beginning to swell, he sternly shepherds the devotees into the humble, cream-and-buff-colored, mix-and-match space. Bare compact fluorescent bulbs hang above the aisles, and strips of tiny LED bulbs stripe each column spaced at twenty-foot intervals. The overall impact remains dreary, but it serves its purpose. The priest marches through the liturgy with a short sermon, Communion (which few devotees take), and a sprinkling of holy water on the attendees at the beginning and end. In less than an hour, the eager pilgrims and their families are back at the bodegas loading the support vehicles and decorating them.

Raúl's bright-orange, large fruit truck stands at the end of a row of bodegas, newly washed and swept clean. In Mexico this kind of vehicle is called a *torton*, the hulking workhorse of the fruit-and-vegetable trade. It rests, cheery and glossy, with its custom wooden bed and cinched tarpaulin cover, as the buzz of preparations take place all around it. This type of vehicle is, in fact, emblematic of pilgrimage and local commerce. If countries had national trucks, like they have national birds, Mexico's would be the torton, due to its ubiquity, utility, and expressive variation. Characterized by a standard heavy-duty truck engine and cab paired with customized, heavy, brightly painted, wooden cargo beds, they are easily adapted to different loads: everything from fruit to family. Adding planks parallel to the floor creates a double-decker cargo bay; attaching arched metal tubing to the top and spanning the space below with taught, burly tarps protects merchandise and pilgrims. It is common to see tortons grinding their way along Mexico's highways brim full of vegetables and fruit or crammed with seemingly miserable livestock. Craftsmen in Acatzingo, Puebla, in fact, enjoy recognition throughout the region for their expertise in building these custom cargo holds. Pilgrims then festoon these workhorses with streamers, flowers, banners, and images. In some instances, devotees grace the crown of their cabs with stunning, handwoven palm-leaf arches. Torch-bearing relay pilgrimages attach metal staircases to the back so that runners can hop on and off with ease.

Caminando Juntos only has Raúl's torton, and this single vehicle carries most of the group's supplies during the journey to Juquila. The larger the pilgrimage, the more numerous the tortons and pickups. Kino stands in the tailgate opening, pondering his colleagues' frenetic preparations from above, ready to accommodate luggage, bedding, and supplies. Although lighter in hue, mounds of fresh oranges (the truck's usual cargo) and heaps of pale, yellow grapefruit sit to one side, edible berms shielding Raúl's bodega. Shimmering above the piles of citrus, an array of large, traditional star-shaped piñatas beckons purchasers and passersby, a seasonal attempt to move additional merchandise alongside fruit. Above the truck's cab, a pair of slogans broadcast Raúl's religious sentiments and hint at merchant livelihood simultaneously: "Dios es Amor" (God Is Love) and "Fruto Bendito" (Divine Fruit).

Raúl doesn't seek a leadership role, but he commands respect by virtue of his quiet, steady demeanor. At meals or on the trail, he is happy to talk about Juquila's role in his life. He points out that commercial success and a public association with Our Lady of Juquila sometimes attracts new devotees. Some individuals embrace pilgrimage in hopes of an immediate uptick in their fortunes. Raúl, as evidenced by his gleaming torton, understands these feelings, but he warns against facile connections. Juquila, he suggests, doesn't work that way. Her intercession unfolds gradually and mysteriously.

Although he lends his truck, Raúl hires Mario to drive throughout the pilgrimage, dons a wide-brimmed hat, takes up the emblematic walking stick, and makes his way to the shrine on foot with the rest of the group. He assures me that embracing pilgrimage helped him recenter his life. Juquila's guidance and protection, he attests, allow him to focus on work and family, model probity for his children, and embrace life as a dutiful husband.

In short order, peregrinos, alongside friends and family members—a hodgepodge of men, women, and a few teens—encircle the poppy-colored torton and a pair of pickup trucks and begin decorating. They tenderly tie framed images of Juquila to their grills and fix bountiful, fresh floral arrangements to the big rig's heavy-duty bumper. They also run strings of multicolored pennants across the sides and unfurl custom-made vinyl banners. Bodegeros are adept and efficient when it comes to tying down virtually anything, but when it comes to the banners, they take their time: tugging, talking, stepping back, tightening, and conferring anew—gradually they make each banner taught, secure, and straight. If hung hastily, banners quickly end up as roadside litter.

Meanwhile, within Silvio's bodega, Santiago and Gustavo, a young itinerate vendor who spends his days driving a pickup truck laden with fruit to outlying villages, start rigging a do-it-yourself carrier for the group's copy of the Virgin of Juquila. Many pilgrim groups commission artisans to make portable glass-covered cases, vitrinas, to house their images while they trek to the shrine. Caminando Juntos had not gotten one in 2016. (They would in 2018, although it broke en route to Juquila.)

Other groups display hand-painted or embroidered cloth standards, which they commission or fashion themselves. Placed on a cross-like pole, many walking pilgrims carry these almost heraldic emblems to keep the group together and broadcast their origins. For example, the walking devotees from Coscomatepec, Veracruz, led by Don Carlos, carry a standard featuring Juquila, which they call *La Generala* (the lady general). She always leads their pilgrimage, and another standard, de-picting their town's patron saint, John the Baptist (San Juanito, they call him), brings up the rear. At each stop, every pilgrim pauses and kisses the Juquila standard before seeking a place to rest.

Throughout the pilgrimage, devotees identify other groups by their standards, T-shirts, and banners (see plate 8). In a sense, it is how they know and remember each other, and it is not uncommon for them to encounter the same groups every year. Naturally, there is a touch of com-petition involved, although unacknowledged. Pilgrims notice attractive sportswear, vitrinas, and standards, as well as impressive truck altars and decorative innovations. Public recognition can, in turn, spur ob-servers to upgrade their own symbols and décor in subsequent years. Of course, ornamental improvement is a matter of aesthetic taste. The hand-painted banners and standards typical of relatively new groups are often attractive, but more established pilgrimages usually opt for the glossy vinyl alternatives with showy computer-generated graphics.

Although Caminando Juntos usually does not bother with standards, in 2016, Santiago and Gustavo improvise a sedan chair for their Juquilita: they tenderly tie the small plaster image from Silvio's bodega to a simple, bulky, unpainted wooden chair, deploying a few wooden wedges positioned under her pedestal to force her firmly against the backrest. They also screw a set of wide leather straps into the chair frame, so individuals can take turns carrying her like a backpack. In the same manner, they attach a hip belt, hoping to make the weight easier to bear. The belt did not work well, however, so the pilgrims simply let it dangle uselessly.

By the time they finish, the sun has set, but, as with so much related to pilgrimage, the task isn't complete without some decorative touches. Ramiro (Kino's brother) and Juan join Santiago and Gustavo to accessorize Juquila's improvised litter with sprays of artificial poinsettia blossoms in glossy pink, gold, green, and silver. Below the Virgencita, shimmery in a petite gilt crown and a sequined white, red, and gold gown, they affix a pair of petite LED cycling lights that I had brought along to the chair's rear crossbar: a slow flashing red bulb on the left and a frenetically flickering white bulb on the right to mark Caminando Juntos for passing vehicles and straggling pilgrims alike.

Watching this group of men work intently and tenderly to prepare and adorn their copy of the Virgin Mary for the pilgrimage recalls broader questions about masculinity and piety (see plate 5). It remains a cliché in Mexico to imagine fervent devotion and participation in ritual as primarily female activities. In my research on earlier periods, I noted that priests in Oaxaca in the early twentieth century often commented on the underrepresentation of men among Mass attendees and parishioners taking sacraments.[13] Indeed, it was a common fear among Catholic leaders in many countries that modernity and secular ideologies brought on a withering of the faith among men.[14] The long hours and weeks of planning that go into pilgrimage organizations, as well as the affectionate decorative efforts male participants lavish on *Nuestra Madre* (Our Mother), remind us that there are different ways to be religious. Men may not gravitate to priest-led liturgies or find the sacraments personally meaningful, but a significant subset of Catholic men clearly finds pilgrimage, and the collective devotional labors it entails, attractive and fulfilling.

It is not so much anticlerical as extra-clerical. This expression of religious belief and devotional commitment emerges from lay effort and ingenuity without significant clerical involvement. Thus, priests and outside observers do not seem to note the overrepresentation of men among long-distance pilgrims. In addition, pilgrimage (at least those cycling, running, and walking) includes a strong element of masculine camaraderie that clearly appeals to some devotees. Stated differently, beyond the relatively staid forms of observance, such as hearing Mass, pilgrimage offers a flexible group project that also involves travel and sightseeing; team-like, goal-oriented exertion; and pleasant socializing, alongside multiple opportunities for relatively free-form religious expression and ritual observance. It is also an environment in which participants value the array of skills honed among laborers, truckers, and market vendors.

With the vehicles decorated and the Virgencita secured to her improvised litter in shimmery finery, Santiago herds everyone into Silvio's overstuffed, now-crowded bodega to set forth loose guidelines and pray. Juan leads with a reading. Silvio's sister, who stays behind to mind the bodega, initiates a Rosary and guides the call and response. When she finishes, Santiago reminds everyone, "This is not a race. The point is to arrive . . . and arrive together."[15]

# CHAPTER 7

# How Traditions Begin

"Every year we live an adventure," muses Vicente, a tired but enthusiastic cyclist pondering Acatzingo's pilgrimage in December 2018. He and four friends, two of whom are cousins, lounge in the evening outside a tiny, crowded *micelánea* (corner store) in Tecomavaca, Oaxaca, stocked with soft drinks, snacks, cigarettes, soap, sugar, and candy. Lately, along this route, shops also branch out a bit, selling wireless internet access. Pixel-hungry pilgrims, however, quickly overwhelm the network. Sprawled on the curb and leaning on a pickup truck, Vicente, Andrés, Emilio, Jacobo, and Cruz, all in their twenties, have just ridden a whopping 111 miles (180 km). It is the first and longest leg of their journey, although others offer long, punishing climbs that make mileage comparisons meaningless. Still, they've earned a rest.

Friendly, gregarious, and polite—the customary, welcoming *mexi-cano, esta-es-su-casa* (welcome-to-your-home) polite—Andrés quickly offers me a drink and darts into the tiny shop to procure beer. Andrés brings me two dark-green sixteen-ounce cans of Indio, a lager. "One for now and one for later," he says with a grin. Andrés and his colleagues also offer to share their cookies and a gamut of flavored chips—chili with lime, jalapeño with cheese, Worcestershire, and habanero. Without realizing it, I break the group's rules on the first night—no drinking en route, although a tipple or two in Juquila, once the riding is done and the festivities begin, is fine.

Word travels fast. Thirty minutes later, Domingo, one of the organizers, starts needling me, "¿Ya estabas pisteando, eh?" (Already boozing, huh?).

These young men look forward to the pilgrimage every year, and they've taken part in several already. In their view, it is an important, yet entertaining, outing, an annual adventure, as they say, yet it represents only a part of the fiesta-driven rhythms punctuating their lives. On Facebook, they share photographs and commentary documenting their participation in religious events throughout the year. For example, a few months after the pilgrimage, during Holy Week, Vicente proudly posts pictures of himself as a centurion: spear in hand, attired in red with a golden belt and matching sandal straps, he plays his part in Acatzingo's reenactment of the Passion.

The trip to Juquila, essentially, is only partially a hometown custom. For these young men, it is a friend-group ritual. Besides their faith, they follow competitive cycling, often setting aside Acatzingo's pilgrimage attire of T-shirt and pants—and thus, setting themselves apart—for racing jerseys, with their bold stripes, corporate logos, and contrasting color schemes. Moreover, they stick together for the duration of the journey, whether riding, eating, or sleeping in plazas or under parked semitrailers.

Pondering the mobile chapels across the street, we take in the scene (see plate 11). Each altar wedged into its pickup-truck transport seems to vibrate with color, the genre of color afforded by an LED-palate of valentine pink, cool green, radioactive blue, and admonition red, alongside effusive faux-floral splendor. Spread out before the truck altars, over two hundred fellow cyclists gradually bed down on Tecomavaca's basketball court or socialize around its perimeter. As we talk about their experience and drain our beverages, they casually take it all in. Maybe someday, they agree, they'll join the organizing committee. They certainly seem the type. Charismatic, confident, and friendly, they already take trips together to different shrines and festivals closer to home throughout the year. In fact, Vicente and Andrés, the most talkative of the group, make the connection without prompting: their friendship, love of cycling, and propensity to arrange journeys to shrines and festivals: "This is how traditions begin," Andrés muses.[1]

Lamentably, the lethal realities of present-day Mexico can destroy the most earnest dreams, and they caught up with the amiable Vicente a few months after we met. Acatzingo, beset by violence linked to the illicit fuel trade, faces a scourge of murders and gun fights. Vicente, the eager pilgrim and Passion-play centurion, also worked as a DJ, performing at late-night parties and clubs—often a high-risk, wrong-place-wrong-time occupation. A few months after riding to Juquila in 2018, Vicente and a close friend, both innocent bystanders, died in cross fire at one of their shows.

The shock spread quickly on social media. "Se nos adelantaron dos" (Two have gone ahead of us), the initial doleful post announced. Quickly, the Facebook page of Acatzingo's cycling pilgrimage became an archive and online gathering hosting an outpouring of grief among Juquila's devotees and a hub of information about funeral arrangements. Vicente's personal page almost immediately became a virtual shrine where friends posted messages and memories. They continued to do so for over a year. His girlfriend's anguished posts immediately afterward and in subsequent months were particularly heartrending.

Many pilgrims joined the young men's families at the subsequent funerals, accompanying the coffins and adorning the graves. The most moving post appeared on Vicente's Facebook wall, a photograph featuring two side-by-side, empty graves: rectangular concrete niches framed in the earth where the young men's remains would soon reside.

Naturally, friends marked Vicente's passing on the Day of the Dead the following November, and as the fortieth-anniversary pilgrimage to Juquila got underway in 2019, his closest companions lamented his absence and posted grieving shout-outs as if he could still read them.

Perhaps many large modern-day pilgrimages have emerged from groups of close friends like these young cyclists. The uncomplicated, small-circle, social origins of the phenomenon certainly accord with what I have learned talking to devotees. A group of young adults, usually male, seeking adventure concoct a trip to a distant shrine, and gradually a tradition takes shape. This concords with oft-repeated old-timers' stories of "the pioneers" walking or riding in small groups, long before anyone thought of organizing committees, donations, and fleets of support vehicles.

This male-bonding-seed-crystal model seems particularly apt for cycling pilgrimages. Not a single woman, apparently, had ever ridden in the Acatzingo group in 2022. In addition, despite observing dozens of cycling pilgrimages over the last several years, I have seen only a small handful of female riders participating. Long-standing gender norms regarding physical sports and intense exertion are clearly in play. But more is at stake. Women in Mexico, and other Spanish-speaking countries, who enjoy biking face considerable criticism, and even public harassment. Some also note that they feel unwelcome among male cyclists. But in some communities, particularly in cities, women refuse to be deterred. In fact, cycling has become a symbol of feminist resistance for some riders in Mexico City who frame their resistance as a battle against the *patriarcarro* (patri-CAR-chy).[2]

I have yet to see evidence of this kind of defiance among Juquila's followers, but incipient change is afoot in Acatzingo. On November 23, 2023, a local social media entrepreneur (the same individual that films and uploads the town's pilgrimage videos to YouTube) posted a clip and photograph on Facebook of a dramatic bike delivery.[3] As he moves through the streets of town, he narrates how a young woman named Conchita (pseudonym) long dreamed of joining the town's pilgrimage to Juquila, and finally she'd secured a bicycle for the group's forty-fourth journey to the shrine. But only a handful of weeks before the group's December 2 departure, someone stole her bike, leaving Conchita heartbroken. Posts decrying the theft and recounting the would-be *peregrina*'s bitter disappointment reached an Acatzingo native working in the US. Moved, he wired money to friends in Mexico, inspiring the video gradually leading viewers through town to Conchita's door as the narrator tells the story as he walks the boldly striped green-and-white bike. Naturally, Conchita breaks down in tears of gratitude and praises her angelic benefactor. In 2023, Acatzingo would have its first woman rider.

Groups may have begun with clunky cargo bikes, beat-up work shoes, and improvised meals, and they may have initially battled rutted dirt roads, but large, recurring pilgrimage traditions must move beyond the happy-go-lucky friend group if organizers hope to endure. In other words, pilgrimages like Acatzingo's are about planning, logistics, and coordinating labor, a lot of labor. At a distance, outsiders imagine an instinctive collective piety, communities rising as one to converge upon an ancient sacred locale. But pilgrimage is more of a subgroup practice, a gritty but often ebullient subgroup practice. The Acatzingo organizers, La Comisión, as lettering declares on matching black jackets, are a loose group of fifteen to twenty individuals headed by three officers—president, secretary, and treasurer—operating amid an abiding, simple ethos: keep the riders safe, and feed and entertain the group in a modest but generous manner. This devotional tradition, in other words, is supposed to be fun. It isn't about Bible study or liturgy, so to say, although participants express their devotion frankly and publicly. There isn't even much ritual aside from a Mass at the start, another in Juquila, and a homecoming service in Acatzingo seven days later (see plate 3).

Veterans acknowledge the pilgrimage's less-than-Sunday-best realities and warn me that cursing, insults, and unruly arguments mark the journey, but this hardly dampens their pride. For the Comisión, the pilgrimage means work. They spend months hat in hand, cultivating donors and sponsors. They approach butchers for meat and vegetable and fruit vendors for produce. They coax different business owners to sponsor meals and each year's matching sportswear; and, when they do, they make sure the items boldly broadcast the business's name and logo.[4] On a smaller scale, individuals and humbler families donate such things as fifteen-kilo bags of rice. A general scramble to secure provisions dominates the weeks before departure. Once underway, the Comisión faces seven days of unrelenting convoy management. They joke about the volume of coffee, cigarettes, and pharmaceutical stimulants that keep them going. Maybe the young riders should've said, "This is how traditions are *maintained*."

## Peregrinación Nuestra Señora de los Dolores

Before I sat down with Vicente and his friends on the road to Juquila, I knew nothing about their hometown, Acatzingo, Puebla, although I had passed by dozens of times on the highway. According to census data, it is a bustling roadside town of over sixty thousand residents, where about eighty-three individuals still speak Nahuatl, the Indigenous language that once dominated the region.[5] Like most of the towns in the Tepeaca Valley, it isn't famous among Mexicans or foreigners. The oversight speaks to Mexico's surplus of ancient towns and communities, because Acatzingo is indeed quite old. The area has received relatively little attention from archaeologists, despite the fact that it was home to a handful of small Indigenous cities in the first millennia of the Christian era.[6] In the fifteenth century, it was an important market center along the pre-Columbian trade route to the Gulf Coast and was politically subject to the city of Tepeyacac (now Tepeaca) within the tributary empire of the Mexica (Aztecs). After the Spanish conquest, it became a regional center of Franciscan missionary efforts, as the massive sixteenth-century convent on the town's main square attests. The monastery's baptismal font, a large carved stone basin, is allegedly the oldest in Mexico. In addition, the colonial administrators forced many nearby residents to relocate in Acatzingo as epidemics and exploitation hollowed out native settlements in the region in the mid-1500s. "Reconcentration," as the crown's agents labeled this policy, sought more efficient governance and control of the increasingly disperse Indigenous populations amid catastrophic demographic collapse.[7] In the eighteenth and nineteenth centuries, Acatzingo was home to several large haciendas dedicated to commercial agriculture.[8]

In a basic sense, the town's economic role has not changed that much. Acatzingo remains a producer of fresh produce for local and distant markets and a transit zone along one of Mexico's most important arteries. There are important differences, of course. In the present day, many locals have migrated to the United States, and the Mexican government estimates that Acatzingo received $7.8 million in remittances in 2022.[9] These figures echo my experiences talking to young men from Acatzingo in 2018. During the pilgrimage, several inquired about travel to the United States. In subsequent months, a couple of pilgrims contacted me via direct message to describe their sense of vulnerability amid limited

Plate 1. Juquilita. Pilgrimage groups often bring along copies of Our Lady of Juquila as they travel, and devotees consider it an honor to carry her. In 2016, Caminando Juntos used a repurposed wooden chair for this purpose. Although the famous statue's origin remains contested, the devotion's emergence coincides with the fluorescence of Mexico's baroque Catholicism in the late 1500s and early 1600s. By the late 1700s, Juquila drew perhaps twenty thousand pilgrims and two thousand merchants to her feast each December 8. Today estimates suggest over two million people visit Juquila each year. Photograph by Mike DuBose.

Plate 2. *En camino*—On the move. For Caminado Juntos the first two days of walking take place in the valley south of Oaxaca City. As the sun rises, the vanguard of the group accompanies Juquilita, as they affectionately call her. The devotion historically revolved around interactions between Oaxaca's populous central valleys and communities in the mountains and along the Pacific coast. For centuries, the pilgrimage doubled as a regional trade fair. In the last fifty years, however, thousands of devotees from beyond Oaxaca have embraced the Juquila's devotion. Photograph by Mike DuBose.

Plate 3. *La partida*—The departure. After a farewell Mass in Acatzingo, two different sets of mariachis serenade the images housed within the group's mobile truck-chapels, visible at right. They include town's patroness (Our Lady of Dolores), a Passion-themed representation of Christ, and the Virgin of Juquila. Many of the town's habitants celebrate alongside the cyclists, consuming over two thousand tamales and Styrofoam cups of *atole* (a sweet, hot corn beverage). Subsequently, hundreds of riders and over a dozen support vehicles depart amid considerable fanfare. Photograph by the author.

Plate 4. *La ruta*—The route. Walking pilgrims spread out along a gravel road leading toward Juquila. In the late 1700s, a Oaxacan priest named Joseph de Ruiz y Cervantes backed by Catholic authorities published a guidebook and history promoting the pilgrimage that includes maps tracing a route from the city of Oaxaca to the shrine. Although, in truth, there are many different paths to the shrine, walking pilgrims approaching from the north still follow the route sketched by the colonial cartographers. Photograph by Mike DuBose.

Plate 5. *Entre hombres*—Among men. Contrary to stereotypes about machismo, Juquila's pilgrimage reveals the men of Caminando Juntos embracing an array of devotional roles within the group. Their unabashed, tender expressions of piety remain largely invisible to outsiders. In a warehouse space in Oaxaca's main city market—where the group's Juquila resides much of the year—devotees carefully decorate and secure the image to a chair they have retrofitted with shoulder straps. Photograph by Mike DuBose.

Plate 6. *Huevos al comal*—Eggs from the griddle. Along the route to Juquila, entrepreneurs hope to cash in on traveling devotees. In some cases, they represent the epitome of improvisation—for example, selling drinks and popsicles out of a backpack. In others, they span the spectrum of the Mexican entrepreneurial spirit: from open-air, mountain kitchens and rough-cut, homemade tables and benches beneath plastic sheeting, to cement-floored, metal-roofed, roadside restaurants with pulsing sound systems. Fried eggs off the griddle, with salsa and coarse salt, in a warm tortilla, represents a classic pilgrim staple. Photograph by Mike DuBose.

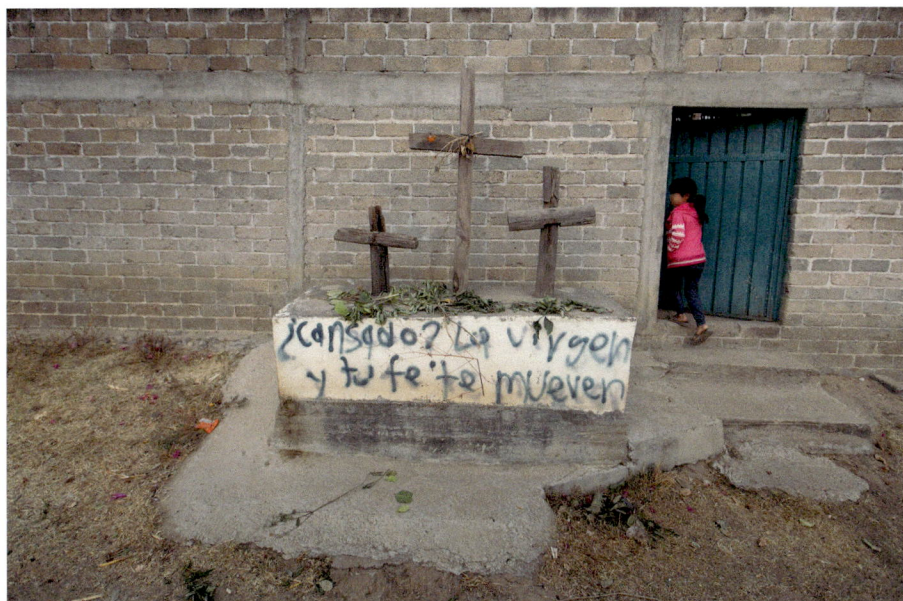

Plate 7. *La Virgen te mueve*—The Virgin moves you. "Tired? The Virgin and your faith move you," announces some graffiti near Zimatlán. Along the route, devotees leave messages for their fellow pilgrims. On the surface, they emerge from the supportive ethos many pilgrims embrace. On a deeper level, the signposting, trailside testimonials, and the folklore about different landmarks reveal devotees giving the landscape an overlay of sacred meaning. Photograph by Mike DuBose.

Plate 8. *Flores y camisetas*—Flowers and T-shirts. Like the trucks and buses making their way to Juquila, cyclists decorate their bikes in honor of the Virgencita. Usually, this means a tiny, framed photograph, or Marian figurine attached to the handlebars amid sprays of artificial flowers. In addition, many groups commission matching, boldly colored T-shirts to commemorate their pilgrimage, and distinguish themselves as they ride. Photograph by Mike DuBose.

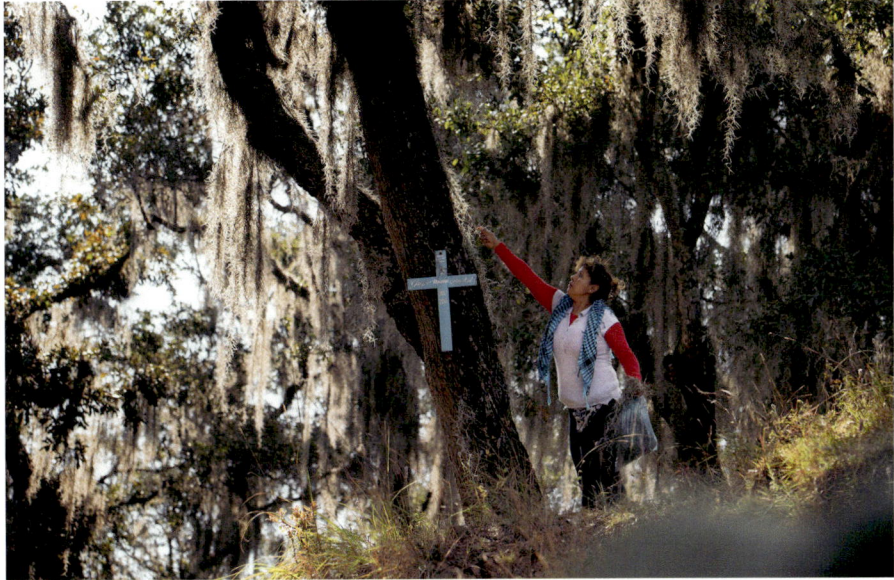

Plate 9. *En el cerro*—In the mountains. At the higher elevations, the path to Juquila becomes a rugged mountain trail. These wetter altitudes support forests swathed with soft, grey tendrils of Spanish moss. Devotees enjoy congregating at scenic high points and leaving behind testimonial objects like this blue cross commemorating a four-year run of pilgrimages. Aside from leaving mementos, devotees also take reminders of the traversed landscape home. Here a pilgrim collects moss to decorate a home nativity scene. Photograph by Mike DuBose.

Plate 10. *Buscando su ritmo*—Finding your rhythm. As Caminando Juntos approaches Yolotepec in the late afternoon of their fifth day, two pilgrims lead the way. Certain activities punctuate each day: waking before dawn, drinking sweet coffee or *champurrado* (a chocolate-based, corn beverage), and resting at different food stands and crossroads. Once on the move, pilgrims spread out as individuals find their own pace. For some, conversation or devotional music leaven the exertion. Others prefer silence and contemplation. Photograph by Mike DuBose.

Plate 11. Nuestra Señora de Dolores—Our Lady of Sorrows. Dedicated to Acatzingo's local patroness, strips of red and blue LED lights set off Our Lady of Dolores's mobile truck-chapel accompanying cycling pilgrims. In fact, it fairly vibrates against the surrounding night. In many cases, chapels allow for various presentations of their images. Some have removable display cases that double as palanquins shouldered at the shrine. In this instance, there is an elemental symbolism at work: Dolores represents the faithful of Acatazingo, and she, like them, visits Juquila every year. Photograph by the author.

Plate 12. *Los árboles del Pedimento*—The trees of the Pedimento. Be it stone, wood, metal, or plastic, devotees create and commission objects to convey pious appeals and testify to their faith. Vinyl banners of all shapes and sizes drape trees around the votive chapel called the Pedimento on the outskirts of Juquila. There they offer a testament to the expanding geography of Juquila's devotion as they flutter in the breeze. They vary widely, featuring text, portraits, vehicles, marking both community and family pilgrimages and commemorating decades of devotion. Photograph by Mike DuBose.

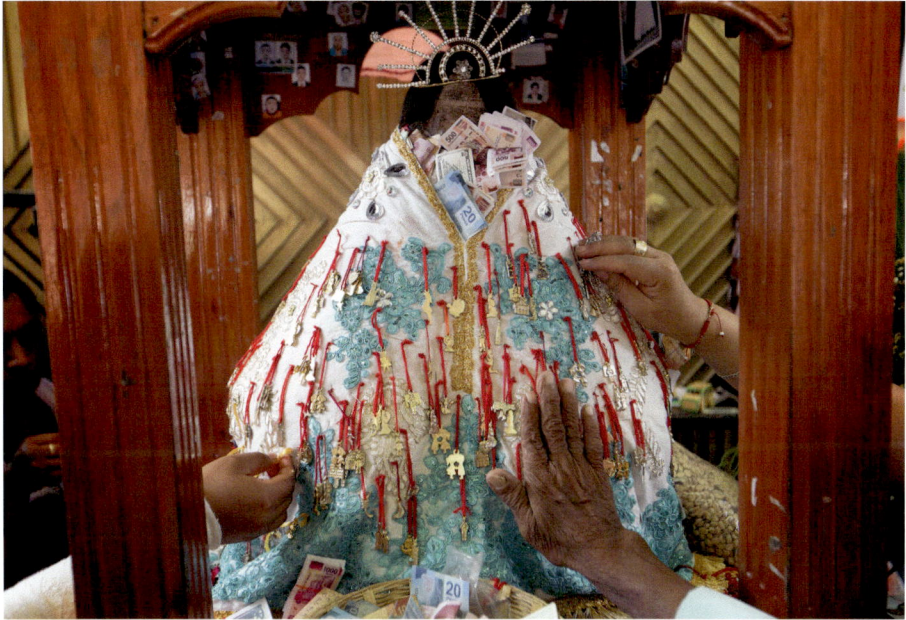

Plate 13. *Tocando*—Touching. Despite traditions centered on personal contact with sacred objects, Catholic authorities forbid touching the original Virgin of Juquila. But the Pedimento's stone copy serves as a stand-in. Pilgrims brush candles against the image and then rub them along their bodies. Individuals stroke the Virgin's vestments, touch her mantle, and pin milagros to her cape. They also leave real and imitation money. And then, amid whispered supplications they make room for other devotees. Nearby the faithful affix tokens of their pleas to the walls and columns of the chapel. Photograph by Mike DuBose.

Plate 14. *El campamento*—The encampment. After four days of riding and two weeks of walking, respectively, Acatzingo's cycling and walking pilgrimages converge in Juquila. As the two groups progressed toward the shrine an increasing number of families driving in separate vehicles caught up with the caravan, swelling its footprint at successive stops. On a school playing field the sojourners set up tarps and start cooking, and laborers erect a large stage. At night the more than five hundred devotees enjoy a live *cumbia* band. Photograph by the author.

Plate 15. *La procesión*—The procession. Amid salvos of fireworks, Acatzingo's pilgrims stage a climactic procession to the shrine and a special Mass in Juquila's basilica. Despite some grumbling from the cyclists, walking devotees in blue-and-white T-shirts take the lead. They bear a display case housing Acatzingo's patroness, Our Lady of Dolores, alongside the Virgin of Juquila, and churn through a set of cheers celebrating Juquila and their hometown. The cyclists, led by mariachis, follow carrying a banner and images of Dolores, Juquila, and Christ. Photograph by the author.

Plate 16. *El atrio*—The atrium. During peak pilgrimage season from November to mid-January, a constant stream of processions crams the basilica's atrium every morning. Crowding within the sanctuary during Mass keeps many devotees outside listening on loudspeakers and, flowers in hand, hoping to approach the famed image Virgin of the Juquila. In 2017, the church added a large television screen to the outside of the basilica so pilgrims could watch the service as well. Photograph by Mike DuBose.

opportunities and periodic violence. They wondered if the risks and uncertainties of migration could pay off, and they were hoping I would have good ideas, connections, or suggestions. Sadly, I don't.

Perhaps characteristic of recent technological and cultural transformations, it was social media that led me to this region of Mexico. Searching for pilgrimage videos on YouTube in 2016 and 2017, I made a list of towns where groups seemed to post annual videos. It seemed crucial that I understand how large groups functioned after having visited the shrine alongside the smaller, comparatively intimate, Caminando Juntos.

I went to the region in the summer of 2018, visiting Huixcolotla first because of its fame as the largest group pilgrimage to Juquila, but I couldn't find the groups' leaders. I then made my way to Tepeaca and faced the same issue. After a few hours, I moved on to Los Reyes Juárez, where I spoke to some devotees. One of them complained that the town's pilgrimage group and the organizers of its annual patron-saint festival essentially taxed residents. They go door-to-door pressuring residents for weekly contributions, he claimed, which they calculate according to employment and reputed wealth. He showed me his receipt.[10]

Finally, I squeezed into one of the overcrowded Volkswagen microbuses that shuttle people between these towns and made my way to Acatzingo. At the parish offices, a priest mentioned Luis, the longstanding president of the Comisión, although he couldn't tell me how to find him. As I soon learned, Luis had recently stepped down after twenty years of leadership, but he remained the most knowledgeable person regarding long-distance cycling pilgrimage. It was only when I fortuitously inquired at a butcher shop named Carnicería Juquilita that I began to make concrete inroads. There, amid dangling chorizos and cuts of beef, the shop owner sketched Acatzingo's tradition and described how he often donated meat to the group. He told me that I could find Luis at the town's health clinic, where he worked as a technician. Luis could not talk during the workday, but he gave me his number, and we spoke over the phone at length about the Acatzingo's pilgrimage, named in honor of the town's Marian patroness, Peregrinación Ciclista Nuestra Señora de los Dolores (Our Lady of Sorrows Cycling Pilgrimage).

This pairing of Marian devotions is interesting and profound it its simplicity. Much of the expressive content produced by Acatzingo's devotees represents a connecting of their local patroness, the Virgin of Dolores, to the distant Juquila, or bringing the two advocations (versions or distinct depictions of the Virgin Mary) together. It appears on their T-shirts and banners and in their climactic pilgrim procession in Juquila, when they carry images of Our Lady of Dolores into Our Lady of Juquila's shrine every year (see plate 15). Essentially, they establish a bond between the images and sacralize a metaphorical relationship through symbolic travel and reenactment. Dolores stands for Acatzingo, and devotees demonstrate their faith by reverently carrying her from their hometown to the more famous image in Oaxaca year after year. Moreover, they broadcast the existence of this bond, and their charge as devotees of both advocations, for all to see as they journey to the shrine.

Luis assured me that I could accompany the group to Juquila in December, but I would need to secure formal approval from the Comisión and its officers. After our conversation, I joined the pilgrimage's Facebook group, and we stayed in touch via What's App. We agreed that I would return in the waning days of November 2018 to meet the organizers and request permission to join the pilgrimage.

As planned, I arrived in Acatzingo on November 29. Wandering the streets and the main plaza, I immediately noticed vinyl banners advertising pilgrimages attached to the wrought-iron fence surrounding the town's imposing parish church. This large handsome eighteenth-century structure combines ornamental brickwork; blue and white tiles; smooth, orange-colored surfaces; ornate balustrades; baroque bell towers; angels; and a blue-and-yellow tiled dome. It may sound like a busy mess, but it works.

One of the banners promoted a torch-bearing, running relay to the Virgin of Guadalupe's shrine, scheduled for mid-December. The other announced a walking pilgrimage that had departed for Juquila a few days earlier, November 24. As I would learn, these walkers and the bicyclists I joined collaborate; they synchronize their respective arrivals in the shrine town, camp together on a rented athletic field, and organize a joint procession and Mass at the basilica. I also stumbled upon a pair of detailed informational posters for the 2018 cycling pilgrimage pasted on a large electrical transformer a few blocks away. On another thoroughfare, I noticed a bike shop named Juquilita and a store displaying custom T-shirts produced in previous years for Juquila and Guadalupe pilgrimages.

Luis directed me to the pilgrimage's offices the following evening, promising to introduce me to the Comisión. I was at first surprised to hear that the group had an "office," but large established pilgrimage groups indeed should be understood as local institutions. It was a modest rectangular space, a short walk from the plaza, with the roll-up metal door typical of retail businesses in Mexico and a large walled backyard where a lone torton had been parked. Inside, the room's mint-green walls and overhead fluorescent lights combined to give a sickly pallor to all its occupants.

Salomón, a stout, bespectacled trucker and the Comisión's president in 2018, explained that the property belonged to him. He decided to use it for the group during his term and quickly set it up for the pilgrimage. On the walls, a sampling of the previous decade's glossy pilgrimage posters and a pair of calendars provided makeshift décor. A handwritten sign alerting devotees to a 600-peso, no-exceptions fee loomed high on the back wall, and a poster-sized task list sat near the backdoor. Nearby sat a large electric coffee urn filled with hot water, accompanied by a respectable supply of instant coffee, a box of tea bags, a plastic jar of sugar, and a sleeve of Styrofoam cups. Periodically, individuals ambled over and served themselves. Around the room, gray metal shelving units held various boxes, supplies, and miscellaneous objects. Eventually, someone arrived with a large plastic bag of *pan dulce* (pastries) and passed it around the room. Soon, nearly everyone was nibbling on pan and sipping coffee.

A long table against one wall of the room hosted a pile of clear plastic bags containing the matching red-and-white shirts as well as red baseball hats and pants custom-made for that year's pilgrimage. The back of the shirt features a line drawing of the town's sorrowful patroness, Dolores, with a quartet of cyclists traversing a mountain on their way to Juquila. On the front, a small, logo-like Juquila appears at left, crowned by the words "Peregrinación Ciclista" arching over her head. Underneath, tiny bikers seem to ride toward the date, 2018, and another row of text states, "From Acatzingo, Puebla to Juquila, Oaxaca." Opposite, at right, in bold black letters, the shirt acknowledges the family that donated the shirts.

A second table, where the Comisión officers typically sit during meetings, jutted into the center of the room. A pair of handwritten announcements hung from the front of the table. One reiterated the message on the wall about the mandatory fee, and the other listed the times for the special Masses associated with the event: 6 a.m. departure Mass on December 2; a 12 p.m. liturgy in Juquila on December 6; and, finally, a 12 p.m. homecoming Mass in Acatzingo on December 8. This pilgrimage, in other words, represents a full week of activities.

When I first spoke to the Comisión, several men smoked as they sat in folding chairs set against the office walls. I was offered both coffee and cigarettes and faced a murmur of mockery when I declined both in favor of chamomile tea. I described my project and explained how I had walked with Oaxacan pilgrims in 2016 and was hoping to join a large cycling group. As I looked over the gathering, I realized that establishing personal connections with Acatzingo's pilgrims was going to be harder than I expected. A wariness, almost prickliness, characterized their demeanor.

Figure 7. The organizing committee. On the first night of their cycling pilgrimage, Acatzingo's Comisión gathers to discuss responsibilities and supplies. In truth, they have been working for months. Considerable effort goes into reserving campsites, fundraising, and budgeting. In transit, they must supply clean water, food, and fuel, as well as address mechanical issues (both for bicycles and vehicles) and provide first aid. Photograph by the author.

Members of the Comisión were blunt and direct. They asked if I planned to sell photographs of the pilgrimage and if I had brought my own vehicle, and they stressed that I would have to accept sleep deprivation and discomfort, like they and the riders, for the duration of the journey. Domingo, Salomón's brother and a fellow truck driver, was emphatic. (He would prove, ultimately, to be among the friendliest members of Acatzingo's Comisión.) Under no circumstances, he said, could I expect "American food." There would be no pizzas or hamburgers, he cautioned. Leonardo, the Comisión's secretary, was still more pointed, looking at me directly and saying, "You must eat what we eat. If you don't, we'll be offended."

In my previous trips to Juquila, I had come to understand the vital importance of meals among devotees. These simple acts of communion and leisurely socializing are central to the experience. A group of pilgrims eats together repeatedly during their sojourn, and these moments of fellowship multiply over time. I was startled, however, by the explicit focus on my response to their food. In fact, throughout the pilgrimage individuals took a surprising level of interest in what I ate. Did I really eat the celebratory tamales and drink *atole* on the first morning? How many? Had I eaten tacos on the evening before arriving in Juquila? Why didn't I go back for seconds? The irony, from my perspective, was that the meals were generally excellent: in addition to the tamales and tacos, on different days they served such things as chicken in mole and pozole. Acatzingo's pilgrims, essentially, enjoy classic Mexican dishes at every stop. Moreover, mealtimes were always cheerful and pleasant. In other words, I found eating alongside the town's pilgrims easy to embrace, except maybe for the devotees' practice of deploying tortillas as edible spoons. I attempted to, but I was obviously bad at it. On a few occasions, individuals simply sidled up and handed me a plastic spoon, saying only, "Here."

These exchanges, though, left me thinking that Acatzingo's devotees have felt the sting of condescension and prejudice regarding their culture and traditions before. In addition, heated political dynamics in the United States, as filtered through the Mexican media, likely seasoned my reception. Donald Trump's contemptuous comments about Mexicans, and the general mistreatment of hardworking migrants, came up repeatedly in conversations. These are not theoretical issues for Acatzingo's devotees. As the remittance data suggests, almost everyone has relatives in *El Norte*. A handful, like Domingo, took time to discuss their views on US attitudes toward Mexican labor. Young cyclists, alternatively, shared stories of uncles and cousins, some of whom they'd never met in person, enjoying success north of the border.[11]

Outside of food and cigarettes, another measure of distance was that most of the devotees simply called me *Güero* (a term meaning light-skinned or blond). This term isn't a slur, unless paired with certain adjectives. In fact, it is a common nickname bestowed on many Mexicans. A few young pilgrims attached a respectful honorific, calling me *Don Güero*, which I found charming. Still, it marked difference. Individuals who sought greater connection, even friendship, reinforced this fact; they chose to call me by my name.

In sum, the time I spent with the pilgrims of Acatzingo underscored the limits of my attempts to fit in. Cycling pilgrimage simply does not facilitate the loose, unhurried fellowship typical of walking groups. In retrospect, I should have borrowed a bike to better share the experience with Acatzingo's young riders. In any case, the Comisión allowed me to join the group, but they made it clear that they would not cater to me. I could tag along, but I would have to adapt. I paid the 600-peso fee, received my T-shirt, and commenced talking to individuals, taking pictures, and observing the preparations.

On the following night, the eve of the pilgrimage, it was clear that a new level of frenetic, jovial activity was in motion at the office. Several large tortons and tractor-trailers were parked on the street getting a decorative makeover. Boisterous devotees yammered while fitting them with the group's thirty-ninth anniversary vinyl banner, which pairs a large representation of Acatzingo's patroness with Juquila's official, post-coronation image depicting her surrounded by silver angels and trampling the red serpent of sin encircling the globe. The two advocations of Mary bookend the group's name, "PEREGRINACIÓN CICLISTA." Finally, the banner acknowledges another local sponsor, a business specializing in engine lubricants.

Aside from matching banners, many trucks also boasted strings of pendants in Juquila's colors of blue and white and handcrafted palm arches bending over the entire cab. Each one of these trucks would eventually be loaded with specific cargo that night. Within the office, a steady stream of young men arrived to sign up. They greeted members of the Comisión, paid their fee, and left with their commemorative sportswear. In many instances, entire families, bundled up against the cool night air, accompanied eager pilgrims as they joined the pilgrimage. Simultaneously, donors and their families coalesced in the streets, dropping off boxes of athletic drinks and food items. A local bike-shop owner also arrived to deliver a new road bike, which he contributed for a raffle in Juquila. I left after a few hours, but members of the Comisión stressed that they would be signing up cyclists and organizing cargo well into the night.

The next day, cyclists, families, and supporters began coalescing in the parish's church atrium on the main plaza before dawn amid a full peal of the temple's bells and fireworks announcing the impending start of the special departure Mass (see plate 3). Pickup trucks and Acatzingo's illuminated truck altars began arriving and parking along the road in front of the sanctuary, and royal-blue-clad mariachis serenaded the sacred images ensconced in the traveling chapels. Carefully, devotees removed the images and reverently carried them into the sanctuary as the musicians followed, still singing and playing.

As the sun rose, it illuminated scores of freshly cleaned bikes resting against the parish church or carefully leaning on each other outside the church's main door and in the plaza across the street. Clumps of cyclists wearing their T-shirts and supporters wrapped in blankets shuffled inside. Some riders were already carrying bulky penitential candles and images, items they bore on their backs throughout the journey to Juquila. When the pews were filled, many devotees remained standing outside or at the back of the sanctuary as the Mass began.

Parked nearby, members of the Comisión worked frenetically out of a canopy-covered pickup, signing up last-minute participants and collecting fees. As soon as the service ended, the entire throng converged

Figure 8. Bearing the cross. Cycling pilgrims undertake the entire journey on Mexico's busy, two-lane highways. Protected by support vehicles and mobile truck-altars accessorized with sirens and flashing lights, bikers have adapted long-standing penitential practices to cycling. Many ride with a crucifix or a framed image of Juquila strapped to their backs. Photograph by Mike DuBose.

on a duo of trucks next to them, where several women handed out plates of tamales from large metal cauldrons and served Styrofoam cups of hot *atole* (a sweet corn beverage) from steaming stockpots and plastic pitchers.

As the gathering began to wind down, Salomón, the president of the Comisión, asked me to move to the far corner of the plaza to take photographs of the pilgrimage's departure. After waiting for perhaps an hour, the choreographed procession of truck altars, cyclists, pickup trucks, and an ambulance with its siren blaring and the group's nursing team inside, executed a slow lap around the plaza, passed me, and headed out of town. Members of the Comisión and supporters were still packing the support trucks. Salomón conferred with the other officers and directed me to climb in the cab of the torton set aside for the mariachis. Jacinto, a hired driver (i.e., not a member of the group), proved a stoic, occasionally surly, companion. By night fall, we had crossed the state line into Oaxaca and set up the first encampment in Tecomovaca.

# CHAPTER 8

# Walking Together

When Caminando Junto's trucks are finally packed and decorated and after a farewell Mass and group Rosary, the *caminando* (walking) begins. Winding through the market as it slowly shuts down for the night, the pilgrims plunge into the urban neighborhoods encircling the city's commercial heart at about 7:10 p.m. Within minutes, we pass another group of Juquila devotees in their predeparture prayer circle. Subsequently, Caminando Juntos finds the main road leading out of town. Juan carries Juquilita, in her improvised sedan chair, on his back. Her lights blink in a slightly disconcerting, arrhythmic, slow-red–fast-white tizzy, producing a feeling of low-level, unwavering agitation.

In daylight, the dense, gritty fringes of Oaxaca represent a somewhat unpleasant part of the city characterized by loud trucks, dangerous street crossings, and the inescapable blaring music. In many cases, pilgrimage includes withstanding periods of sonic assault, but that isn't the only sensory challenge. In this early stretch, passing the old Atoyac River channel, the stench of exhaust fumes, garbage, and wafts of urine and sewage are relentless. The evening, however, is much safer than a daylight trek in this busy area, hence the timing of Caminando Juntos's departure. From the outset, the fellowship of peregrinos begins to stretch out, and individuals unwittingly sort themselves by physical conditioning and frame of mind. The same set of pilgrims, Alicia, Francisco, Chabela, and Pablo, tend to form the vanguard, walking alongside their Juquilita throughout the entire sojourn. Santiago, Silvio, Juan, and Ramiro coordinate their respective locations, spreading out within the group to provide guidance and support.

Dispersal facilitates conversation. Beto and Tere initially engage in the usual get-to-know-you banter with me. The former, a boyishly sweet seventeen-year-old who likes to try out English phrases, calls Tere *madrina* (godmother). This honorific title announces what anthropologists call "fictive" kinship relations among pilgrims, an example of the *madrina de velacíon* (a.k.a. *comadre de levantada*: pilgrimage godmother). Tere, in other words, initiated Beto during his first pilgrimage. Alicia refers to Silvio as *padrino* for the same reason.

Tere, age twenty-eight, is also the mother of Miguel, the youngest member of the group at eight years old. Cheerful and prone to bright laughter, she cooks and serves meals in front of the bodegas, alongside many fruit-and-vegetable vendors who, like her, work in semi-temporary stands colonizing what once served as a broad thoroughfare between the bodegas and a set of brick-and-mortar shops in the back of the market. Several pilgrims eat with her regularly. She jokingly calls her improvised stand a restaurant, Los Cuatro Vientos (The Four Winds).[1] However, although quite friendly, approaching voluble, in relaxed group settings, Tere avoids personal interviews.

Beto, in contrast, loves to talk. Young and guileless, he works at his parent's market stand selling paper products and school supplies in a different neighborhood market. He is also a distracted high school student. His grandparents live in a Zapotec village in the mountains above Oaxaca's Central Valleys, but his parents moved to the state capital in search of greater opportunity decades ago. Beto sometimes arranges custom orders of traditional *papel picado* (the colorful decorative-paper cutouts strung together in long festive streamers common in Oaxaca and Puebla, and currently a symbol of Mexican national identity) from the ancestral pueblo. Mostly, he focuses on standard teenage-boy interests: social media, motorcycles, and girls. To my shock—but not surprise—in 2018 Beto withdrew from Caminando Juntos because his girlfriend was pregnant. His frustrated parents noted that he had to step up to adult responsibilities.

Manuel, Beto's uncle, perhaps thirty or so, works a few stalls away at La Merced and also takes part in the pilgrimage. He tends to boss Beto, which his affable nephew respectfully endures. Manuel occasionally plays the jester on the way to Juquila, uncorking full-voice, off-color jokes in a pun-laden mockery. Jests directed his way, however, generate gruff, curt warnings, suggesting insecurity. Flashes of sadness and disappointment flicker in fleeting references to his time as an undocumented laborer in the United States.

As Caminando Juntos progresses, it becomes obvious that some individuals approach the trip differently than most of their fellow pilgrims. On the more challenging stretches, they steal naps in one of the trucks, a common occurrence for the younger participants but rare among adults. Are these participants less committed to the devotional experience?

Maybe, or maybe not. Outsiders tend to imagine pilgrimage as a religious time-out where devotees step out of society to complete a serious religious act. However, for many individuals a single trek to the shrine can represent one of many during their lifetimes, some more serious than others.

Kino, limping due to new blisters, provides nuanced perspective on individual motivations that probably extend to many of Juquila's pilgrims. Many members of Caminando Juntos, he claims, although they may not realize it, take part to escape the stress of work. Of course, they believe in the Virgin of Juquila and acknowledge her miraculous powers of intercession, but, in his view, escaping stress and family obligations often spurs participation. Selling at the market represents an unrelenting, unbounded work-life existence, characterized by considerable competition and tension between vendors (some of whom are relatives). Abastos is a frenetic, crowded space where there is little escape from constant engagement with customers and colleagues. The six-day journey to the shrine, in this context, provides a socially acceptable reprieve. Kino's analysis rings true, considering the various activities at rest and rendezvous stops and the leisure-centered tone of certain parts of the pilgrimage. This practical facet of the Juquila phenomenon makes more sense than uninformed assumptions about thousands of people engrossed in unmitigated fervor for days on end.

Most adults, even as they mix devotion and leisure, don't skip portions of the journey, especially those *cumpliendo la manda* (fulfilling a vow). Pilgrims who "owe," as it were, Our Lady of Juquila limp and labor for miles. They climb into a support vehicle only as a last resort. For example, within Caminando Juntos, Doña Meche, a soft-spoken and kindly woman of fifty-four, was on her third pilgrimage to the shrine in 2016. A latecomer to this mode of devotional practice, Meche had promised the Virgin to complete the walk to Juquila for three consecutive years, a standard votive commitment. She struggles during the climbing portions, huffing and puffing, although usually aided by one of her doting nephews, Kino, Ramiro, or Santiago. Doña Meche occasionally apologizes for slowing Caminando Juntos down, but she remains determined to fulfill her vow, and the group finds her resolve inspiring.

Pilgrimage organizers, like Coscomatepec's Don Carlos, stress the importance of facilitating members' individual *mandas*. He sees it as one of his chief obligations and will only intervene in extreme circumstances. For example, he describes coaxing a woman to set aside her vow for a time after she was bitten by a dog along the route and her wounds became infected. He was able to get her to a nurse and secure antibiotics, but she rode the rest of the journey to Juquila in a car.

Members of Caminando Juntos note that aside from devotion, Doña Meche's fortitude stems from difficult family dynamics. Most of the year, she is the sole caretaker of her elderly father. Pilgrimage offers her an escape from the grinding monotony of home health-care labor. Apparently, her husband mocked her initial interest in the pilgrimage, alleging that she would never make it. Thus, in completing the trek, Doña Meche proves to herself, her pilgrim companions, her spouse, and, naturally, Our Lady of Juquila, that she can meet the challenge.

In sum, a spectrum of commitment within any group of pilgrims is normal. Likely some participants may become more serious in later years after initially taking part casually. They are devotees in training, as it were. Personal histories hint that this dynamic is indeed at work. Santiago, for example, who embraces the part of medic, masseur, and facilitator of pious vows, recalls visiting the shrine when he was Miguel's age (eight years old) in the mid-1970s, a time when Juquila remained beyond the reach of paved roadways. His family took the bus from their home near Ocotlán to the asphalt's end at Sola de Vega and walked to the shrine from there.

Chema, Marta's nephew and the driver of the group's pickup, offers yet another perspective: outright skepticism and disbelief. A veteran of previous walking and cycling pilgrimages to Juquila, he no longer bothers with Catholicism or places any faith whatsoever in the Virgin Mary. Instead, he professes a personal, churchless faith influenced by a brief flirtation with evangelical Protestantism. Chema talks to God directly. He describes crucial moments of divine intervention in his life but without intermediaries or shrine visits. For example, amid hardship after his parents separated, and feeling obliged to support the whole family, he desperately asked for divine help. He proceeded to experience four consecutive days of extraordinary sales at the market. His Catholic relatives find his break with tradition troubling, he claims, but they respect him. He, in turn, cheerfully accompanies them on the pilgrimage, keeping his doubts to himself, and they pay him to drive one of the support vehicles.[2]

In other words, despite stories about strict, pious norms during pilgrimages, there is an acknowledged spectrum of commitment. This underscores what scholars have long pointed out about religious social environments: unthinking, monolithic belief and action is rare.

There are other discrepancies within Caminando Juntos. For instance, Alicia and Francisco represent outliers in one regard, while also being among the most fully committed to the ritual, quasi-liturgical dimensions of the pilgrimage. They were boyfriend and girlfriend in 2016. At the time, she was twenty-eight, and he was forty-two, although both conveyed an infectious youthful energy. Alicia may have not been able to convince her siblings and friends to join her, but she succeeded with Francisco. They are both professionals who work for the state government, and they understand that this sets them apart from most other pilgrims. Regardless, Alicia, both in word and action, is a particularly fervent devotee of the Virgin of Juquila, and this fact is part of her identity among family and friends.

Like many other pilgrims, Alicia knows the Juquila folklore. Perhaps the most common thread in the cautionary tales attached to Oaxaca's diminutive image of Mary Immaculate centers on her role as a punisher of impieties. On many occasions, I've been told by Oaxacans, including some who have no interest in the pilgrimage, that Juquila is dangerous. She is famously touchy, and legend holds that she makes those without faith suffer for approaching her casually. Likewise, she allegedly castigates those who behave immorally during the pilgrimage, backtrack on promises, or whose devotion proves fickle. In some stories, the repercussions are lethal. In my case, after I become sick to my stomach during the first day of walking, Alicia gently chides me, "It is because you came without faith."[3]

Caminando Juntos's improvisational ethos gives the group an easygoing flexibility but can also lead to uncomfortable situations. In 2016, they did not make prior sleeping arrangements like many other pilgrimage groups do. Instead, they figured it out as we went, heading for well-known towns along the road and searching out a free patch of ground among other pilgrims. For example, arriving after midnight in Zimatlán on the first night of the pilgrimage meant hastily parking in the center of town and making camp on the sidewalk in front of the village square. The trees surrounding the plaza were full of keening, roosting grackles. Worse yet, any sharp noise startled the birds, causing them to take flight, and defecate, before returning to their roosts. Making matters still worse, the following day was Zimatlán's market day. By two in the morning, an army of vendors had swarmed the plaza and began setting up their booths. Irritated by our presence, they embraced every opportunity to spook the chattering flock, making sleep impossible. In the end, bird droppings speckled both pilgrims and bedding. Remarkably, much to my relief and surprise, it shook off easily.

In truth, no night during the pilgrimage is restful. Fitful sleep amid snoring colleagues and considerable, almost ceaseless, ambient noise marks every stayover. In addition, the most disciplined groups begin setting off fireworks at 3 a.m. to wake their members and commence their advance on Juquila. These are not small rockets, either. They are *cohetones* (large rockets), designed to screech and explode with considerable force. Most of Caminando Juntos sleeps right though these barrages, anyway, until Silvio and Juan rouse everyone.

Notably, although the devotees of Caminando Juntos believe in Juquila's power as an intercessor, none seem to approach the pilgrimage as an act of austere reverence. Their tradition is nothing like the Opus Dei backpacking trip I went on as a teenager in Jalisco in 1982, during which youth leaders pushed campers to focus on faith and pause at specific times to recite the liturgy of the hours. Neither does it resemble the priest-led Spanish Catholic youth camp I attended in 1985, during which guides admonished us to hike in silence for long stretches, offering pain and fatigue to the Virgin Mary. Each of these religious immersion experiences featured expressions of piety cultivated by Catholic conservatives internationally. There is some overlap, naturally. Juquila's devotees often speak of toil and suffering as a penitential offering too. However, the attitude of rigid, pious seriousness is foreign to the pilgrims from the Mercado de Abastos.

The members of Caminando Juntos, for the most part, enjoy socializing as they travel. During each leg of the journey, the group spreads out and then reconvenes at previously agreed-upon locations. These interludes bring out a leisurely dimension of the pilgrimage. At food stands, hundreds of which span the route, pilgrims begin ordering various dishes. On the simpler side, these include *huevos al comal* (fried eggs) and *memelas* (thick, tortilla-like corn cakes flavored with lard, beans, and cheese). But at some locations, devotees enjoy *barbacoa de chivo* (pit roasted goat), *carne frita en salsa roja* (fried beef in red chili sauce), and stacks of tortillas. Pilgrims also order rounds of beer and soft drinks, and on one occasion Santiago procures a bottle of local mescal. He uses it as a cure-all, energy boost, and topical massage aid. In short, their pilgrimage evinces a rhythmic pattern: hike for a few hours, stop, eat, drink, socialize, and then commence walking. These interludes often include friendly exchanges with other pilgrims from different groups. Much of the repartee centers on casual conversation and easygoing verbal jousting and joking. No one, in my experience, gets drunk. On a more basic level, pilgrims commonly take naps while waiting for their colleagues, nodding off in a chair or lying down in an available shady spot.

The pilgrimage, of course, is a much bigger phenomenon than Caminando Juntos. They represent only one group among many streaming across the landscape during peak periods, especially from November to mid-January. Indeed, at times it seems as if human tides surge into small towns along the route every evening. Sola de Vega, roughly the halfway point for Caminando Juntos, offers a good example, residing at the end of a physically demanding day. Grimy and charmless, it bears no resemblance to the mescal-distilling idyll depicted in recent state-sponsored Juquila tourism advertisements. In the late afternoon and into the evening, exhausted devotees descend on the town. They gradually fill plazas, basketball courts, sidewalks, breezeways, alcoves, and arcades. They bed down in clumps, claiming their space with brightly colored acrylic blankets featuring Disney characters or superheroes, items readily available at markets like Oaxaca's Abastos. As night falls, the early arrivals are already asleep despite continuing boisterous socializing. They are likely the more organized pilgrims who will be gone well before dawn. Later arrivals plop down alongside the sleepers and proceed to organize quick *taquizas* (a taco picnic): tortillas filled with whatever unheated preparations (*guisados*) fill the plastic receptacles arrayed before the tired pilgrims: perhaps scrambled eggs and green beans, chorizo with potatoes, or *chicharrón* (pork rinds) in green chili. Many devotees try to spend as little money as possible, which entails avoiding Sola de Vega's many food vendors.

Caminando Juntos takes a different tack. Setting up camp along the river paralleling the main road where their support vehicles find space, several men seek out restaurants where they can catch the championship tournament of Mexico's professional soccer league. Others seek out showers at one of the establishments catering to pilgrims' needs for toilets and a rejuvenating encounter with soap and water. I chose the latter.

Overall, towns like Sola de Vega depend on the flow of devotees, but residents live amid a nightly carnival atmosphere when the pilgrimage is in full swing: plazas, sidewalks, and churchyards fill up every evening and empty out every morning from mid-November through early January. Imagine it in time-lapsed, drone footage: First, Sola de Vega appears relatively quiet, with only faint radio programs and pop music spilling out of windows, tortilla mills whirring in the distance, and a passel of dogs and roosters contributing a seemingly episodic animal banter. Then support vehicles rumble into view, music blaring, and park. The trucks begin coloring the town with their bright paint jobs, tarps, and pilgrimage decorations fluttering in the breeze. As the afternoon ripens, groups of pilgrims start to flow in, perhaps in twos, threes, or fours. Gradually, the travelers spread out comforters and blankets, adding still more color to open public spaces until almost none is left. The soundtrack of this imagined film would feature a mounting sonic assault. As trucks and pilgrims fill up the town, sellers bark out menu highlights, and the small shops pump out loud, come-hither-and-spend party music. Constantly moving through the frame as the evening falls, clusters of pilgrims nursing blisters and sore muscles amble gingerly back and forth in search of water, bathrooms, medicines, provisions, and internet service. Several hours later, the approach of dawn offers this footage in reverse: fireworks punctuate the pre-twilight as the puddles of pilgrims and their vehicles gradually begin to evaporate, and the town regains a measure of quiet for a few hours. Then the cycle begins again.

The trail exiting Sola de Vega inaugurates a new round of hiking and intense climbing, but it also features perhaps the most pleasurable portions of the journey, as hundreds of pilgrims from different groups make their way into the cool, cloud-covered, higher elevations. In 2016, Caminando Juntos often walked alongside perhaps one hundred devotees from Ocotlán wearing long-sleeved red-and-blue T-shirts celebrating their twenty-second pilgrimage to Juquila. The Ocotlán group offers a veritable snapshot of the Juquila pilgrimage, as it includes many adults who appear in their everyday work clothes (jeans and T-shirts) and well-worn athletic shoes, a handful of Zapotec women in traditional skirts and blouses and wearing cheap plastic flats on their feet, and a healthy number of adolescents in Mexican versions of on-trend athleisure: tights and tops, as well as Converse Chuck Taylors or other brands of gym shoes, quite likely local bootlegs.

During these portions of the journey, it proves nearly impossible to keep the group together; we splinter and spread out as individuals, couples, and small groups find a suitable pace (see plate 10). Caminando Juntos simply agrees to reconvene at a series of rendezvous points during the day, usually at the top of a pass, a distinct landmark, or one of the clusters of food stalls at certain trail junctions. Sometimes large crowds of pilgrims congregate in the same locations, taking breaks on the damp ground, looking for seats in the improvised restaurants with their open, wood-burning stoves, and tending to blisters with needles, string, and mescal amid clouds of pine-scented cook-fire smoke.

In previous centuries, writers like Ruiz y Cervantes described traversing virgin forest during this part of the journey. Such claims would be preposterous now, but in comparison to Ocotlán, and the streets surrounding the Mercado de Abastos, the patchy forests of these mountains may as well be an untouched natural setting. Every so often, a pair of parrots on the wing or roosting in a distant tree evoke a wilder past. But that is it. There is a certain sad irony in their scarcity; Juquila was once known as a place where vendors sold parrots in the bustling market set up during the Virgin's feast. Scant wildlife remains today, and instead heaps of pilgrim garbage—much of it plastic—clutter the edges of the trail and slump down the hillsides, a sad testament to the copious flow of visitors and the lack of basic services in the countryside.

One of our rendezvous points, called simply La Cruz (the Cross), features a large wooden cross set in a concrete pedestal at the top of a ridge. Festooned with bright red and white plastic streamers in 2016, it occupies the center of a modest clearing, and many pilgrims pause there. Some steadfast devotee probably carried it up, quite likely in compliance with a vow. Someone else then garlanded the large cross with streamers. Additionally, many pilgrims have crammed several small crosses commemorating their own journeys into its base, and a few have simply tied their crosses to the front and back of the larger crucifix. La Cruz merely marks the crest of a forested ridge. There is no grand view, although the large surrounding trees draped with Spanish moss give the space a sanctuary-like feeling (see plate 9).

These kinds of devotional monuments, continually and gradually reshaped by the accretion of personal mementos, are common in the mountainous portions of the route. As Caminando Juntos advances, we encounter many commemorative markers, wooden crosses, banners, and testaments of gratitude fashioned in metal and plastic. Almost always they announce a devotee or whole family's name and town of origin. In the logic of this mode of Catholic practice, to identify oneself, to be counted, to publicly proclaim fealty to the Virgin of Juquila is a central facet of devotion. These parts of the pilgrimage route also feature symbolic locations with specific meanings attached to natural features alongside the trail and landscape. For example, in these mountains we pass a spring where many women take a drink and leave a token of gratitude if they hope to get pregnant. *El cerro de la mujer preñada* (The mountain of the pregnant woman), pilgrims call it.[4] Some devotees collect this water to help a friend or sister conceive. In a sense, these portions of the pilgrimage reveal shrine making and the gradual construction of devotional meaning that becomes fused to the landscape in the process. In this case, near a trickle of water crossing the trail, a partially upended tree root revealed an area where devotees noticed a dark-colored splotch that vaguely delineated the Virgin's silhouette. Over time, stories emerged about the water's fertile efficacy, and a tradition developed.

Pilgrimage groups and families take turns getting their picture taken at markers such as La Cruz and make small talk while they rest and wait for stragglers. A woman who lives in New Jersey asked me to pose for a picture with her, conveying a distinct attachment to her adopted home in the United States.

Perhaps the most touching interaction of this type, however, involved a family from Ayoquezco, Oaxaca, that paused to discuss their life in the agricultural heartland of Washington State. They embody the poignant complexities many migrant families experience as they sustain ancestral ties and traditions while putting down cultural and economic roots in the United States. Although the parents are Oaxaqueños, their twelve-year-old daughter was born in Seattle, and their eight-year-old son proudly proclaims Toppenish, Washington, as his hometown. The father remains relaxed but stays silent; the boy's mother, however, beams as her son speaks to me in fluent, unaccented English.

Another recurring interaction I experienced at such places entailed individuals from different pilgrimage groups pulling me aside to illuminate the depths of devotee commitment. For example, while Caminando Juntos milled around La Cruz, an elderly gentleman led me behind the large crucifix to ponder a particular pilgrim tribute. Made of concrete and rebar, fashioned into a heavy, squat cross, the offering was indeed unique. Offerings expressing gratitude are common along the route, but they are usually smaller and much lighter. This testament to pilgrim fortitude and commitment, however, is broken at the base. It lies on its back in two pieces, rebar visible, like bones exposed by a compound fracture. The skeletal metal has begun to rust. Etched in bold black letters on the dappled concrete, the damaged cross proclaims, "Thank you Virgencita for having come fifty consecutive months walking to visit you."[5] In other words, this offering memorializes four years and two months of repeated journeys to the shrine. Such a feat must have involved a serious, maybe desperate, plea for miraculous assistance. If the devotee was from the Central Valleys of Oaxaca, it meant leaving home almost every three weeks to take these trails to Juquila. Such an undertaking would also mean making the journey in the rainy season, a colder, muddier, more difficult proposition. The final journey, moreover, which entailed climbing the ridge with the heavy offering in tow, must have been especially challenging. Regardless of the effort, now fragmented and broken, the cross risks being trampled and eventually covered with dirt and grass. Like so many other petitionary mementos, it may become forgotten devotional debris.

Additional rituals take place simultaneously as groups stage photographs around La Cruz—including Caminando Juntos. Several pilgrims move up the ridge to collect understory brush and fern fronds to make large bouquet-like hand brooms with which to swat themselves on the legs and feet. A common explanation is that this gentle flogging eliminates fatigue. It is also an Indigenous purification practice. As we wait, Beto explains to me that in his mother's Zapotec village in the Sierra Norte, this is a venerable tradition, a *limpia* (cleansing ritual) designed to banish bad spirits clinging to the body. At the same time, many pilgrims collect Spanish moss from the trees to use in the nativity scenes at home.

As pilgrims get closer to Juquila, stopovers often include landmarks associated with cautionary legends or locales known for devotional activities. El Pocito, a small collection of houses and food stands where a mountain spring emerges, is one such place. Although I've seen no mention of its pools in documentation from the 1800s or early 1900s, some believers claim that the truly faithful can see the image of Our Lady of Juquila, dressed in red or blue, where the water emerges. Several pilgrims I've met claim to have witnessed the marvel, but others admit they perceived nothing on the spring's rippling surface. In any case, clusters of devotees often stand peering into the pool below the spring hoping for a glimpse of Juquilita. Caminando Juntos mostly focuses instead on sodas, beer, and food. Further along, pilgrims pass *la piedra de los compadres* (the godparents' stone), a large rock outcropping in the middle of a field and the subject of cautionary pilgrim lore. The oft-repeated legend revolves around the tale of two pilgrims who couldn't resist an extramarital tryst while traveling to Juquila. As the story goes, they were turned to stone for their impious transgression, but the rock in question is much bigger than the combined mass of two libidinous pilgrims. According to Juan, the pillar kept growing until a local bishop performed an exorcism. The massive stone and the colorful story warn pilgrims against unrestrained lust and untoward behavior while traveling to the shrine.

On the last morning of the pilgrimage, Caminando Juntos wakes up in Yolotepec, a Chatino Indigenous village about ten miles away from the shrine, only a half-day's walk. Like so many pueblos in this part of the Sierra, Yolotepec seems to tumble haphazardly down the mountainside as if the homes, twisting and turning paths, and humble yards have been tossed from above. During the pilgrimage season, although on a slightly smaller scale, it experiences the same kind of inundation-evaporation cycle as towns like Sola de Vega.

On the cusp of departure, a new enthusiasm ripples among the devotees. The exertions and rough sleeping arrangements are nearly over, and the festive atmosphere surrounding the shrine awaits them. Unlike the other mornings, the pilgrims muster next to Raúl's torton and form a circle while Alicia and Juan lead the Rosary and a series of prayers, much like on the first night in Silvio's bodega. The last leg of the trek is also different; no grueling climbs remain. The hike up to the main road from Yolotepec offers the most demanding pitch. Afterward, the group follows the meandering paved road to Juquila, taking a few shortcuts. In other words, on the last morning Caminando Juntos coasts.

The peregrinos make no effort to conceal their excitement. A spring enlivens their progress, although some limp or walk gingerly. Breezy chatter and picture taking mark the final miles. In addition, even the children—Sofi, Nora, and Miguel—take turns shouldering Juquilita in her DIY sedan chair. As they do, adults smile and praise these youngsters for taking a turn leading Caminando Juntos.

However, aside from the sense of accomplishment, relief, and anticipation, another shift occurs. As the members of Caminando Juntos leave behind the toiling rhythm of the preceding days, they turn their attention to an array of traditions that will occupy the coming afternoon. As we get closer to the shrine, Chatina women selling armloads of flowers appear, and then we come upon lines of parked tour buses, cars, and rows of vendors in haphazardly constructed stands. These individuals sell various souvenirs, but mostly they specialize in the bewildering array of symbolic objects that devotees use to convey their votive and testimonial appeals to the Virgin of Juquila. For the most part, items purchased here will be left behind within a couple of hours.

Doña Meche now carries Juquilita on her back and leads the Mercado de Abastos pilgrims for the first time. Juquila appears to look back at them from her improvised backpack litter, the blocky unvarnished wooden chair from Silvio's bodega. Meche takes Caminando Juntos through the noisy crowds milling in the parking lot and up to the long line of pilgrims. Many of those gathered wear the hats and T-shirts of their respective pilgrimage groups. Clusters of young men linger, tour buses disgorge friends and coworkers, and extended families pick their way through the throngs and try to stay together. Here, perhaps three miles from Juquila, a cross section of southern Mexico comes together. Doña Meche, the devotee who struggled most but never wavered, finds the end of the queue, and takes her place in line. The members of Caminando Juntos crowd in behind her. Slowly, we inch our way into El Pedimento.

# CHAPTER 9

# A Festival on Wheels

Imagine a train of vehicles, a motley modern-day caravan, a potpourri of the wheeled conveyances that ply southern Mexico day in and day out. Trucks predominate, large eighteen-wheeled tractor-trailers with their fifty-three-foot containers in tow, hulking fruit rigs, small-ish box trucks, and a panoply of pickups, heavy and light, stock and retrofit. Add a couple of cars, an SUV or two that is getting on in years, a motorcycle, and, of course, 265 road bikes and riders, and you have the Acatzingo's 2018 cycling pilgrimage. But really, these are just the basics. There is a logic, a choreography, at work. Modern (dare I say, "mechanized"?) pilgrimages progress as a structured convoy with coordinating moving parts. At least, that is how they are supposed to work. I stress "supposed to work" because, as they say in Mexico, "Del plato a la boca, se cae la mejor sopa" (From bowl to mouth, the best soup spills). Trucks and bikes break down, drivers make unplanned detours, cyclists of varying fitness levels spread out over dozens of strenuous miles, and individuals sometimes fail to follow directions.

At first glance, perhaps amid a few muttered curse words if they are slowing your progress to Oaxaca's beaches, the train of devotee-travelers just seems like more traffic, a thickening of the everyday congestion that clogs Mexico's arteries. This group represents a more-or-less standard large cycling pilgrimage. A few are bigger, but many take to the highway with fewer than one hundred bikers or perhaps only a dozen. Relay-style running pilgrimages, although similar, work differently due to their unique approach: They send a truck or two ahead, dropping off runners every few hundred yards, while another vehicle inches along in the rear, picking up individuals who have handed off the torch to the next pilgrim after completing their leg of the journey.

All of these groups make their way along *la libre*, the old free highway, avoiding *la cuota*, a newer toll road, where wealthy drivers and first-class buses zip between major cities. The objectives, obviously, are different. Acatzingo's cycling pilgrims do not sweat a few extra hours on the road, and their budget doesn't include tolls. In truth, securing the permits for *la libre* is enough hassle, and pilgrimages, with their tendency to gum up traffic, are almost certainly prohibited on *la cuota*. From another perspective, the old highway is more suited to pilgrimage. Modest restaurants, workshops, and local stores line the route, should any need arise. Also, pilgrimages are meant to be public, to be seen, heard, and witnessed. *La libre* traces the roads marked by mule drivers centuries ago. It also runs along a path reworked by railroad surveyors in the nineteenth century and then by postrevolutionary highway engineers in the twentieth century. Crucially, unlike the toll road, it doesn't avoid Mexico's pueblos, with their dusty plazas and colonial landmarks. *La libre* targets them, one after another. Hence, the devotee caravan lurches through farmscapes, arid pasturelands, and the grimy strip-mall tendrils of recent unplanned development stretching tentatively from larger towns toward Mexico's main transportation arteries. Then, the pilgrim train chugs into the heart of ancient pueblos like Tecamachalco.

Locals immediately differentiate between regular traffic and the pilgrimages that frequently rumble into their towns from mid-November through the Christmas holidays, which in Mexico reaches January 6, the Feast of the Three Kings—Epiphany—simply *Reyes* (Kings) in Mexican shorthand. For one thing, pilgrimages sound different, and, for another, they don't obey the ebb and flow of workday, or weekend, transit. Sometimes they pass through at midday, in the dead of night, or at daybreak. Regardless of the hour, though, they bring along a wall of sound.

In the strictest sense, we could say that the soundscape of each pilgrimage is unique, depending on the sirens they deploy and the blaring music that moves participants, as well as their distinctive symphony of hydraulic hiss, exhaust-note reverberation, gear grind, cargo clatter, and insect-like click-whir-whoosh of cyclists by the score. However, the patterns, and even the musical repertoires, are remarkably similar from one to the next. In fact, so consistently analogous are the various pilgrimage caravans that it is clear an informal network dynamic undergirds this facet of Mexican culture: the sharing and copying of organizational and aesthetic ideas, adaptable traditions, and innovative approaches to logistics, praise music, and decoration are rapid and widespread. There is also, in some cases, a simple historical reason.

Indeed, participants reveal that there has been a good deal of what we could call mentorship and emulation among groups. Quite likely, much has been transferred from the pilgrimages to Our Lady of Guadalupe and other venerable image devotions peppering heartland regions like Puebla and Veracruz. There are also a handful of progenitor pilgrimages, well-established pilgrimage traditions in which individuals experience veritable apprenticeships. Thus, we can almost sketch genealogical linkages between Juquila groups: pilgrimages in towns like Huixcolotla (see Don Valentín's family history, chapter 4) and Acatzingo, to a lesser degree, constantly spawn offshoots.

Huixcolotla sets the standard. In 2018, the president of their nearly sixty-year-old cycling pilgrimage boasted of his group's 630 cyclists and countless support staff and vehicles.[1] Their Facebook posts reveal seven elaborate mobile chapels, more than twice Acatzingo's.[2] Spending about 1 million pesos ($52,000) each year, and incorporating participants from several neighboring communities, this thriving market town remains the almost universally acknowledged champion of the Oaxacan Virgin's devotion. In Juquila, individuals in the new state tourism office, established expressly to stoke shrine visitation, and members of the municipal government note how Huixcolotla has successfully carved out a distinct niche on the shrine calendar. In mid-November each year, the town sends a semitrailer full of flowers to decorate the basilica before their group's arrival. In addition, they carefully coordinate the convergence of very large walking and cycling groups and stage a large festive gathering featuring well-known dance bands. Again, over time satellite communities break off and form separate pilgrimages. It can be an amicable break, as in the case of Coscomatepec's pilgrimage, a scion of Huixcolotla's venerable walking group.[3]

Acatzingo's pilgrimage has gone through a similar process, although the organizers do not seem pleased about it. At its peak, the Acatzingo cycling pilgrimage surpassed six hundred riders, but a gradual splintering brought the number down to its current two to three hundred cyclists.[4] In some cases, offshoot groups even copy the itinerary, almost to the day. Hence, they sometimes park alongside Acatzingo's pilgrims at the same meal stops, eliciting vaguely sullen comments from members of the Comisión. This was the case of San Sebastián Villanueva, which in 2018 had been on its own for only two years. Smaller, and likely with a limited budget, they did not decorate their support trucks with glossy banners. However, their carefully crafted, hand-painted banners depicting the dramatic martyrdom of their patron saint—the always forlorn San Sebastián, bound to a tree and riddled with arrows—were unique and attractive.

Acatzingo's pilgrimage, when moving as planned, resembles a caravan with three distinct sections. The first two sometimes proceed together as a single long convoy, and at other times they uncouple into separate columns, which alternate in the lead: the larger group focuses on the immediate needs of the riders and protecting the cyclists as they make their way to Juquila; the smaller section carries most of the laborers, equipment, mariachis, and provisions. A third section can hardly be called a convoy, which suggests a semblance of order. It is little more than a scattered herd of camp followers, a varied assortment of vehicles carrying the cyclists' friends and families and gradually catching up with the formal caravan as it progresses. In the strictest sense, they are not part of the organized pilgrimage; however, they become increasingly prominent, and numerous, as Acatzingo's cyclists approach Juquila, where they rendezvous with the town's walking pilgrimage.

For most observers, the main convoy is the focus of interest because of the uniformed cyclists, the alleged reason for the group's existence and the symbolic heart of the endeavor. They inaugurate the pilgrimage each year with a slow half-lap around Acatzingo's *zócalo* (main plaza), and they bring it to a close with a triumphant parade ride into the same square seven days later. The lead vehicle is a 1990s-vintage ambulance van that once served the city of Puebla. White, with a custom elevated roof, a dull gold stripe circumnavigating its midsection, and mismatched hot-rod wheels, the aging rescue vehicle announces the pilgrim's arrival with a full complement of red, blue, and white lights and the full-throated wail of its siren. Inside, a nurse and medical technician accompany the driver, prepared for injuries. This is no idle concern. Although scrapes, cuts, muscle aches, stomach upsets, and a broken bone every so often represent the standard first aid challenges, approximately twenty-five years ago one of Acatzingo's cycling pilgrims died after drifting into oncoming traffic.[5]

Following the ambulance, though, is a seemingly less practical but equally important vehicle—a fifteen-year-old white Chevy Silverado ingeniously transformed into an imposing mobile chapel, although in some ways it suggests a Passion-themed float akin to the mobile allegorical tableaux used in religious processions of the early 1900s.[6] Upon close inspection, its conversion has been achieved simply by spanning the entire vehicle, literally bumper to bumper, with a modified cargo frame, creating a high white canopy above the entire vehicle. The six tall supports sustaining this shelter reside inside heavy-duty clear plastic pipes creating columns. These, in turn, have been threaded with interior lights that glow yellow, orange, and red within a white sheath of translucent plastic with embossed letters, relief-stamped images of the Virgin Mary, and geometric cutouts. In the darkness, the columns radiate a warm flame-hued splendor, and the lettering spells out the name of the family sponsoring the chapel. Beneath the canopy and facing forward, a forlorn yet luminous *Ecce Homo*—the suffering, tortured Christ—looks down from a flower-decked frame above the truck's cab. In the back, a still more generously garlanded image of Nuestra Señora de Dolores (Our Lady of Sorrows, Acatzingo's colonial-era patroness, who enjoys a local miraculous reputation) holds center stage facing the back of the pickup, so cycling devotees can see her as they ride. Aside from the extra flowers, Dolores also seemingly receives the pious attentions of a pair of stylized snow-white swans that double as overstuffed flower bearers with artificial blossoms cascading from their elegantly curved necks and winged backs. The avian courtiers appear to swim toward the *Madre Dolorosa* in unison on a blood-red velvet carpet, which they share with a pair of floor monitors—speakers, like those used onstage at concerts. Overhead, hanging from the canopy's ceiling, small white lanterns with delicate butterfly cutouts, each one dangling a coral or sea-green pendant, illuminate the altar scene. Finally, a special banner spans the tailgate, celebrating the pilgrimage's thirty-ninth anniversary and acknowledging the chapel's sponsors. As you might expect, the anthemic, devotional pop emerging from the speakers battles the ambulance's screaming siren for aural supremacy as these vehicles pass.

In a slightly jarring contrast, the next section of the caravan brings roughly one-third of the group's cyclists, perhaps eighty riders, attired in Acatzingo's pilgrimage kit. Perhaps 10 percent of these riders carry penitential images on their backs: framed photographs of the Virgin, statuettes of the baby Jesus and various saints, large crosses, or thick, heavy votive candles. This tradition allows ample room for self-expression. The rectangular frames and crosses often feature homemade rag or rope straps, but the candles and images of the Santo Niño usually travel in dainty hand-crocheted backpacks or slings.[7] A few riders bear personal, modest vitrinas. Most of these individuals have promised Juquila to carry these images throughout the journey, either out of gratitude or in hopes of securing her intercession, or both. As part of their vows, they remain inseparable from the image or candle throughout the pilgrimage; even if they are eating meals or resting at the planned stopovers, it stays on their back or stands next to their plate on the tables assembled from long planks and metal sawhorses.

On the heels of the first peloton, a second mobile chapel rolls into view. Close inspection, however, reveals that this extravagant exemplar of mobile pilgrimage architecture was designed for a different pilgrimage. Stenciled letters on the chapel's front facing panel, above the Ford F-150's cab, announce the sixty-second anniversary of the Los Reyes Juárez's Virgin of Guadalupe torch relay. In other words, this truck altar

Figure 9. The boys. After lunch and an hour of rest, a cluster of young men dressed in Acatzingo's pilgrimage T-shirts prepare to climb on their bicycles and renew their journey. Two of them stand with penitential offerings strapped to their backs: at left, a thick, votive candle ensconced in a crocheted sling; at right, a sizable, plaster Christ Child declaring, "I will Reign." Photograph by the author.

was borrowed and repurposed for the occasion. The famed brown-skinned image remains visible under Acatzingo's patroness. In a way, it is fitting. It offers us a visual representation of devotional layering and the connections between distinct pilgrimage devotions. Moreover, many poblanos visit Guadalupe, the national patroness, long before embracing devotion to the more distant Juquilita.

Retrofit and ready, the structure rises impressively from the pick-up's cargo bed, looking like a miniature basilica. Crafted of sheet metal given a deep auburn patina, it looms above the truck's cab. Below Juquila's image, large mosaic-like ovals of snuggly fit peach, pink, and red roses surround streaks of purple gerbera daisies and encircle the truck bed. The effect is quasi-funerary, which is not surprising given that the same artisans accept commissions from mortuaries and families of the deceased. Like the preceding chapel, it also deploys light and sound to round out its pious flamboyance. In this case, another set of speakers reside beneath the Virgin Mary, but here they feature integrated multicolored lights that pulse and churn to the beat of a devotional playlist. Above, strips of green, white, and red LEDs trace the dome's seams, arches, and bell towers, complete with tiny bells (see plate 11).

Immediately following, a second flock of cyclists flies along, awash in the praise songs, and among them purrs a lime green Chevy Spark, one of the few subcompact cars taking part in the pilgrimage. Outfitted with a modest set of warning lights spanning its factory roof rack, this vehicle functions as Acatzingo's chase car. It has no fixed place in the caravan but surges ahead or lags behind to buy parts, ingredients, medications, or whatever else is needed. There are other vehicles that also lack an assigned place in the caravan. They simply forge ahead and wait at stipulated meal stops. For example, a small, refrigerated box truck carries fresh meat from animals donated by sponsors only must keep up with the group. The little Chevy Spark is much more important.

In 2018, it carried Luis, my chief contact and one of the most important members of the Comisión. In the little hatchback, he zips up and down the caravan, cheering or chiding as needed, calling on riders to get moving after meals, and admonishing them to stay between the mobile chapels. He stands out among the other members of Acatzingo's organizing committee. He lacks the rough-cut, macho, road-warrior exterior that characterizes several others. It makes sense: most of his colleagues are truckers and tradesmen, so it is hardly surprising that they project a kind of don't-mess-with-me, gruff exterior. On another level, many of them also exhibit the can-do, keep-it-moving improvisational spirit I had witnessed among members of Caminando Juntos.

Luis, however, is a professional, a technician at the hometown health clinic. He seems professorial in his unassuming navy blue crewneck, cotton sweater, jeans, and sensible short haircut and neatly trimmed mustache. Although he doesn't shy from calling attention to problems, he doesn't bark orders or slide into off-color verbal jabs that are commonplace in the melee of semitrailers, bikes, and pickups or amid the set-it-up-and-tear-it-down whirlwind of mealtimes. He speaks with measured calm to cyclists and fellow organizers alike. He commands respect subtly, a respect born of years of dedication and leadership.

Luis enjoys his role and the respect he inspires among the young cyclists, but once we reached Juquila, I sat with him and his wife for a relaxed midday meal, and they detailed how taxing leadership had been over the previous years. His father founded and led the pilgrimage for two decades, and then Luis followed in his footsteps for almost twenty more years, finally passing the baton to others for the thirty-ninth anniversary in 2018. It had been an inherited honor and obligation, he claimed.

His wife, Adriana, argued that his leadership of the pilgrimage had gradually become the cause of significant marital strife. Luis was often at meetings with the Comisión, working on tasks for the group, or simply absent from the home while spending time with the *muchachos*, Acatzingo's young cyclists. Luis acknowledged that he felt a deep affinity for them and informally mentored several individuals. Adriana, though, maintained that she and their children felt abandoned. The two of them fought and approached the verge of separation. She joked that at one point she threatened to lead girls' activities that would require her to be absent from home too. Leading the pilgrimage year after year was simply too much. Luis eventually agreed, although he admitted it was hard to let go.[8]

Originally, he told me, he had not planned on going to Juquila in 2018. He tried to just step back, but he wanted Acatzingo's tradition to endure, and the Comisión had struggled in his absence. Therefore, he agreed to accompany the group to provide support and coaching. He noted that the trip was much more pleasant and relaxing with his wife in tow and without all the president's responsibilities; Adriana agreed.[9]

In short order, the third and final truck-chapel emerges just ahead of the last group of pilgrims. Subdued in comparison to the others, it resembles a parish church fashioned from metal in the same mahogany tones as the mini-basilica from Los Reyes. Dedicated to Our Lady of Sorrows (Dolores), as you would expect, it too sports strings of LED lights accentuating architectural details: neon red for the central arch and the three small crosses gracing the bell towers and plastic dome, blue for the neoclassic roof lines, and white underlining the Juquila and illuminating the plastic cupola from within. Beneath the roof, the chapel's floor functions as a stage for simple floral arrangements, artificial lilies, carnations in blue and white, and a large speaker. The builders expanded the space available for display by adding a copper-hued metal extension along the sides of the pickup bed; its stamped, faceted surface reflects both sunlight and the LEDs. Facing forward, on the wall opposite the Virgen de los Dolores, a traditional (i.e., not the likeness promoted by the archdiocese since 2014) framed photograph of Juquila dressed in white completes the Marian duo at the center of Acatzingo's celebration. Juquila appears against a classic baroque backdrop of textured gold. This image is perhaps the most common likeness appearing on pilgrimage vehicles, regardless of their geographic origin. In a sense, Juquila, a representation of the Immaculate Conception, and Dolores, a grieving Mary at the foot of the Cross, represent two sides of the devotional coin: triumphant purity alongside obedient, pious sorrow, a pairing symbolically connected by Acatzingo's pilgrims in this truck altar.

Almost immediately, the last group of riders comes into view, accompanied by a modestly decorated black motorcycle sporting a small-scale, framed image of Juquila affixed to the handlebars and flanked by two bouquets of red and white artificial flowers. Its rider keeps track of stragglers.

Finally, a pair of tractor-trailers brings up the rear. Each displays the group's thirty-ninth anniversary banner on their expansive flanks and Juquila's image on the grill. The first is a mostly vacant, cavernous cargo space. During the pilgrimage, cyclists who are too tired, hurt, or lazy take refuge inside. It also stores bicycles that cannot be repaired and ultimately will hold hundreds of bikes on the return trip. The final truck, another eighteen-wheeled behemoth, serves as a traveling workshop. Ernesto, a bike-store owner in Acatzingo, and two mechanics, Gustavo and Octavio, spend the journey inside the cargo bay repairing bicycles and then putting pilgrims back on the road as quickly as possible. Ernesto also donates an expensive road bike for a raffle at the dance party that Acatzingo hosts in Juquila. Pleasant and stippled with grease stains, this trio works hard and charges riders for repairs. Sometimes, the flow of bikes needing their attention is overwhelming, but at other times, they doze, fiddle with their cell phones, or simply stare out the open tailgate, watching the landscape recede as the pilgrimage advances.

Ernesto is quite thoughtful. As is often the case, during occasional quiet moments, the more mature, usually older participants explore the deeper questions involved in Juquila's devotion.[10] Not surprisingly, health issues are often central. For Ernesto, it is a timeless philosophical question, "¿A qué se debe?" (Why are things as they are?). He ruminates for a long moment, staring out the wide-open cargo bay toward distant mountains before turning his gaze back into the cavernous trailer, "Why are some people wealthy and others poor? Why are some blessed with good health, and others suffer continually?" Ernesto doesn't come across as pious, and he distances himself from devout certainties. People claim, he says, "God sends us tests," but, "doctors tell you this isn't true."[11] Then Ernesto shifts gears and speaks of his eight-year-old daughter's battle with liver cancer. He recounts how doctors cautioned him, "Don't waste your money."[12] They advised him to just take her home and take care of her until the end. He lets the cruel reality of this advice linger for a dozen long seconds without elaboration. The noise of the semitrailer laboring up the mountains and rattling with each bump in the road fills the void.

Undaunted, Ernesto sought out different doctors who carried out a difficult hours-long surgical procedure. Today, his daughter is healthy. Ernesto, however, doesn't explicitly make the connection between devotion and miraculous cure, as so many pilgrims do, yet the implication is clear in his parting comment, "I owe the Holy Virgin and God a great deal."[13]

In fact, the themes of pious debt and doubts about modern medicine come up in many discussions. Domingo, the sometimes-foul-mouthed trucker and member of the Comisión, speaks in similar terms. Doctors, "the good kind," he stresses, counseled his wife to terminate a pregnancy due to their detection of profound birth defects. Anguished, she refused, but sometime later, still fretting about her unborn child, she managed to touch the hem of Acatzingo's famed Virgin of Dolores's mantle while the image was on public display. As she handled the fabric, she quickly asked for a miracle. Domingo, puffing a cigarette, pulls out his phone and begins scrolling with his free thumb. Eventually, he finds what he is looking for and turns the screen toward me, showing a series of pictures of his daughter's *quinceañera* (fifteenth birthday party). She is "totally normal," he assures me. Domingo looks at me intently, and his words emerge calmly amid a cloud of smoke, echoing Ernesto: "I owe the Virgin a lot."[14] In fact, the Virgin of Juquila inspires several members of his family. Domingo also donates the use of his tractor-trailer and helps organize the pilgrimage with his brother, Salomón, the president of the Comisión. His son, he told me, was driving a support truck for Acatzingo's walking group in 2018.

The second section of the pilgrimage represents the group's quartermaster corps, rolling pilgrimage worker hotel, and mobile mess hall. It is made up of four hefty decorated tortons. In Acatzingo's case, each truck has been earmarked for specific essentials: One carries the mariachis, along with their outfits and instruments, as well as a few male laborers. Another is packed with cooking gear—huge stockpots, field stoves, gas tanks, massive griddles (*comales*), tools, all manner of cooking implements, and tableware, as well as a dozen or more long wooden tabletops and folding steel sawhorses to create makeshift counters where pilgrims can eat while standing. A third carries *víveres* (victuals), including many large sacks of vegetables, crates full of fruit, large jars of spices, and huge plastic tubs holding everything that goes into rustic Mexican fare. Finally, the last truck serves as both transportation and accommodations for the ten-woman cooking crew and an equal number of their children. It also must fit their luggage, bedding, and a 1,200-liter water tank. Each truck boasts cheerful decorations as well.

Carrying nearly all the provisions, laborers, and musicians, this truck quartet must move independently to keep the whole pilgrimage progressing smoothly. Typically, it must surge ahead of the riders and mobile chapels to arrive at the preplanned stopovers, quickly set up a field kitchen, extend tarps to shade incoming cyclists, and prepare hot meals. The mariachis are on hand to celebrate the riders' arrival and to enliven meals with *ranchera* classics, devotional ballads, and party favorites. For the morning and mid-afternoon stops, they remain in street clothes, often tucked into a corner or space between trucks. In the evening, they don full *charro* outfits: the nineteenth-century ranch-dandy costumes

with black-ribbon ties, snug bolero jackets, and tight pants sparkling
with faux-silver buttons and chains. If it is cold, they wear cowboy pon-
chos over their outfits. They position themselves to serenade the images
within the mobile chapels, which are always lined up carefully with their
altars facing the congregating riders at the end of each day.

For this set of trucks, meeting their obligations often means setting
out well after dark, when the riders are bedding down for the night, so
that the kitchen crew can set up and cook in the hours before dawn.
Subsequently, the tortons remain behind when the bikers and support
trucks return to the road. The cooks and workers clean up and stow
equipment, and then this group races ahead, passing the main convoy
and making haste to the next stop. While on the move, the mariachis and
staff do their best to sleep in their own torton.

Finally, perhaps forty or more vehicles bearing friends and families
of all ages follow the cyclists, organizers, and support staff to Juquila.
Here, there is no evidence of coordination whatsoever. Typically, six
to eight revelers are packed in old tarp-covered pickups crammed full
of cooking gear, foodstuffs, bedding, and nesting sets of plastic stools.
Were it not for their irrepressible cheer, they could be confused with
refugees. On the first two nights, few of these tagalongs appear; however,
knowing Acatzingo's itinerary, which hasn't changed for decades, several
materialize on the third morning of the journey at El Vado, where the
cooking crew is serving a hearty pork mole to cyclists. When the entire
group finally reaches Juquila, they are legion. Even a charter bus mate-
rializes and nestles itself in alongside the sundry rattletraps parked in
front of the rising bandstand. Of course, these travelers bring their own
kitchen gear and food, creating a touching scene in the encampment
with Juquila's shrine visible a couple of kilometers away: many groups
of three, sometimes four, generations relax and socialize around the back
of their vehicles. They envelope the core group of support trucks and
their tarps in a patchwork quilt of family gatherings. Quickly, fan-like
patterns of plastic stools and upended plastic buckets spread out from
glowing *anafres* (braziers), from whence emerge *gorditas* (stuffed tortilla
snacks), *albonigas en mole* (meatballs in mole), and *huevos a la Mexicana* (scrambled eggs with tomatoes, onions, and chili). Additionally,
pilgrims consume a fair amount of *pan dulce* (pastry), *atole* (hot corn
beverage), and Coca-Cola.

As coordinated from the beginning, in Juquila the cycling pilgrimage joins forces with a spirited group of walking devotees who left
Acatzingo a full week beforehand. They number perhaps sixty pilgrims
and travel with their own support vehicles, including an ornate wooden
mobile chapel and two carved miniature backpack temples carried by

a rotating cast of pilgrims. For the next forty-eight hours, the swelling number of families, walkers, riders, and neighbors take part in a veritable village festival—one that has been crated, carted, and reconstituted almost 300 miles (500 km) away from the plaza and parish they call home. The devotional climax of the entire event is a procession in which the cycling and walking pilgrims, their respective organizers and support personnel, and all the additional devotees that have coalesced in Juquila, carry Acatzingo's images—those that arrived in the mobile chapels and those carried by pilgrims—amid fireworks, chants, and mariachis.

Although it causes some consternation within the cycling Comisión, for the past few years the walking group has led Acatzingo's march from the encampment to Juquila's basilica. They grumble that in the past the different groups took turns, but now the hikers have laid permanent claim to the vanguard. Although smaller in number, the hiking devotees dwarf the cyclists in enthusiasm, and that seems to be the foundation of their precedence claims. They've chosen Juquila's traditional colors for their group and hence distinguish themselves in blue-and-white T-shirts. Four of them carry a large wooden display case with both Juquila and the Virgin of Dolores and follow on the heels of a few rocket-wielding young men announcing the procession's advancement. They, in turn, are followed by a handful of standard bearers and two young men wearing the small backpack chapels that accompanied the walkers on their journey. Behind them, the rest of their group processes, with a handful of family members mixed in, belting out call-and-response *porras* (cheers) reminiscent of sporting events and political rallies, such as the basic, "María aclamamos, por eso caminamos" (Mary we praise, that's why we walk), and, of course, the protest movement classic, "Se ve, se siente Acatzingo está presente" (roughly, "You see, you feel, Acatzingo's here for real"). However, my personal favorite remains:

| | |
|---|---|
| Estamos todos tristes? | Are we all sad? |
| NO, NO! | NO, NO! |
| Estamos muy contentos? | Are we all very glad? |
| SI, SI! | YES, YES! |
| Entonces cantaremos todos nuestra porra | In that case, then let's sing out our cheer |
| Entonces cantaremos todos nuestra porra | In that case, then let's sign out our cheer |
| ¡Maria Reina! | Mary Queen! |
| ¡Maria Reina! | Mary Queen! |
| ¡Maria Reina! | Mary Queen! |
| ¡Reina, Reina, Reina!" | Queen, Queen, Queen! |

Their dedication to maintaining these chants during the procession to the shrine is impressive, and, privately, they criticize their cycling compatriots for not showing similar spirit. However, riding for four days, often spread out over several miles, can't foment the same level of group cohesion as a grueling two-week trek over a rugged swath of the Mexican countryside.

In any case, a series of porters carry the cyclist's images behind the blue-and-white-clad chanters: a single individual goes first, holding up a cloth standard of the Virgin of Dolores; then, a series of paired bearers bring the Marian images and, finally, Acatzingo's suffering Christ. Behind these icons, the mariachis appear in their white outfits and turquoise ties, reprising the repertoire of devout rancheras they've been cycling through for the entire journey. Trailing them, the cyclists process in their red-and-white riding kits. As with their walking counterparts, many of them carry votive candles and floral offerings, and several also lug the images they've borne personally throughout the journey. And finally, just as when they were on the road, a large number of the relatives and friends who have followed the pilgrims bring up the rear. Acatzingo's combined pilgrimages and their entourage easily fill the sanctuary for the special Mass that the organizers previously commissioned. As the Mass begins, some members of the Comisión appear visibly relieved and totally exhausted. The group's secretary finds an out-of-the-way buttress toward the back of the basilica and slumps to the floor. His eyes half open and his arms crossed, he can barely stay awake. All that remains is the evening's dance and a slow, triumphant drive home.

Curiously, in pursuit of efficiency and practicality, the Acatzingo cycling pilgrims visit Juquila's Pedimento chapel on their way home, instead of pausing there before approaching the shrine. In doing so, they depart from the crescendo-of-arrival practices that most groups sustain. It would indeed be difficult to safeguard hundreds of bikes if tired riders arriving in dispersed groups paused, parked, and joined the crowds entering the famed votive chapel. Instead, Acatzingo's pilgrims visit the Pedimento all together with their bikes safely stowed inside their tractor-trailers as they depart. This decision—anticlimactic, but understandable—hamstrings the powerful devotional theater of pilgrimage. For most other groups, the Pedimento stop offers a crucial precursor scene in the staged, dramatic arrival at the shrine in Juquila.

Pondering the phenomenon as a collection of convoys, and the mulling levels of coordination involved, brings into focus the remarkable complexity of the endeavor. Viewed closely, the work required of the Comisión in the months, weeks, and days preceding the event is astounding. Perhaps the only cultural events similar in terms of mass movement and festive encampments in North American society are music festivals and the tailgate-party practices connected to some universities' football teams.

Large Mexican pilgrimages like Acatzingo's maximize economy. In fact, merchants along the road, and in Juquila, complain about how little pilgrims spend. To put it another way, the goal is to put on the best celebration for the lowest cost, without being "cheap." Ease and efficiency hardly seem important, but a local notion of excellence guides the organizers. Again, they have a simple, powerful tool at their disposal: labor. Many individuals work hard and ignore fatigue for the pilgrimage's duration. From a distance, or to anyone outside this religious culture, it may seem irrational, extravagant, or excessive. Indeed, fiesta-centered piety in Mexico has faced such criticism for centuries. Some commenters within the Catholic Church, as well as those within certain intellectual and political circles, have labeled such customs as wasteful, backward, and fanatical in the past.

On another level, members of the Comisión, although defensive about its unpolished nature, remain committed to their vision of the pilgrimage experience and collective celebration. These organizers could perhaps seek out lighter, smaller equipment, employ labor-saving shortcuts, cease hiring mariachis and dance bands, or scale back the elaborateness and number of hot meals, but such actions would clash with the pilgrimage's ethos, in which participants construe exertions and preparations as pious offerings and believe that a truly festive experience is important. However, they organize their trips within a deep do-it-yourself pueblo tradition common in Mexican towns. For example, it appears as if the Comisión approaches each challenge with a list of the available individuals, tools, materials, social connections, and expertise in mind and then surpasses obstacles by deploying a mix of these resources and exerting greater effort.

To a certain degree, this is evident in the equipment the Acatizingo pilgrims carry for the camp kitchen. The standard made-in-Mexico "appliances" that are unremarkable in a public market's food court seem excessively cumbersome for travel; they are hulking and awkward. Apparently, metal workers designed them to last forever. For example, one pickup truck's only purpose is to carry a large donated gas-powered corn mill to grind the *nixtamal* for fresh, handmade tortillas, which works in tandem with a trio of waist-high, hand-operated tortilla presses and a large—approximately six feet long and four feet wide—gas griddle. Taking culinary dedication to a still higher level, the Acatzingo pilgrims also bring along two large spits (*trompos*), which are anchored to a large portable steel counter, hence providing the full experience of *tacos al pastor* (shawarma-style pork tacos) for over three hundred people. The twin spits only emerge for a single meal and remain in the torton for the rest of the journey.

Eating well remains of central importance and a symbolic measure of celebratory grandeur for participants. In fact, veterans reminisce about particularly elaborate meals and festive activities when the pilgrimage celebrated its twenty-fifth anniversary in 2004. Fermín, the driver of the refrigerated truck that carries Acatzingo's supply of meat during the journey, speaks nostalgically of roasting dozens of sheep for the occasion.

Many participants simply couldn't enjoy this kind of experience outside a collective endeavor. Ostensibly, then, the pilgrimage is organized for the cyclists, yet it remains a largely open event, attracting a mostly working-class cross section of Acatzingo to enjoy an escape from their daily labors, a chance to see other parts of Mexico, and a visit to a famed shrine. The current contribution for cyclists in 2018 was 600 pesos (thirty-one dollars), up from 400 pesos a few years earlier, for a week-long excursion, but these fees don't come close to meeting the pilgrimage's costs. Doing that requires an extensive effort to solicit donations, in cash and kind, from individuals and businesses. Of course, the truckloads of camp followers that ultimately join the pilgrimage in

Figure 10. Tacos. Sharing food is a key part of the pilgrimage experience for many groups. Acatzingo's Comisión, for example, plans excellent, varied meals for each day of their journey, which requires the hauling of special equipment, such as, the gas-fired spits visible here. On this evening, hungry pilgrims enjoy tacos al pastor, a Mexican favorite, with all the fixings. Photograph by the author.

Juquila incur their own costs in food and fuel. In addition to the obvious expense of provisions, the group's stopovers along the way sometimes entail fees. Renting the large playing field from Juquila's high school is perhaps the most crucial. All the riders' and support personnel's meals are included, and the cooking crew generously gives away meals to others outside this circle. The one trick that makes stops easier entails securing sponsored meals. For example, on two occasions, different patronesses along the route treat the entire group to a meal, arriving at the prearranged location in their own trucks with the food already prepared. This gives the supporting cast a much-needed break and smooths logistics by removing the need for a full setup and breakdown of the mobile kitchen.

Heading the list of outlays, the Comisión also hires a well-known cumbia band from Puebla for celebrations in Juquila. The dance also draws pilgrims from other communities whose groups are too small for such extras, and, by all appearances, Actazingo's organizers proudly host fellow devotees.

Essentially, pilgrimage groups cultivate a symbolic drama that requires additional time, energy, and expense. For example, Acatzingo's Comisión long ago decided that their group will depart each December 2, followed by a dramatic return on December 8, the actual feast day of Our Lady of Juquila, but the group doesn't need a full week. The riding portion takes only four days and three nights, and they spend two nights in Juquila before loading all the bikes into one of the large trucks and heading home. Acatzingo's pilgrims, however, drag out their return, spending a night in Oaxaca, where they enjoy another donated meal and pastries in the main market. Finally, they stop for an additional night within a few miles of Acatzingo on December 7. This last stop allows the group to pull all the bikes back out at first light on December 8 and stage a parade ride into the main plaza for the Feast of the Immaculate Conception. There, in the same space where they began, they file into the pueblo's historic church for a homecoming Mass. Clearly, the scheduling and staging suggest that the point is to create a memorable week, mixing devotion, celebration, entertainment, and leisure, topped off with a triumphant cycling procession at home on Juquilita's official feast day.

# CHAPTER 10

# Arriving at Your Feet

Only two or three miles distant from Juquila's basilica, the Pedimento occupies a modest promontory with an expansive view of the shrine and surrounding pueblo in the distance. Juquila appears as a jumble of angular structures scattered haphazardly across the steep mountainside. Nestled in the center and rendered in the colonial basilica style (although rebuilt in the twentieth century), the imposing sanctuary compound presides over the overgrown village—its prominence a fitting metaphor for its local importance. Were it not for the four-hundred-year-old image of Mary Immaculate, and episodic promotion, Juquila may have remained a nondescript Chatino village, like others in the mountains above Oaxaca's Pacific coast. Instead, the bustling, chaotic town drives regional economic growth. The shrine town even draws transplants from other regions, at least it did prior to the COVID-19 pandemic. For a time, with business shuttered and devotees staying at home, residents faced hard choices like many Oaxacans in less dynamic communities. In 2022, however, waves of pilgrims returned in force.

El Pedimento is an apt name, formed by making a noun of *pedir* (to ask or petition), resulting in, essentially, "the place to plead." In some ways, the Pedimento seems more important than even Juquila's basilica, the ostensible end point of the pilgrimage. Here, with the shrine visible in the distance, devotees address Our Lady of Juquila directly. Here, they pause for long visits and leave behind symbolic items: their messages, their requests, their promises—evidence we can view and, to a certain degree, "read."

The Pedimento's history is murky, and its future is suddenly—and bizarrely—uncertain. One of Oaxaca's main newspapers claims it dates from the 1700s but offers only a vague nod to church sources.[1] It also asserts that 7,800 different pilgrimages make the customary stop at the

Pedimento each year. Father Ruiz y Cervantes, however, never mentions it in *Memorias* (his 1791 book on the pilgrimage), and I've never come across a reference to the chapel in nineteenth- and twentieth-century archival documentation. Veteran pilgrims assert that no such chapel existed in the 1960s and report that in the 1970s a simple cross appeared there, inspiring some devotees to leave offerings.[2] The chapel, in other words, is a relatively recent innovation. Presumably, arriving pilgrims walked directly to Juquila's sanctuary in previous years. For devotees, these questions hardly matter. For the last few decades, most devotees have begun their celebratory arrival in Juquila at El Pedimento.

In a sense, the chapel is just one part of a set of attractions that have sprung up along the route over time. We can list it alongside the oft-repeated legends tied to natural landmarks in locations like El Pocito, where present-day pilgrims pause in hopes of seeing Our Lady of Juquila in burbling pools, or the trailside mountain spring where women hoping to become pregnant leave special offerings. The addition of such stops over the years, and the evolution of practices linked to them, underscores pilgrimage's dynamic nature. This is also part of what anthropologists characterize as the ever-evolving "moral geography" of many pilgrimages, referring to the processes by which devotees attach special significance and instructive narratives to specific locations and pass these meanings on to others and subsequent generations.[3] Periods of increasing popularity and expansion are particularly suited for these innovations within changing traditions. Over time they can lead to complex landscapes infused with sacred associations that are often reinforced as pilgrims recount the legends and stories linked to stone outcroppings, peaks, springs, mountain passes, and chapels.

It is tempting to suggest that the controversial Father Bourguet, while pastor from the 1940s to the 1980s, had a hand in the Pedimento's emergence, but I've seen no evidence of this in church archives, and he does not mention it in his reports. Newspapers report that before 1984, the Catholic Church controlled the site and the donations collected there.[4] Therefore, it likely began as a simple, final stopover for devotees as they approached Juquila and saw the shrine in the distance. Devotees probably began pausing to give thanks, and, subsequently, leave offerings. Its location, with easy access to the road connecting Juquila to Oaxaca City and the Pacific coast, was likely a crucial factor: devotees walking, cycling, running, driving, or riding in chartered buses could converge at the Pedimento. When I first visited in 2001, it was relatively large but still modest. A plaque at the site announces a substantial renovation in 2010, adding an additional side chapel, a pair of storage rooms, and a new roof for the main chapel. Likewise, another plaque declares that between 2011 and 2013, local authorities added stairs and paved the pathway connecting the Pedimento and Juquila. Not surprisingly, these years coincide with mounting governmental efforts to stoke religious tourism.

Unlike many religious monuments in Oaxaca, there are no baroque works of colonial art on its walls. It isn't attractive in a conventional sense, but architectural beauty is not the point. Built on a steep slope, it appears as a curious, single-level chapel from the front, opening upon a large, shaded waiting area and a sprawling parking lot. From the opposite direction, it looks like a multistory unwieldy ship preparing to sail into the valley. Close inspection reveals a practical design attuned to the site's function: a simple chapel facing the road and a series of yellow retaining walls and paved patios connected by stairs facing Juquila. This layout keeps the Pedimento chapel from tumbling into the valley, naturally, but it also offers many places for pilgrims to relax, socialize, and express themselves. The tall butter-colored walls invite votive graffiti. In fat flare-tip markers of black, blue, and red ink, in pleading paragraphs and staccato avowals, they fill the available space. In another respect, the Pedimento's architects met devotional practices with box-like niches set into a curving retaining wall, and they often house handmade petitionary offerings to poignant effect. At times, it appears like an uncoordinated exhibit of popular ritual art.

In truth, the Pedimento represents a complex of outdoor settings and indoor spaces rather than a single structure. It offers a set of stages where loosely established, expressive practices unfold. On one level, they are nearly all the same. Almost all devotees give thanks or make a pious request, and many do both. From another perspective, each individual's communication with Juquilita is unique—a customized variation on classic pious themes. In other words, at the Pedimento we encounter a keyless symphony, a layering of fugues, and an accretion of songs to the tune of need, plea, promise, hope, fear, and thanks.

Groups, like Caminando Juntos, generally arrive from the road. We follow Doña Meche as she makes her way toward the main chapel carrying Juquilita. Market stalls line the main road and beckon with glossy images of Juquila and piles of votive merchandise. As visitors turn onto the drive leading to the chapel, still more vendors appear. In concert, they display a glut of statuettes, portraits, key chains, rosaries, stickers, paperweights, pens, necklaces, scapulars, and a stunning diversity of gilded milagros. Each of the latter symbolize a specific ailment—from illnesses to loneliness—or some economic need. More surprising are teetering stacks of small, wooden houses. Many declare, "Virgin of Juquila, Grant me a Home" above their tiny entryways.[5] Alongside the mini-dwellings, vendors position toy cars, tiny fences, and plastic livestock. Nearby, small crates display artificial pesos and dollars. In sum, merchants sell an array of items to help devotees convey their messages with objects, objects that "speak" (like milagros) or that represent a different, hoped-for material reality.

The central chapel retains an open-air quality, functioning as a series of articulated spaces. Formal rituals seldom occur here, at least in my experience, and during peak periods, pilgrims must be patient: an hour or more wait is common. A covered patio serves as a large waiting area where devotees sort themselves into two parallel lines leading into the chapel. Long benches on either side accommodate resting pilgrims, many of whom have already completed their devotions. There they chat and await friends and family or simply watch new arrivals. On the edges of this covered area, individual devotees and pilgrimage groups have taken their messages vertical: banners, mostly made of shiny vinyl, cloak the trees and stretch between nearly every post, trunk, and railing surrounding the Pedimento. For the most part, they are positioned so pilgrims can examine them as they advance toward the chapel (see plate 12).

According to Frank Graziano's study of votive practices, the leaving of banners is unique to Juquila's Pedimento.[6] Thanks to technologies that allow printing on large sheets of durable, glossy vinyl, devotees enjoy a range of options. As you might expect, the aesthetics of local commerce carries over to devotional banners. Some feature large blown-up portraits of individuals or family photographs superimposed on dramatic landscapes. A fair number commemorate an individual devotee's recent passing. Others incorporate photo collages, or fan-like sprays of pictures, in combination with computer-generated graphic art. For example, in 2016, two couples, Julia and Ángel, from Córdoba, Veracruz, and Rafaela and Abel, from Playa del Carmen, Quintana Roo, left a simple sign stating, "We celebrate 6 years that you've let us arrive, we thank you Virgencita of Juquila."[7] Likewise, the fireworks artisans of La Posta Xiutetelco, Puebla, celebrating their second cycling pilgrimage, offered a banner featuring a white-clad, resplendent Virgin of Juquila, flanked by stylized red figures riding bikes, against a backdrop of digitally simulated blue and green pyrotechnic explosions. Bold red lettering at the top and bottom announces the group's provenance and a pilgrim slogan, "The faith on wheels leading to you."[8]

In some instances, banners appear in tiers, as pilgrims, finding easy-to-reach spaces filled, shimmy up tree trunks to find higher, unoccupied vantage points. Some remain taut and straight, while others drape off balance; still others, torn after months of exposure, flap loudly in the breeze. Most are made of tarp-like vinyl, but some visitors, including La Escandalosa, a band from the small Zapotec village of Quioquitani, leave hand-painted, cloth banners. Using a blue marker on a white sheet, they adorned their sign with a hand-drawn musical staff, stenciled red rosettes in each corner, and carefully drawn block lettering listing successive trips to Juquila in 2014, 2015, and 2016.

In addition, devotees seed the ground with a thick understory of commemorative crosses made of stone, metal, wood, and cement. Some must have been costly, and they usually represent large, established pilgrimage groups. For example, a stout marble cross embossed with a golden Juquila at its apex commemorates the twenty-fifth cycling pilgrimage from Palmarito, Puebla. Toward the bottom, it lists the business patron who paid for the cross, Hermanos Rodríguez's furniture rental business, and then acknowledges the pilgrimage's original founders.

At the end of the waiting area resides the main chapel, a medium-sized space with a handful of pews, which devotees almost never occupy. Some visitors pause to kneel and pray on the steps as they enter, but mostly they wait to approach the copy of Juquila inside. The panorama inside offers a mix of permanent ornamentation and devotee offerings. On the ceiling, rustic paintings recount the Virgin of Juquila's official history and legendary miracles; for example, one panel depicts the famed image's legendary emergence from the church fire in Amialtepec. Pilgrims inch forward, some talk quietly, and some crane their necks to examine the paintings above. Typically, several devotees are taking pictures and recording videos, their phones held above their heads as they near the image. The replica of Juquilita remains impassive at the heart of the chapel and centered within multiple phone screens. She stands on a stout pedestal, a minimalist stone carving arrayed in sequined finery, sheltered by a wooden canopy.

Nearly everything within the chapel changes constantly due to the relentless depositing of offerings, testimonial objects, and tokens of gratitude. Some of the decorations are quite unique. For example, in 2017, pilgrims from Huamantla, Tlaxcala, placed a striking earth-toned mosaic made from various seeds and beans over the main doorway. More commonly, large floral or balloon arches frame the Pedimento's Juquila. Fresh flowers, usually dahlias, carnations, gladiolas, and lilies, fill large vases arrayed on the floor before the image. Occasionally, more expensive arrangements including roses and birds-of-paradise nestle among them. In addition, devotees often deposit small bouquets on whatever unoccupied surface they can find.

The chapel's stone likeness of the Virgin of Juquila serves a crucial purpose and has much to do with the Pedimento's importance. Like the original, she wears a wig, flowing garments, and a golden diadem, although her dark, scarcely delineated face offers a shadowy, blank visage.

She is also much larger, perhaps two-feet tall. Crucially, however, this is an image visitors can touch. To make physical contact with sacred images has long been a vital facet of Catholic devotional tradition. Although sought passionately, it has long been impossible to touch the original image, which resides encased in thick glass above the altar in Juquila's basilica. She is too old and fragile to withstand devout caresses.

The Pedimento, however, offers devotees a chance to give their tactile inclinations and attendant hopes free rein. Pilgrims gently press hands to the image, stuff real and fake money into her robes, affix portraits to the sides of the canopy, and pin written messages and gilded milagros to her white robes. They also brush votive candles over the bedecked replica, which they then rub over the body of a parent, child, or fellow supplicant. The Pedimento, in other words, provides something devotees cannot find at the basilica, intimacy.

As with image devotions in the Catholic tradition elsewhere, leaving ex-votos (narrative testaments of faith and gratitude) and petitionary objects drives a shrine economy; in this instance, an economy that has been booming for the last few decades. In fact, it is not uncommon for visitors to observe workers at the Pedimento emptying baskets of pesos into bags, which they then carry away. Such scenes lead to assumptions about *millionadas* (untold millions) flowing through the chapel and into corrupt hands. They also explain why controlling the votive chapel has become a perennial flashpoint in local politics.

The conflict centers on who gets to sell at the site and collect alms, rent space, charge fees, and deploy the accumulated capital. Such struggles are common in shrine communities; rarely, however, are they as public as they have been at Juquila in recent years. In truth, they expose the unseemly side of the town's economic dependence on pilgrimage. Quite simply, conflict within the community has long centered on what faction, and which institutions or individuals, can profit from popular fervor. At the Pedimento, the clashes occasionally turn violent. Threats, roadblocks, organized protests, and periodic brawls are common. Individuals have died in the more intense skirmishes, and arsonists occasionally torch vendors' stalls.

For years the struggle appeared to be mostly a three-way tug-of-war between church officials, Juquila's municipal government, and a popular citizens' organization from Juquila's barrios, the Comisariado de Bienes Comunales (Public Goods Association), usually just called *comuneros* (communards). In the last few years, the clash has become more complex as another group of comuneros from the neighboring Chatino pueblo of Yaitepec asserts that Juquila illegally took the land where the Pedimento resides from their village. In a sense, they have inserted the chapel into the complex and historically fraught terrain of Indigenous land rights. Not surprisingly, juquileños argue these claims are specious. That hasn't stopped Yaitepec from aggressively occupying the site (allegedly armed), destroying merchandise, evicting vendors, blocking the main road with burning tires during pilgrimage season, and skirmishing with the police and national guard troops who forcibly ousted them on December 1, 2019. Yaitepec's activists claim that police killed a seventy-seven-year-old woman in the operation. The government denies these allegations.[9]

In any case, the conflict seems to have no end. For a time, Juquila's comuneros retained the Pedimento. News reports indicate that control has shifted back and forth between them and the municipality in the past, and representatives of the archdiocese claim the church holds the legal title to the chapel. In 2013, the comuneros forcibly occupied the site and wrested control from municipal officials, whom they accused of corruption and malfeasance, a reprise of accusations aimed at the polemical pastor when the municipality pried the site away from the parish and Father Bourguet in 1980s.[10] Municipal authorities claim that they managed the Pedimento for the common good, allocating the estimated 7–10 million pesos collected annually to social programs and infrastructural projects, but critics countered that officeholders surreptitiously pocketed large sums. Recently, municipal and church representatives have reworked the script, accusing the leaders of the comuneros of embezzlement.[11] Not surprisingly, church officials claim that they are the appropriate stewards of the Pedimento and related income simply because it is a religious site. In addition, they argue that funds donated by Juquila's followers should be reserved solely for religion-related expenditures.[12] But given the allegations of venality that led to Bourguet's ouster and common suspicions about church wealth, many locals scoff at the archdiocese's claims.

Of course, no one foresaw the COVID-19 pandemic, which closed the votive chapel and Juquila's basilica for months. Yaitepec's aggressive occupations of the site have exacerbated the conflict still more and have kept the Pedimento closed even after the shrine has reopened and pilgrims have begun returning in large numbers. They have also been strategic, framing the conflict as one of a long-suffering Indigenous community facing a long history of depredations from the neighboring shrine town, whom they depict as a grasping mestizo oppressor. Juquila contends that it, too, is a historically Chatino community, even though growth driven by the pilgrimage has drawn many residents from other parts of Mexico. At present, it is unclear if negotiation or a legal ruling could end the stalemate. If the Pedimento remains closed, it seems likely

Figure 11. The Amialtepec road sign, 2016. Only a handful of miles from the shrine, Amialtepec challenges the Catholic Church's official history, proclaiming that the Virgin of Juquila appeared miraculously in their community. In doing so, they raise enduring questions about the legitimacy of the image's eighteenth-century confiscation while calling on present-day devotees to visit sites they developed independently. Photograph by Mike DuBose.

that someone will build a replacement of some kind. In truth, it seems like an opportunity for nearby Amialtepec, the village where the tiny image of the Virgin Mary first developed her miraculous reputation.

Pilgrims are aware of these conflicts and frustrated by the chapel's closure, but they focus on their own immediate goals. The decidedly unholy human foibles rooted in greed don't dent their enthusiasm for Our Lady of Juquila or the Pedimento. It is hardly surprising that groups vie for a piece of a burgeoning shrine economy when the surrounding region offers very few opportunities. Most juquileños understand that the tiny colonial-era image of Mary drives the flow of people, goods, and wealth through their community. A tacit acknowledgment of this reality, especially in the context of the devotion's current popularity, emerges on the local PRI (Partido Revolucionario Institucional, an infamously corrupt political party) Facebook page, which offers a full-throated celebration of Juquila's remarkable recent growth.[13]

The Pedimento, in other words, represents a nexus of cultural, political, and commercial currents. As a result, it affords us a glimpse of political and religious practices in their messy, sacred, and not-so-sacred dimensions. It may seem damning to outsiders, but these dynamics produce little shock in societies where Catholic devotional customs remain ubiquitous. Mexicans, for one, have noted the economic and political ramifications of image devotions for centuries; it is no surprise that money changes hands at Juquila. It is also common among secularists to dismiss shrines as a form of exploitation of the credulous poor.

Devotees bristle at such facile characterizations. It bears repeating: Juquila's followers are aware of the political and economic motivations in play, but it doesn't dim their earnest sentiments and hopes. They remain critical of the opportunism and corruption at the shrine (and elsewhere too), but they focus on their relationship with Our Lady of Juquila. This is what matters when they enter the Pedimento.

Leaving these clashes to one side, it pays to remember the nature of image devotions. As Doña Fina's testimony reminds us (see chapter 1), there is an eminently practical ethos among many of Juquila's followers. Individual pleas tend to coalesce around three key topics: home (shelter, safety, and family harmony), health (illness, disability, and emotional struggles), and well-being (jobs, land, professional goals, education, and success in business), or a combination. Then there are general requests for overarching divine protection.

In other words, a candid focus on everyday struggle, need, and gratitude flourishes at the Pedimento. It may offend sticklers for sacramental piety, but the unabashed humanity on display remains understandable and, at times, moving. Even if the tenor of devotee petitions remains static, repeat visits to the Pedimento reveal an evolving expressive creativity. It isn't just the profusion of entreaties and offerings and what they "communicate" that inspires admiration. It is the dynamism, the unplanned bricolage, the ceaseless agglomeration, and the layering of devotee expression. It is pondering all of this and the simultaneous flurry of devotee activity that proves arresting.

To put it another way, the Pedimento, when it is open, offers a charged "found art" experience. Votive crowding amplifies Catholic devotionalism's elemental pathos and earnest sentimentality and gives it an intense, cacophonous quality—as if the multitude of pleas forms a jumbled, atonal chorus. For example, the surrounding hillsides seem to be a curated installation of expressive devotion, with three-dimensional collages of vinyl banners affixed between trees, the ground crowded with metal and stone crosses, the branches thickly festooned with smaller wooden crosses, and votive dioramas clustered here and there. Then there is the matter of the texts often accompanying these objects or scrawled on the sites' walls. The complexity of which also merits close, detailed examination.

When members of Caminando Juntos reach the Pedimento's image of Juquila, they carry out their personal devotional obligations. Tere mouths inaudible supplications, gazing earnestly at the image with Miguel at her side. Marta and her daughter, Sofi, do the same. Alicia pins milagros to the Virgin's vestments for her mother and father's health problems and prays. Gradually, other pilgrims press forward and members of Caminando Juntos move around a screen-like wooden barrier behind the image to an area under the image's long red mantle. There, additional images of Mary reside, and more offerings accumulate. Some of the toy cars and tiny wooden houses purchased outside appear at the foot of these images. Tere, Marta, and Sofi all reach out and gently tug on the Virgin's red, sequined mantle, allowing it to slowly pass through their hands, a lingering gesture of wistful affection. Then, one-by-one, they find the backdoor (see plate 13).

Devotees have different needs and thus different strategies. Some place their requests for help as close as possible to the carved image, often wedged into whatever spaces or cracks they can find in the wooden canopy or affixed to her clothing with a safety pin. Since proximity is often sought by other pilgrims, too, these items are the most likely to be removed as devotees deposit their messages and offerings in subsequent days. It is common to see school photos and diplomas among the offering. Others tape pictures and texts to columns nearby.

Many of these are simple expressions of gratitude, but some are more complicated. One devotee named Manuel deployed blue-and-silver glitter tape to leave three photos of a house in Orizaba, Veracruz, and his personal request: "Holy Virgin of Juquila, I ask you to grant me the miracle that the shack sells. . . . I ask you with great faith that you send a good client."[14] Manuel's message, of course, is not only for Our Lady of Juquila. He also speaks to fellow devotees, providing hand-copied, tear-away strips with his contact information, photos of the property he hopes to sell, a street address, and his name.

Manuel's plea is quite specific, but many more are broadly aspirational, occasionally cryptic. For example: "I ask for health, love, and hope, I love you very much and I ask that you help me achieve my dream of becoming a lawyer, and I want you to help me forget what happened, Amen."[15]

Nearby, Valeria R.F. writes in teal-blue marker (paired with a sketch of a girl in pigtails and a heart): "Virgencita: I know that I am not your best daughter, but I try to be a good person, for that reason I am daring to ask you that you don't abandon me in my struggle to secure my dream of being a doctor and being able to help others, help me achieve my dream, that it becomes real, I want to be a doctor and will never forget the reason for my goals."[16] Petitions like the forthright Valeria's remain anchored in youthful angst about life choices and livelihood. It is understandable that they are instrumental and future oriented.

Others, however, seek atonement. For example, a wooden plaque from February 2017 alludes to a husband's penance after an extramarital dalliance: "Virgin of Juquila: Thank you for allowing me to remain with my family after the careless act of mine on 17 September 2012, thank you for your miracle, José."[17]

Among the members of Caminando Juntos, Santiago left a very specific and unique votive offering at the Pedimento in 2016. After waiting his turn in line, he prepared a deeply personal, modern version of the traditional votive offering expressing his profound gratitude. Like so many Oaxacans, he has moved back and forth between the United States and Mexico seeking a steady livelihood and a safe place to raise his children. After working in various jobs over the years, he established his own heating and air conditioning business in the United States, not long before the pilgrimage in 2016. Santiago, like others, spent some time before the Pedimento's stone image of Juquila, but he then moved to the back of the chapel and sought out a high, blank space near the exit. From his backpack, he fished out a pen, glue, and a large manila envelope. He then extracted a photocopy from the Texas Department of Licensing and Regulation. (He had clearly planned for this moment.) In blue lettering on a bright yellow background, it declares him a licensed technician and states the name of his business. He then scrawled across the top, "Thank you Virgencita for giving us health and the tools to work and provide food for our family . . . 4 December 2016."[18] In sum, Santiago credits Juquila with his family's security. He then spread glue on back of the document and stuck it high on the wall near the exit. A year later, in 2017, his offering remained attached to the wall, still proclaiming Santiago's abiding gratitude. A part of him, so to say, still remained at the shrine.

When I first visited Juquila in 2001, the variety and volume of offerings outside the Pedimento's chapel, and the personal, narrative customs of display, stunned me. In fact, I initially passed by many of the vendors lining the road and parking lot without attending to the merchandise on offer. Having examined markets at other shrines, I expected to see candles, flowers, milagros, and a variety of keepsakes. Those items indeed abound, but it wasn't until I spent a few hours walking the grounds and noting the unique array of offerings that I circled back to examine the market wares more closely. The stands overflow with items that help devotees communicate their hopes and needs. Essentially, they sell visual aids. Such dynamics are not totally unique, but the variety of expressive aids and devotee interest in this medium of communication is particularly intense at Juquila's Pedimento.

Just outside the main chapel, to the left and right, is a pair of elongated one-room cinder-block votive chapels for leaving candles (*capillas veladoras*). To the uninitiated, they appear like dreary bunkers: dark narrow spaces lacking doors and nothing but an eight-inch-tall slit near the ceiling passing for a window. But again, form truly follows function: these chapels are simple, seemingly indestructible, impervious to fire, and maximize the space for hundreds of burning candles and multiple devotees to enter, pray, and deposit personal offerings.

The chapels also illustrate a commonly overlooked facet of image-centered religiosity. They don't make sense without ongoing, sustained devotional practice. Active devotion gives them meaning and dispels the blunt austerity they otherwise communicate. Wide, waist-high ledges for votive candles span a wall in each *capilla veladora*. During the height of pilgrimage season, hundreds of burning votives fill the shelf space, producing a soft, wavering glow, filling the air with their waxy warmth, and chasing gloom from the windowless enclosure. A potpourri of photographs, handmade drawings, messages, and images affixed to the walls speaks for devotees alongside their candles. These mementos fill the space above the flickering flames emitting a different register of heat and light, hope, anxiety, loss, and determination. In addition, individual devotees and groups enter, set their candles among the scores of others, and pray quietly.

Thus, you may come upon forty-year-old men like Caminando Juntos's Francisco, humbly communicating with Juquilita, his arms prayerfully crossed over his chest, and a few feet away encounter adolescent boys in Virgen de Guadalupe T-shirts with wide *guadalupana* bandannas on their heads leaving lit candles. Then, you may spy a small group of cyclists in matching bike-racing outfits kneeling on the cement floor, heads bowed. The sensory impact is memorable, to say the least—tremulous candlelight, the scent of smoke and wax, clusters of pleading pilgrims, and the unplanned collage of votive objects. The steady flow of offerings, the accretion of deposited messages and personal tokens, the overlap of tattered and discolored items and newer objects is also crucial to the evolving collage of hope. Additions suggest broader credence, enduring faith, pending pleas, and prayers answered. Without a flow of new offerings, the space would perhaps communicate a very different message: fading, seemingly forgotten devotional ephemera suggest despair.

Below one of the *veladora* chapels, several meters from the main chapel along a slope leading into the valley below, a simple, thatched ramada shelters a pair of narrow worktables where pilgrims fashion clay replicas representing their petitions and devout sentiments: for example, mud houses speak to a longing for simple, safe homes, and earthen hearts express hopes for well-being. Often several devotees work side by side, trickling water from refilled plastic bottles as needed to work the clay. Looking beyond this shaded space to the surrounding hillside, countless holes remain where pilgrims dig for clay. Many diorama-like petitions remain nearby or reside in more sheltered places, like the niches in the retaining walls.

But devotees do not rely solely on their ability to work clay. Here, the destination of many toy-like items sold by nearby vendors becomes clear. Pilgrims deploy these items, sometimes in combination with their clay creations, to stage scenes of bucolic stability and prosperity: a roof over one's head, a sturdy truck parked out front, and plump farm animals in the yard. Sometimes, devotees also stuff wads of toy money into the doors, under the roofs, and along the sides of their imagined *ranchitos*. In sum, the slopes surrounding the Pedimento reveal miniature communities of yearning.

Nearby, still more votive offerings fill the trees. In this area, however, it is no longer banners that predominate, but rather hundreds of simple wooden crosses—which vendors also sell—attached to trunks and branches by various means: twine, shoelaces, and even a necktie. In some cases, there are so many crosses that the trees appear beset by a parasitic infestation. Alternatively, the thick agglomerations along the trunks and spreading to the branches approximate an avant-garde art piece featuring living trees sprouting frantic profusions of Christian symbols.

Indeed, the Pedimento affords a stunning glimpse of popular religious expression, as if it were a collective outdoor exhibit. Its power comes across through accumulation, excess, and repetition: adamancy in the face of struggle. However, large piles of devotional trash amassed by laborers are unavoidable. In other words, many offerings end up in trash heaps, especially those made from ephemeral materials. Piles molder on the slopes, next to sheds, and even a few feet from new offerings. Presumably, workers cart a portion of this detritus away at some point, although the sun-bleached heaps suggest a lack of urgency.

Pilgrims notice this, too, but it doesn't seem to bother them. Like reciting the Rosary, singing a hymn, or counting the miles en route to the shrine, permanence isn't the point. It is about saying the words, expressing appreciation, and demonstrating faith. As with pilgrimage traditions more broadly, return and reiteration provide the stubborn rhythm of practice. Its cyclic, seemingly perpetual nature represents part of its power. The offerings, and the feelings experienced at the moment

Figure 12. Messages. Jumbled, as if a work of abstract art, hundreds of crosses jockey for space in the Pedimento's trees. Attached with twine, shoestring, cloth, and even neckties, they seem to cling fervently to the branches. None of them on their own are particularly profound. Their written messages offer straightforward pious declarations. However, in the aggregate, in their density, in their commonplace, earnest simplicity, they speak to a deep well of hope and need. Photograph by Mike DuBose.

of their deposit, reflect devotees' sentiments, even if the objects themselves are later discarded as trash. From a believer's perspective, Juquila knows. She doesn't need them to last forever.

## In Juquila

Heading away from the Pedimento, individuals take turns carrying Juquilita on her retrofitted chair. The trail drops down deep into the valley, running alongside a creek, before bringing the devotees to the dusty, winding streets of the town surrounding the shrine. Here Caminando Juntos pauses to regroup. For a time, Miguel, the youngest pilgrim, carries the Virgin, with Tere, Silvio, and Santiago beaming behind him and the rest of Caminando Juntos clustered together beyond them. This is the most tightly packed formation of the entire pilgrimage.

Perhaps a kilometer into town, we pause at a small open-air chapel alongside the street, featuring an image of Christ on the Cross. Many pilgrims stop here to pray briefly and leave behind a particular set of offerings. On the trail, walking devotees share the idea that an individual's walking stick absorbs their troubles and sins as they travel toward the shrine. Typically, individuals begin purchasing them from trailside vendors and using them when the path enters the steep slopes of the Sierra Sur. Veteran pilgrims caution newcomers not to pick up anyone else's staff; that would mean taking on their failings, sorrows, and struggles too. In a sense, this bit of pilgrim folklore speaks to the possibility of personal renewal.

At the street chapel on the outskirts of Juquila, the tradition is to stop, pray, and discard your walking stick. Some pilgrims also cast aside their wide-brimmed sun hats. Metaphorically, then, devotees are setting aside their pain, flaws, and troubles; they shed what has been holding them back. As a result, a large pile accumulates on the tiled floor of the street chapel. This seemingly innocent ritual act also signals an important shift in the journey, and it offers a moving tableau: a pile of staves and hats representing a longing for rejuvenation, a clean slate, a new start.

For Caminando Juntos this moment also signifies the end of the pilgrimage, as individuals discard the material trappings of this sweaty, kinetic mode of devotion. We have arrived.

However, for a few individuals, a final, strenuous offering remains. Alicia volunteers to lead a penitential procession through the streets of Juquila and all the way to the Virgin's altar, walking on bended knee while reciting the Rosary during the final stretch, perhaps a mile or so.

Figure 13. Your staff and your struggle. Walking sticks and wide-brimmed hats have been emblematic accessories for centuries. Within Juquila folklore, each rod absorbs its owner's personal struggles as they progress toward the shrine. When weary pilgrims reach the streets of Juquila, they pause at an open-air chapel, ponder the crucifix, and abandon their staves—and sometimes their hats too—before proceeding symbolically unburdened. In another sense, this moment presages devotees' return to Mexico's mundane realities. Photograph by Mike DuBose.

Two other women from Caminando Juntos agree to join her. Others, particularly the men, embrace supporting roles, sustaining a frenetic relay of blankets and pads to cushion their progress.

There is hardly a more venerable expression of pious humility in popular Catholicism. In fact, the image of the knee-walking penitent is a staple of devotional representation, and it remains a common practice at Mexican shrines. For some pilgrims, it represents a fitting conclusion to their *manda* (their vow), when they promise Juquilita to *llegar a tus plantas* (arrive at the *soles* of your feet.) But in a broader sense, it is simply one type of devout procession common at the end of a pilgrimage. Many groups organize public, pageant-like parades through the streets of Juquila as the final act of their journey. In nearly all cases, they involve expressions of joy, humility, and love; they can be quiet, intense, and penitential or cacophonous and triumphant. Often you can witness both types taking place simultaneously on the streets of Juquila.

Large groups comprised of hundreds of devotees and hired musicians (particularly the brass bands) are the most noticeable. They marshal impressive parades of their members decked out in matching outfits. For example, the cycling and walking groups from Acatzingo, Puebla, begin their respective pilgrimages at different times, but they meet in Juquila and then process to the shrine together for a special Mass booked months ahead of time. They carefully remove the large religious images from their truck altars and array them in the vanguard. In some instances, important sponsors/donors serve as bearers. A group of young men precede the assemblage, launching large exploding rockets above Juquila's rooftops, announcing their progress. Each group has its own traditions, but the basic format is relatively standardized. Groups wend their way through Juquila's streets led by their respective standards and their *imagenes de bulto* (statues). Individual pilgrims often carry floral bouquets or, occasionally, heavy penitential offerings such as thick four-foot-tall candles.

During peak periods, streams of processions converge on Juquila's shrine throughout the day. As the basilica looms larger, the streets narrow thanks to the encroachment of vendors' stands on both sides of the town's main arteries. The bands, particularly the drummers, appear engaged in a call-and-response contest with the pyrotechnic salvos, providing Juquila with a seemingly constant concussive soundtrack. These reverberations mix with recorded music wafting out of storefronts, the periodic tolling of the basilica's bells, and the amplified liturgy emanating from the sanctuary's PA system. Pilgrimage, at least this pilgrimage, concludes amid sonic excess.

Its visual aspect is no less arresting. Since organized groups often wear matching shirts, athletic pants, baseball caps, reflective vests, or custom tracksuits, the throngs, like an unplanned flash mob, form a swirling, multicolored human mosaic. In addition, their cherished images installed in elaborate vitrinas—many stylized as miniature churches—bob on an undulating sea of humanity flowing inexorably into the basilica. Many individuals clutch recently purchased souvenirs: typically, gilt-framed photographs of Juquila and small copies of the legendary statue. Above the amassed devotees, fluttering blue and white plastic steamers connect the atrium's fence to the upper reaches of the shrine's facade, tracing a quaking wedge of color.

In this manner it continues, almost incessantly, from November to early January, during Holy Week, and periodically throughout the year. In waves, roughly coinciding with the Mass schedule, processions reach the basilica. The new arrivals fill the sanctuary, replacing the preceding groups filtering out the shrine's side doors and making their way to additional attractions, such as the pathway leading under the Virgin's mantle, an additional votive chapel, and an open-air stage-like chapel where priests bless newly purchased images and lead individuals in making devout *juramentos*. Priests announce over the basilica's PA system,

Figure 14. The sanctuary. Pilgrims amass in the plaza and atrium in front of Juquila's basilica. They await their turn to enter and approach the original colonial-era image. She presides in sumptuous finery high above the altar behind thick glass. Many pilgrims will later process along a walkway behind the altar leading beneath the Virgin's long mantle. It is the closest they can get to the fragile image. Photograph by Mike Dubose.

however, that they will not consecrate tourist mementos, such as key chains and pens.

Many devotees return to the main plaza to take pictures of themselves in front of the basilica, which they promptly share on social media. Since 2020, and Juquila's designation as a *pueblo mágico* (magic town), large capital letters spelling out J-U-Q-U-I-L-A have become a popular backdrop. Not surprisingly, a few enterprising photographers work the scene. With printers and laptops nearby, they provide paying devotees with nearly immediate photographic souvenirs.

Behind the pilgrims within the sanctuary, new arrivals clog the outdoor atrium spreading out in front of the basilica's main entrance (see plate 16). Above the doorway an unattractive, plain white vinyl banner shouts "ENTRADA" (Entrance) in red letters. On the busiest days, visitors fill in much of the town's plaza as well. Church officials removed all seating many years ago to accommodate more devotees, but Juquilita's popularity guarantees many must remain outside. Acquiescing to this new reality in 2017, officials placed a jumbotron and speakers against the basilica's facade, allowing amassed pilgrims to "see" the four-hundred-year-old image of the Virgin on screen and hear the Mass amplified. Monitors on pedestals also reside at intervals within the shrine, communicating information and directives. The practical reasons for these adaptations are understandable, but the aesthetic impact remains jarring. Pilgrims do not seem to mind. They await their chance to enter the basilica and greet Our Lady of Juquila.

Amid the shrine town's churn and commotion, Caminando Juntos begins its final approach. Vanesa carries Juquilita. The men work together lining up blankets and a foam pad pointing toward the shrine, a set of long rectangles end to end. Alicia, in black joggers and a white long-sleeved shirt, takes a black-and-white patterned shawl and artfully wraps it around her head and over a bun, an improvised, appropriately modest head covering. She produces a small, printed prayer book and a rosary, clutching both in her left hand as she kneels at the leading edge of the first blanket. Tere joins her in jeans and a pink zip-front sweatshirt with a blue New York Yankees logo. Her hair is pulled back too. Finally, Pati, a mere teenager who didn't walk with us but caught up with the group on the outskirts of Juquila, kneels behind them. She wears jeans and a striped, green T-shirt incongruously accessorized with a lace collar. Alicia begins to recite the Rosary; her companions provide the responses. Together, they start their slow progress to the basilica, praying as they advance, while the men sustain a frenetic relay. Each time Pati moves beyond the last blanket, they roll it up and pass it, hand to hand, to the front, where the last man lays it down carefully. Vanesa treads slowly ahead with Juquilita; Meche, for a time, accompanies her. Others simply amble patiently alongside the penitent trio. They pass houses, market stalls, and shops from which proprietors and staff occasionally survey the street, paying scant attention to Caminando Juntos. As the three women progress, the men carve out space for them in the crowded streets. At one point, a different pilgrimage group in matching red shirts passes the penitents led by their brass band. Cars, cabs, and moto-taxis going in both directions glide by, as does a funeral procession with pall-bearers carrying an ornate coffin. In the town's plaza, other pilgrimage groups are waiting with their images and offerings. When they enter the basilica, Caminando Juntos traces a gentle arc to the atrium gate with their blankets. More pilgrimage groups appear behind them, led by stoic men carrying their image-bearing vitrinas on their shoulders. Gradually, Alicia, Tere, and Pati arrive at the temple's entrance and pause; they remain on their knees, waiting.

Alicia's mother, who rode to Juquila in a minivan, has joined the group. She makes her way through the crowd and sidles up to her daughter, putting an arm around her. She closes her eyes in prayerful contemplation. They wait together.

Finally, they get their chance and enter the sanctuary, leaving the blankets behind. Vanesa, still carrying Juquilita, leads. As she does, other pilgrims open a path for Caminando Juntos. The trio, still on their knees, splits up as family members accompany them toward the altar. Alicia holds Francisco's hand as she inches forward, and her mother walks alongside her. Miguel puts his arm around his mother, Tere, and they follow. Silvio eventually steps forward and takes her hand. They gradually arrive at edge of the altar. Vanesa sets the group's image down, still strapped to the repurposed wooden chair from Silvio's bodega. She faces the arriving devotees. Alicia, Tere, and Pati stay on their knees beside this replica of Juquila. The famed one-foot-tall four-hundred-year-old original image towers over them above the altar, perched on her new gilded pedestal behind thick protective glass.

Mass begins. The officiating priest doesn't acknowledge Caminando Juntos's penitents. He marches through the liturgy; the standing pilgrims respond at the traditional scripted moments but appear detached. Many devotees seem to tune out the priest, focusing on Juquila and murmuring their personal supplications.

Shrine sermons are typically forgettable. Perhaps the most common homily focuses on the Virgin Mary as a model of devout behavior, unquestioning faith, and self-effacing obedience. On a couple of occasions, I've heard more pointed messages centered on individual morality and personal responsibility. In simplest terms, this kind of sermon is a stern admonition directed at tired pilgrims, asking, "Why bother to walk, cycle, run, leave offerings, and proclaim pious devotion to the Virgin of Juquila if you're unwilling to abandon your sinful habits and selfish inclinations?" Flowers, milagros, vows, sweat, and struggle mean nothing without a firm individual commitment to change. Personal calamities, fears, unemployment, health crises, poverty, migration, and nagging uncertainties go unacknowledged. When I've mentioned this kind of sermon to pilgrims, they nod. They've heard it before too.

During the "sign of peace," an exhausted, emotional Alicia gets to her feet and envelopes her diminutive mother in a long joyful embrace. Then she finds Francisco for another heartfelt hug. As the Mass ends and the faithful begin to shuffle out the shrine's side doors, Santiago picks up Juquilita. He slips the straps over his shoulders and carries her out.

Caminando Juntos disperses: some join the queue leading beneath the Virgin's mantle, some slip into the souvenir market next door to the shrine, and others simply enjoy wandering around town amid thousands of other pilgrims. In the afternoon, Marta, her daughter, and few others climb into the back of Don Valentín's pickup truck. Everyone else piles into the back of Raúl's torton. We slowly retrace our steps, over ridges, through dusty towns, past other groups of laboring pilgrims heading toward Juquila, before dropping into Oaxaca's Central Valleys after dark. The return journey takes hours. Many individuals try to sleep. By 11 p.m. we are back in Abastos, emptying out of the truck and collecting our bags in front of the bodegas. Families are there to pick up their returning peregrinos. Many members of Caminando Juntos will be back at work in the market within a few hours.

# On My Skin and in My Heart

In the spring of 2020, amid lockdown and while drafting these chapters, I found myself wondering what impact the COVID-19 pandemic would have on Juquila's pilgrimage. Prior to the virus's emergence, I concluded that my research was done. I wouldn't need to seek out more interviews or track down more documentary leads, a constant temptation for professional historians. It was time to "close the door on sources," as we sometimes say, but I had grown to truly care about many devotees, and we kept in touch via social media. With the virus spreading, I tracked their Facebook posts, we exchanged greetings in the comments, and we communicated individually through direct messages and WhatsApp. Almost without realizing it, I was still researching Juquila's devotion.

The members of Caminando Juntos mobilized to scrub the streets, pathways, and stalls of the market, and they embraced masking to convince their fellow Oaxacans that the main market was safe and open for business. By summertime, individuals and pilgrimage groups were discussing what the pandemic could mean for their respective Juquila traditions. Devotees on social media sought and shared information about road closures and access to the sanctuary. Residents of Juquila were also concerned. With the basilica and Pedimento closed, the town's economy had ground to a halt. Some of them began trying to sell baked goods and tamales to their neighbors, even if they were mediocre cooks. Many just hunkered down, and others left town for the dangers and uncertainties of imagined opportunity in the United States.

Through messages and posts, I learned that church authorities canceled the Virgin's festival in 2020, but they allowed the sanctuary to remain open. In pictures, I could see blue plastic circles glued to the basilica's floor and ample churchyard space to encourage social distancing. Larger pilgrimage groups were expressly prohibited; therefore,

Acatzingo's Peregrinación Nuestra Señora de Dolores had to postpone their forty-first trip to Juquila. Smaller groups, meanwhile, pondered their options. A skeletal version of Caminando Juntos decided to risk the trip, although they reported that it was difficult because most shops and food vendors were shuttered, both along the route and in Juquila. The shrine town, they noted, was also strangely empty. They don't regret going, though.

I kept paying attention to the news and online chatter, but I sensed from the start that the coronavirus represented a hiccup rather than an existential threat. Pandemics and pilgrimages are hardly strangers. Catholic image devotion was essentially built for this moment. Health concerns and healing have long resided at the center of petitionary practices and thus bestow upon devotees a rich and varied repertoire surrounding illness, loss, and grief. Juquila's followers in previous generations weathered cholera outbreaks, the Spanish flu, and two revolutions. A powerful earthquake in 1931 severely damaged the eighteenth-century basilica—the shrine built as Father Ruiz y Cervantes was writing *Memorias* and the colonial-era church was devising the pilgrimage's first full-fledged marketing campaign. Father Bourguet organized its reconstruction in the 1950s, and the devotion expanded rapidly afterward.

Devotees and shrine promoters can rework their plans in the face of new challenges, and history suggests they can always just bide their time, waiting for conditions to improve. That is what many of the individuals discussed in this book did during the recent pandemic. Flexibility, again, represents the key adaptive characteristic of pilgrimage devotion. Celebrations and trips to the shrine can be postponed. Devotional traditions can take place locally or be creatively adapted to social media's virtual spaces and communities. Finally, as the faithful often assert, Our Lady of Juquila understands her children's struggles and limitations. If their faith remains strong, she will not abandon them. She accepts improvisations, knowing they are heartfelt and represent the best they can do in the circumstances. Moreover, as we've seen, shrine visitation can even slow to a trickle for decades and then pick up again at a later date. In truth, the COVID-19 disruption may well prove to be much less dramatic than what Juquila's followers have experienced in the past.

What seems more threatening to the devotion are local political and economic conflicts. In particular, the increasingly tense clashes at the Pedimento after the Chatino village of Yaitepec seized control of the votive chapel and skirmished with police. Members of Juquila's political factions and church officials aired their claims in the media. The dispute appears intractable. For periods, Yaitepec even blocked the road to Juquila entirely. Pilgrims openly express their disgust and anger over what they deem a shameless tug-of-war rooted in greed. In the comment section of news coverage, many devotees beg the Virgin to touch the hearts of the various rivals and make them abandon their intransigence, allowing pilgrims access to once again fill the chapel and the surrounding hillsides with their written pleas and personal offerings.[1] The Pedimento, which has been central to the Juquila experience for the last thirty to forty years, remains shuttered, but here, too, echoes of the devotion's history reach us. There is nothing new about factional fights for control of images and devotional spaces. We can also see Yaitepec's occupation of the Pedimento as an outgrowth of native communities' more recent assertiveness after centuries of discrimination and exploitation.

Regardless, by the fall of 2021, pilgrimage groups of all sizes were organizing their annual journeys and celebrations as before, although, of course, different fortunes had befallen individual devotees in the intervening years. Lalo, Acatzingo's charming, impish veteran, perished in the pandemic. He had been a model of perseverance for decades, but COVID-19 halted his streak of forty consecutive trips to the shrine. As his colleagues on the Comisión told me, he just refused to take any precautions.[2] I also discovered that Doña Fina had succumbed to cancer. When I met her in 2016, she was looking for a chance to visit Juquila, waiting for the Virgin to facilitate what would be her ninth trip. I hope she made it.

The last few years have been particularly difficult for Alicia, the energetic devotee and leading figure in Caminando Juntos in 2016. After the birth of her daughter in 2018, she stopped walking to Juquila due to her maternal responsibilities. Her husband, Francisco, however, remained an active participant in the group. Then Alicia faced a series of painful events in rapid succession. First, her mother and father's health deteriorated, and by 2019 both had passed away. The loss of her mother was particularly hard for Alicia. She posted on Facebook about how much she missed her company and guidance as she raised her own daughter. Most tragically, Alicia's sister was murdered in murky circumstances in 2022, and she found herself forced to press local authorities to investigate the crime amid her shock and grief. This cascade of losses left her heartbroken. Her faith in Juquila endures and she still is a member of the group, but the devout joy she radiated previously had dulled.[3]

In contrast, Santiago's business, and his family, have continued to thrive in the United States. In addition, his role as an organizer within Caminando Juntos has expanded. He and I discussed via direct message and phone conversations the peculiarities of college in the United States as his children progressed in school. In 2023, one of them, now a freshman at a public university and working on a class presentation, contacted me through Facebook to discuss the pilgrimage's history and her family's strong connection to Oaxaca and Our Lady of Juquila.

Meanwhile in Acatzingo, Luis returned to the presidency to lead the fortieth-anniversary pilgrimage in 2019, and then he stepped down from the Comisión again, perhaps for good. In 2021, Felipe, a genial young carpenter, stepped forward to lead the pilgrimage. I met the group in Oaxaca City as they were returning from Juquila in 2022. Only about 160 riders participated (a 40 percent decline), but Felipe expressed confidence that he could revive participation.[4]

The pandemic underscored another issue for me. Spending time with devotees and getting to know them made me gradually realize that for many of them it isn't a single year's journey to the shrine that matters as much as the ongoing relationship with Juquila sustained through serial pilgrimage. In other words, many devotees don't seek a simple personal transformation or expect a life-changing miracle after one trip to the shrine. They embrace process, although they would never say it that way. They cultivate an evolving and gradually deepening connection with their devotional mother, their celestial advocate. We could also say that this is where the closer relationships with other pilgrim colleagues and lasting devotional community is rooted.

Miracles, in this context, as Frank Graziano points out, are not one-time events, either. Divine intervention, as described by many devotees, is often identified long after the fact, the result of distinct outcomes and factors falling into place over time.[5] It is a retrospective narrative dynamic, a kind of stocktaking that leads to conclusions that Juquila is responsible for a pattern of events or the sum of happenings. It is this dynamic that leads to pilgrim explanations like, "Yo le debo mucho a la Virgencita" (I owe the Virgencita a lot), which I heard repeatedly.

Indeed, perhaps the core attraction of a lasting commitment to pilgrimage is that it facilitates episodic autobiographical narration. It helps individuals tell their story, building a personal framework to order travails and triumphs, an honorable chronicle of devout perseverance. That doesn't mean a life without fault, failure, or sin. In fact, pilgrimage, metaphorically, is much better suited to a saga of ups and downs, steps forward and missteps, self-improvement and shortcomings, but with a sacred beacon, a saintly figure, a goal in the distance. It is like the walking pilgrims struggling on the trail while carrying Juquila in her vitrina on their backs as they climb a ridge, the cyclists grinding through the miles on sun-blasted pavement while focusing on Juquila's image in the truck altar thirty-yards ahead, or the bus pilgrims singing hymns and reciting the Rosary together as they ride toward the shrine.

If there is one thing that I learned from taking part in pilgrimages, talking to devotees, following Juquila's devotion online, and observing the ebb and flow of devotional activity at the basilica and Pedimento, it is that there is no last word on pilgrimage. Its genius, endurance, and global success reside not in a conjuring of utopian happenings and emotional states, but in its open-ended, remarkably elastic nature and almost stricture-free bridging and blurring of the social realms we mark as sacred and profane. There is an age-old malleability that undergirds the ease with which practitioners reinvent pilgrimage in each passing generation and allows its adaptation to new contexts. Thus, there is no single idea, belief, or meaning to hold in one's mind and say, "Aha! This is pilgrimage."

But sometimes a tattoo gets close. Sometimes a vision incised on skin in shades of gray and black encapsulates a dynamic phenomenon. In truth, it isn't just the tattoo. It is the digital staging and circulation, in this case, that brings history, landscapes, imaginaries, connections, commitments, movement, fluidity, and emotions into focus. Like so many thought-provoking encounters, this one came to me amid the most routine and lamentable of practices, procrastination. Up early on the morning of March 22, 2022, I sat down to write, but then I decided to check social media. There, in my Facebook feed, I noticed a quartet of images arranged in the platform's typical collage format.

The first image, which appears largest, shows a seated, shirtless young man with his back to the camera and wearing a white baseball cap. He almost fills the lower left half of the picture, grounding the composition. He gazes across Juquila's plaza at the shrine's illuminated facade at night. Dark-blue light emanates from the bell towers. A sparkling, stylized shooting star made of artificial lights arcs across the center of the structure above a stained-glass window depicting Our Lady of Juquila and a set of niches occupied by statues of saints. The sanctuary's floodlights overpower the camera, rendering the saints unrecognizable. Outside the churchyard gate and seeming to emerge (almost like a speech bubble) from the young man's mouth, we see the gaily colored capital letters spelling out J-U-Q-U-I-L-A, although overexposed by yet another set of spotlights. Like those visible in tourist destinations across Mexico, this very recently constructed display of the shrine town's name serves as a selfie and portrait station, a backdrop for visitors eager to share their whereabouts on social media. Entrepreneurial photographers often prowl the plaza offering to take devotees' pictures in front of the letters and sell them a framed, printed copy on the spot. Each of them keeps a laptop and color printer nestled against the basilica's wrought-iron fence and plugged into one of the temple's outdoor electrical outlets. A photo in front of the letters and sanctuary essentially declares: "I made it, I'm in Juquila." From a devotee's perspective, there is another message being broadcast: "My vow has been fulfilled."

In these particular images, however, there is more in evidence than a simple arrival post. Under a fanciful account name, Mapache Garcia, the young man proclaims, "Gracias x todas las bendiciones madre mía te yebo en mi piel y corazón" (Thank you for all the blessings my mother I carry you on my skin and in my heart). Doing so, he draws attention to the distinctive tattoo reaching from the top of his right shoulder to middle of his back. Of the four images he includes, three feature his new body art. The fourth simply offers a photograph of the shrine at night.

Figure 15. On my skin and in my heart, March 20, 2022. A young pilgrim poses in front of Juquila's shrine and reveals a new tattoo. It depicts his participation in a cycling pilgrimage and expresses his heartfelt devotional commitment. He proudly shared this image on a religious tourism Facebook page devoted to Our Lady of Juquila.

Devotional tattoos are nothing new. Indeed, pilgrimage and tattooing are both ancient. In the present day, Virgin of Guadalupe tattoos are a cherished tradition (a cliché, really) in Mexican and Mexican American culture, simultaneously celebrating devotion and cultural identity. Likewise, various ink-on-skin representations of the Virgin of Juquila appear occasionally on social media platforms, but this tattoo is different. It represents the act of pilgrimage, cycling pilgrimage to be precise.

The context of this image's circulation matters too. The young, tattooed model (his Facebook page reveals he has many of them) posed for the photograph and posted his images first on his own "wall" and then shared his pictures in a relatively new Facebook community called "Juquila Pueblo Mágico," the shrine town's promotional page. This group also maintains an Instagram page with the same name, inspired by the federal government's conferral of the special "magic town" designation on Juquila in December 2020.[6] Skeptics and purists may disparage the page as a tasteless commercializing of religion, but the page and its companion Instagram account are very popular among Juquila's followers. As of September 2022, it boasted 164,000 members. This stems from its simple, clever strategy, which is essentially an invitation: "In the group you can publish photos and videos of your visit to Juquila or pilgrimage."[7]

Devotees have responded eagerly. New posts appear almost daily, and peak season (November and December) inspires an avalanche of user content. In addition, many of Juquila's individual followers and organized pilgrimage groups share posts from the site on their own social media pages. The flow of content ranges from shrine snapshots to home altars, vehicles with Juquila decorations, and typical regional foods. They include images created by the Juquila Pueblo Mágico's administrators with sharing clearly in mind, featuring simple, sentimental slogans superimposed on well-known locations within the shrine town: "Every day my trip to Juquila gets closer," or "It wasn't depression, all I needed was a trip to Juquila," or "I was about to arrive in Juquila when my alarm clock went off."[8]

Local entrepreneurs have also become frequent posters on Juquila Pueblo Mágico. During the pandemic, advertisements for proxy services mushroomed on this page. Reachable by WhatsApp, merchants offer to deposit floral offerings in and around the shrine and post photographs on the site in the name of their clients. As expected, devotees encountering these pictures add prayers and devout emoji in the comment section. Often, messages have no obvious connection to the original content— they speak directly to Our Lady of Juquila.

When Mapache shared his pictures on March 20, he almost certainly expected to reach an audience of fellow devotees and hoped to inspire likes, shares, and comments. In fact, his post appeared in my Facebook feed because a walking pilgrimage from Tecamachalco, Puebla, noticed it on Juquila Pueblo Mágico and shared it with their nearly five thousand Facebook friends on March 21. I met members of this group as they traveled to Juquila in 2017. I introduced myself at a dusty way station and found them eager to discuss their devotion. Within days, we became Facebook friends, and I subsequently followed them on the platform. The Tecamachalco pilgrims are particularly active on Facebook, often sharing pictures and videos from a variety of different groups' social media and pilgrimage promotional sites. They also reveal interconnections between different devotions, sharing posts from groups traveling to different Mexican shrines throughout the year.[9] Mapache's tattoo photographs appeared in my feed a day after Tecamachalco's pilgrims shared his post, or forty-eight hours after he initially posted them. In that span, he garnered sixty-seven comments and sixteen shares. Only one comment was critical, admonishing him that Our Lady of Juquila doesn't need her followers to get tattoos to show that they are truly devoted.

The tattoo itself brings to life academic discussions of pilgrimage as an embodied, visceral mode of religious practice. It also echoes common statements among participants when they describe pain, discomfort, and exhaustion as part of an atonement process and as an experiential means of unlocking deep, spiritual understanding. Then, it pushes us to think more seriously about social media as a devotional and promotional platform.

The image on Mapache's back is equal parts vision, map, document, offering, and portrait. At its core it is a metaphorical representation of two journeys: the Rosary's spiritual journey via Marian devotion that leads the Catholic faithful toward the divine; and the earthly road inhabited by pilgrim riders, twisting and turning through Oaxaca's rugged mountains and ultimately reaching Juquila. The highway and the rosary appear intertwined at the bottom of the tattoo, drawing the eye, like a cyclist, to the shrine's threshold. Upon the road, the lone rider, our inked Facebook user, labors dutifully. A banner spans the middle distance, indicating that he journeys on behalf of his entire family. Finally, floating on cottony, grayscale clouds massing above the basilica, a resplendent Virgin of Juquila appears flanked by angels.

In concert, the photographs, the tattoo, and the manner of circulation bring together a seemingly effortless, accessible mashup of old and new, ordinary and sublime. What's more, we can perceive the intermingled footprints of perennial fellow travelers—devotion, commerce, and promotion—and the interplay between the wider realm of technology, economics, and culture and the intimate practices and personal meanings that coalesce in pilgrimage.

For a time, Mapache was happily sharing his tattoo design via direct message. And then on December 26, 2024, news began to spread on Facebook—the Pedimento had opened its doors to devotees once more.

# ACKNOWLEDGMENTS

To share a pilgrimage with others is to take part in a powerful act of communion regardless of your beliefs. As I've tried to convey, a real social bonding occurs over the miles and meals. In researching this book, I came to know and truly care for many of individuals who shared their histories of pilgrimage and personal stories of life, labor, hardship, and devotion. This project would have been impossible without their gracious welcome and kindly patience. For the sake of privacy, I created pseudonyms, and hence I cannot thank them by name here. But their friendship and generosity made this book a pleasure to research and write. I owe a great debt of gratitude to pilgrims of Acatzingo, Coscomatepec, and Caminando Juntos. They have forever deepened my personal connection to Puebla, Veracruz, and Oaxaca. I have long studied these vibrant regions of Mexico, but now I feel a more rooted emotional attachment. I'll never look at peregrinos hiking in the sun, running with torches, rumbling along in vehicle caravans, or whizzing past in their cycling pelotons the same way. I will always be able to conjure memories of the trails, roadways, and fellowship that connects devotees across southern Mexico. There are also residents of the shrine town of Juquila who've generously made time to talk to me over the years and thus shaped my understanding of this remarkable, complicated community.

I must add to this list of fellow pilgrims my friend Mike DuBose, who magnanimously agreed to accompany me to Juquila twice and provide photographs. Mike's work has appeared in our local newspaper, the *Tennessean*, and his brilliant visual documentation of the international humanitarian projects and global ministry of the United Methodist Church over the years is truly inspiring. He provided beautiful, moving images for this book thanks to his remarkable attention to light and composition alongside his profound respect for Mexico's devotional traditions. My own pictures that also appear here represent a futile attempt to approximate his images. In addition, Mike is a peerless travel companion. Both during and after visiting Juquila, he helped me process the pilgrimage experience.

As with any academic project, there are colleagues who helped me think through my analysis. In Oaxaca, it is always thought provoking and enjoyable to check in with Daniela Traffano, Paco Pepe Ruiz Cervantes, Pedro Torres, and Perla Jiménez. It was also helpful for me to present and discuss this work at CIESAS in Oaxaca City back in 2017. Beyond Antequera, as Oaxaca is sometimes called, I benefited from discussions with Margaret Chowning, Robert Curley, and Erika Pani. In addition, close colleagues John Lear and Susie Porter were willing to read drafts, have meals, drinks, and go on hikes with me and listen to my ramblings about pilgrimage devotion. The support of colleagues at Vanderbilt was also crucial, particularly my fellow Latin Americanists Celso Castilho, Jane Landers, Frank Robinson, Lesley Gill, and Marshall Eakin. Also, at different phases in the process two research assistants, Ricky Sakamoto-Pugh and Carlota Guadalupe Martínez-Don, helped me deepen my research.

Criticism before publication, as the saying goes, is a gift. Thus, I must acknowledge a crucial reading I received from development editor Carol Higham when I was attempting some structural and narrative experiments. Carol helped me sort out what was working and what wasn't. In a similar vein, albeit with the next iteration of the manuscript, it has been delightful to work with Kyle Wagner at the University of Chicago Press. I am also indebted to two anonymous reviewers who read the manuscript very closely and offered constructive suggestions.

Institutionally, the long trips to Mexico would have been impossible without the sustained financial support of Vanderbilt University and a fellowship from John Simon Guggenheim Memorial Foundation.

Although listed last, family support keeps me grounded and allows me to focus on scholarly projects. First, my wife, Gini, and my children, Elías and Sara, form my day-to-day foundations. My mother and siblings, Doña Teresita, Betsy, Juanito, and Caro, keep me connected. Betsy, an excellent scholar in her own right, has been a crucial sounding board and reader of drafts for decades. Finally, both my father, Richard N. Wright, and my father-in-law, Enrique Pupo-Walker, discussed this project with me in the early days, but passed away before I could finish. The former proofread my dissertation in 2004 and dutifully read the stream of academic publications that followed it. It took me a while to realize that this represented a profound act of love and respect on his part. Enrique was a cherished scholarly mentor and a first reader of two preceding books. I can't replace either of them, but maybe I can emulate their generosity and kindness. It is my turn to support the next generation.

# NOTES

## En camino

1. This description is based on the author's participation in the pilgrimage in late November and early December 2016.

2. "Una cifra récord de peregrinos recibió la Basílica de Guadalupe para celebrar el Día de la Virgen," Infobae, December 12, 2022, https://www.infobae.com/america/mexico/2022/12/12/una-cifra-record-de-peregrinos-recibio-la-basilica-de-guadalupe-para-celebrar-a-el-dia-de-la-virgen/. See also "Mi hija es un milagro que me concedió la Virgen," Univision, December 10, 2022, https://www.univision.com/noticias/america-latina/peregrinacion-virgen-de-guadalupe-2022-ciudad-de-mexico-fotos.

3. Juquila estimates in the two to three million range are relatively typical in news accounts. See, for example, "El lugar de adoración a la Virgen de Juquila ya tiene tres años cerrado," Azteca Noticias, December 7, 2022, https://www.facebook.com/watch?v=464989325587638. However, I've also seen estimates as low as seven hundred thousand. For example, Oscar Rodríguez, "Francisco concede conornación pontificia de la Virgen de Juquila," *Milenio*, September 2, 2014, http://www.milenio.com/estados/Francisco-coronacion-pontificia-Virgen-Juquila_0_242376149.html.

4. Gobierno del Estado de Oaxaca, "Oaxaca cuenta con un nuevo pueblo mágico," December 1, 2020, https://www.oaxaca.gob.mx/comunicacion/oaxaca-cuenta-con-un-nuevo-pueblo-magico-santa-catarina-juquila/.

5. The use of hotel data was confirmed by an official at the state ministry of tourism: Antonio Mario Aguilar López, interview with the author, November 4, 2016. Sebastián (pseudonym), a native of Juquila, took part in surveys in a previous era and suggested that they were unreliable due to hotel owners' tendency to underreport room rentals to escape higher taxes, the mere guesswork involved in occupancy estimates, and an unwillingness to fund a proper survey. Interview with the author, November 5, 2016.

6. Mario Carlos Sarmiento Zúñiga, "Un portento milagroso en época de reformas: La imagen de la Inmaculada Concepción de Juquila en la configuración de una devoción secular," *Estudios de Historia Novohiapana* 56 (2017): 26–39.

7. Brian Larkin, *The Very Nature of God: Baroque Catholicism and Religious Reform in Bourbon Mexico* (Albuquerque: University of New Mexico Press, 2010), 70–92.

8. Originally, "Si tienen voluntad, pueden hacer las respuestas."

# Chapter One

1. Fina, interview with the author, Oaxaca, Oaxaca, November 14, 2016.

2. San Juan Teiticpac Pilgrims, group interview with the author, Ocotlán, Oaxaca, December 11, 2022.

3. Joshua Kurlantzick, "21st-Century Religious Travel: Leave the Sackcloth at Home," *New York Times*, April 29, 2009, http://www.nytimes.com/2007/04/29/travel/29religion.html?_r=0; and Michael George, "Walking the Way," *National Geographic* 225, no. 5 (May 2015), http://ngm.nationalgeographic.com/2015/05/the-way/george-text.

4. Maureen Orth, "The Virgin Mary: The Most Powerful Woman in the World," photographs by Diana Markosian, *National Geographic* 228, no. 6 (December 2015): 30–59.

5. For example, see Timothy Egan, *A Pilgrimage to Eternity: From Canterbury to Rome in Search of a Faith* (New York: Penguin Books, 2019).

6. Virgen de Juquila, Facebook, https://www.facebook.com/pages/VIRGEN-DE-JUQUILA/135430733155318. In 2024, the site featured over eighty thousand likes.

7. See, for example, Jerrihc78, "La Virgen de Juquila en Gilroy, ca. 2013," YouTube, December 12, 2013, https://www.youtube.com/watch?v=3iKDSrI3XbM.

8. Morristown, although small, has a sizable Mexican population and a bakery named after Our Lady of Juquila. The Morristown ICE raid has drawn considerable press coverage. See Jonathan Blizter, "Some Conservative Voters Rethink Trump's Immigration Agenda," *New Yorker*, April 19, 2018; and Miriam Jordan, "The Town Fought Back," *New York Times*, June 26, 2018.

9. Suzanne K. Kaufman, *Consuming Visions: Mass Culture and the Lourdes Shrine* (Ithaca, NY: Cornell University Press, 2004).

10. Victor Turner and Edith Turner, *Image and Pilgrimage in Christian Culture* (New York: Columbia University Press, 1978).

11. John Eade and Michael J. Sallnow, "Introduction," in *Contesting the Sacred: The Anthropology of Christian Pilgrimage*, ed. John Eade and Michael J. Sallnow (New York: Routledge, 1991): 1–29. See also Simon Coleman, "Do You Believe in Pilgrimage?," *Anthropological Theory* 2, no. 3 (September 2002): 355–68.

12. Drew Thomases, *Guest Is God: Pilgrimage, Tourism, and Making Paradise in India* (New York: Oxford University Press, 2019).

13. Eduardo Chemin, "Producers of Meaning and the Ethics of Movement," in *Gender, Nation and Religion in European Pilgrimage*, ed. Willy Jansen, Catrien Notermans, and Ellen Badone (Burlington, VT: Ashgate, 2012), 134.

14. Lena Gemzöe, "Big Strong and Happy: Reimagining Femininity on the Way to Compostela," in *Gender, Nation and Religion in European Pilgrimage*, ed. Willy Jansen, Catrien Notermans, and Ellen Badone (Burlington, VT: Ashgate, 2012), 27–53. See also Anna Fedele, "Gender, Society and Religious Critique among Mary Magdalene Pilgrims in Southern France," in *Gender, Nation and Religion in European Pilgrimage*, ed. Willy Jansen, Catrien Notermans, and Ellen Badone (Burlington, VT: Ashgate, 2012), 55–69.

15. Eade and Sallnow, "Introduction," 15–16.

16. Simon Coleman, *The Powers of Pilgrimage: Religion in a World of Movement* (New York: New York University Press, 2021).

17. For a complex discussion of the recent past arguing for the centrality of religious and philosophical understandings of territoriality and reciprocity among Oaxacan Indigenous groups, see Alicia Barabas, "Cosmovisiones, y etnoterritorialidad en las culturas indígenas de Oaxaca," *Antípoda* 7 (July–December 2008): 119–39. For a helpful overview

of trends in broader pilgrimage scholarship in Mexico, see Alejandra Aguilar Ros, "Transcending Symbols: The Religious Landscape of Pilgrimage Studies in Mexico," in *New Pathways in Pilgrimage Studies: Global Perspectives*, ed. Dionigi Albera and John Eade (New York: Routledge, 2016), 142–62.

18. For example, for an exploration of Nahua indigenous transformations of Catholic ritual in the early colonial period, see Inga Clendinnen, "Ways to the Sacred: Reconstructing 'Religion' in Sixteenth Century Mexico," *History and Anthropology* 5 (1990): 105–41.

19. Kristin Norget, "Popular-Indigenous Catholicism in Southern Mexico," *Religions* 12 (2021): 531. See also Kristin Norget, *Days of Death, Days of Life: Ritual in the Popular Culture of Oaxaca*, New York: Columbia University Press, 2006.

20. Norget, "Popular-Indigenous Catholicism," 532.

21. See Coleman, *Powers of Pilgrimage*, 117–22.

22. Lalo, interview with author, Acatzingo, Puebla, December 1, 2016.

23. Carlos, interview with the author, Coscomatepec, Veracruz, August 27, 2016.

24. Cecilia, interview with author, Zimatlán, Oaxaca, November 10, 2016. Originally, "Para tener una experiencia."

25. Ezequiel, interview with author, Zimatlán, Oaxaca, November 10, 2016. Originally, "Le debo un favor a la Virgen . . . y prometí caminar desde mi casa hasta sus plantas."

26. Ezequiel, interview with author. Originally, "Me han pagado como veinte veces el boleto, mi familia y otros amigos. Pero nunca he querido. . . . Porque mi deseo . . . era para pagárselo en sacrificio en el camino."

27. Alicia, interview with the author, Zaachila, Oaxaca, November 29, 2016. Originally, "El venir caminando a ver la Virgen no solo nos aumenta la fe, o nos hace ver lo que es realmente la fe, nos ayuda en las emociones: a ver las cosas de manera positiva. Allí se conoce la hermandad. . . . Ya cuando uno regresa a la realidad, al trabajo, a la familia, todos los problemas se hacen más pequeños."

28. Carlos, interview with the author, Coscomatepec, Veracruz, August 27, 2016. Originally, "Somos como el azadón . . . puro pa'cá y nada pa'lla."

29. Carlos, interview with the author. Originally, "Cuando la fe es grande, el camino es corto."

30. Carlos, interview with the author. Originally, "Aquí no caminas tú. Aquí camina tu fe, y esto es mental. Psicológicamente si tú dices puedo, vas a llegar. Pero si vas con la idea que 'Eeeh, ya no puedo llegar . . . ,' ya te chingaste, mejor súbate al carro porque ya no vas a llegar. Pero si tú dices, 'Yo promtí llegar,' vas a llegar."

31. Juan, interview with the author, Oaxaca, Oaxaca, November 13, 2017.

32. Javier, interview with the author, Zimatlán, Oaxaca, November 10, 2016.

33. Alicia, interview with the author, Zaachila, Oaxaca, November 29, 2016.

34. Frank Graziano, *Miraculous Images and Votive Offerings in Mexico* (New York: Oxford University Press, 2016). See also Frank Graziano, *Cultures of Devotion: Folk Saints of Spanish America* (New York: Oxford University Press, 2007).

35. Paul Vanderwood, *The Power of God against the Guns of Government* (Stanford, CA: Stanford University Press, 1998), 49–66.

# Chapter Two

1. Gobierno de México, Data México, Santa Catarina Juquila, https://datamexico .org/es/profile/geo/santa-catarina-juquila. They note that approximately 2,609 of these inhabitants still speak Chatino, the region's ancestral language.

2. Joseph Manuel Ruiz y Cervantes, *Memorias de la portentosa imagen de Nuestra Señora de Xuquila* (Mexico City: Felipe de Zúñiga y Ontiveros, 1791).

3. William B. Taylor, *Theater of a Thousand Wonders: A History of Miraculous Images and Shrines in New Spain* (Cambridge: Cambridge University Press, 2016), 502.

4. Mario Carlos Sarmiento Zúñiga, "Un portento milagroso en época de reformas: La imagen de la Inmaculada Concepción de Juquila en la configuración de una devoción secular," *Estudios de Historia Novohiapana*, 56 (2017): 26–39.

5. Fina, interview with the author, Oaxaca, Oaxaca, November 14, 2016. Also Pilgrims of Tonameca, Oaxaca, interview with the author, Yolotepec, Oaxaca, November 11, 2017; and Caminantadefe, "Documental XIX Caminata de Fe Tlaxiaco Juquila 2015," YouTube, September 3, 2015, https://www.youtube.com/watch?v=N4cgLcAESN0.

6. Ruiz y Cervantes, *Memorias*, 2–3 and 34–35.

7. Ruiz y Cervantes, 41.

8. Sarmiento, "Un portento."

9. Louise Burkhart, *The Slippery Earth: Nahua-Christian Moral Dialogue in Sixteenth-Century Mexico* (Tucson: University of Arizona Press, 1989).

10. Archdiocese of Oaxaca, shrine brochure, "Breve historia de la Imagen de la Inmaculada Virgen de Juquila."

11. Ruiz y Cervantes, *Memorias*, 6–8.

12. Ruiz y Cervantes, 10.

13. Ruiz y Cervantes, 8–21.

14. Antonio Rubial García, *La santidad controvertida* (Mexico City: Fondo de Cultura Económica, 2015).

15. Taylor, *Theater of a Thousand Wonders*, 63. See also Larkin, *The Very Nature of God*; and Rubial García, *La santidad controvertida*.

16. Los Guerreros del Sol, "La historia de la Virgen de Juquila," on *Buenos Días Virgencita* (2017), used in the pilgrimage video, Arrazador11010, "Pergrinación Candelaria a Juquila," YouTube, December 5, 2015, https://www.youtube.com/watch?v=USao7u1bjq0.

17. Ruiz y Cervantes, *Memorias*, 21–35.

18. Sarmiento, "Un portento milagroso en época de reformas," 32.

19. Ruiz y Cervantes, *Memorias*, 67–80.

20. Román Alavés, interview with the author, Santa Catarina Juquila, Oaxaca November 5, 2016.

21. Comisión Organizadora, Peregrinación Nuestra Señora de los Dolores, group discussion with the author, Oaxaca, Oaxaca, December 7, 2022.

22. Ruiz y Cervantes, *Memorias*, 36–58.

23. Carlos Sánchez Silva, *Indios, comerciantes y burocracia en la Oaxaca poscolonial, 1786–1860* (Oaxaca: Insitituto Oaxaqueño de las Culturas; Fondo Estatal para la Cultura y las Artes; Universidad Autónoma Benito Juárez de Oaxaca, 1998); and Jeremy Baskes, *Indians, Merchants, and Markets: A Reinterpretation of the Repartimiento and Spanish-Indian Economic Relations in Colonial Oaxaca, 1750–1821* (Stanford, CA: Stanford University Press, 2000).

24. Ruiz y Cervantes, *Memorias*, 58–61. Originally, "negros, mulatos, índios, y cuantas castas contamos en nuestra América, con el ínfimo vulgo de Oaxaca."

25. Ruiz y Cervantes, 56.

26. Ruiz y Cervantes, 56–57.

27. AHAO, Diocesano, Gobierno, Parroquias (DGP), Decretos y disposciones de Ilmo. y Rmo. Sr. Arzobispo Dr. Dn. Eulogio G. Gillow acerca del Santuario de Nuestra Señora de Juquila, February 4, 1894.

28. Ruiz y Cervantes, *Memorias*, 47–51.

29. Ruiz y Cervantes, 40–47.

30. Eric Van Young, *The Other Rebellion: Popular Violence, Ideology, and the Mexican Struggle for Independence, 1810–1821* (Stanford, CA: Stanford University Press, 2002).

31. Margaret Chowning, *Catholic Women and Mexican Politics, 1750–1940* (Princeton, NJ: Princeton University Press, 2023), 17–44.

32. Chowning, 45–72.

33. Wright-Ríos, *Searching for Madre Matiana: Prophecy and Popular Culture in Modern Mexico* (Albuquerque: University of New Mexico Press, 2014), 130–47.

34. Brian Connaughton, *Dimensiones de la identidad patriótica: religión, política y regions en México, siglo XIX* (Mexico City: UAM, Iztapalapa, 2001).

35. Chowning, *Catholic Women*, 58.

36. For example, AHAO, DGP, 1880–81; 1885–87; 1887–88; 1889; and 1890–92.

37. For example, AHAO, DGP, 1868, "Cuenta de limosnas y misas peretenecientes a Nuestra Señora de Juquila," which lists $4,113 in alms and $640 in Mass intentions. See also AHAO, DGP 1870–71: "Año de 1871," $2,964 in alms and $55 in Mass intentions; "Año de 1872," $2,004 in alms and $4,155 in Mass intentions; and "Año de 1873," $3,441 in alms and $950 in Mass intentions.

38. AHAO, DGP, 1885–86, Receipt from Librería y Mercería San Germán, March 5, 1887; and AHAO DGP 1889, Receipt from Librería y Mercería San Germán.

39. *La Voz de la Verdad*, December 17, 1899.

40. Antonio Morales Sánchez, *Romería de Juquila* (Oaxaca: Sedetur, 1997).

41. Edward Wright-Ríos, *Revolutions in Mexican Catholicism: Reform and Revelation in Oaxaca, 1887–1934* (Durham, NC: Duke University Press, 2009), 73–140.

42. Wright-Ríos, *Revolutions*.

43. Morales, *Romería*.

44. Francie Chassen-López, *From Liberal to Revolutionary Oaxaca: The View from the South, Mexico, 1867–1911* (State College: Pennsylvania State University Press, 2004), 45–47.

# Chapter Three

1. Jean Meyer, *El conflicto religioso en Oaxaca, 1926–1938* (Oaxaca: IAGO, 2006).

2. Alan Knight, *The Mexican Revolution* (Lincoln: University of Nebraska Press, 1986).

3. Paul Garner, "Federalism and Caudillismo in the Mexican Revolution: The Genesis of the Oaxaca Sovereignty Movement (1915–1920)," *Journal of Latin American Studies* 17, no. 1 (May 1985): 111–33.

4. See Víctor Raúl Martínez, ed., *La Revolución en Oaxaca, 1900–1930* (Oaxaca: Instituto de Administración Pública de Oaxaca, 1985); and Francisco José Ruiz Cervantes, *La revolución en Oaxaca: el movimiento de soberanía, 1915–1920* (Mexico City: Fondo de Cultura Económica and Insituto de Investigaciones Sociales, 1986).

5. James Greenberg, *Blood Ties: Life and Violence in Rural Mexico* (Tucson: University of Arizona Press, 1989), 59–63.

6. AHAO, DGP, 1914, Ausencio Canseco, "Misas rezadas en la fiesta de la Santísima Virgen de Juquila de diciembre 1914."

7. AHAO, Diocesano Gobierno Correspondencia (DGC), 1940–41, Cornelio Bourguet to Agustín Espinoza, December 20, 1941.

8. *El Mercurio*, December 2 and 13, 1921.

9. This comes through in a Oaxacan satirical newspaper which referred to federal soldiers as parrots because of their green uniforms and quipped, "con tanto perico parece que estamos en Juquila" (with so many parrots it seems like we're in Juquila). See "Entre Manarios," *El Zancudo*, January 27, 1924.

10. *El Mercurio*, November 6 and 24, 1928.

11. Wright-Ríos *Revolutions*, 211–17.

12. This information comes from a trio of letters written in October 1926 to the secretary of the archdiocese. AHAO, DGC 1926, Ausencio Canseco to Agustín Espinoza, October 6, 16, and 28, 1926.

13. Greenberg, *Blood Ties*, 59–63.

14. AHAO, DGC, 1933, Cornelio Bourguet to Agustín Espinoza, September 3, 1933.

15. AHAO, DGC, 1950–52, Cornelio Bourguet to Canon Guillermo Álvarez, December 30, 1950.

16. AHAO, DGC, 1948–49, Cornelio Bourguet to Guillermo Álvarez, December 23, 1948.

17. Thomas Rath, *The Dread Plague and the Cow Killers: The Politics of Animal Disease in Mexico and the World* (New York: Cambridge University Press, 2022), 116.

18. Elin Luque Agraz, "Análisis de la evolución de los exvotos pictóricos como documentos visuals para describer "la otra historia" de México," PhD diss. (Universidad Nacional de Educación a Distancia, Spain, 2012), 507.

19. Jorge Hernández Díaz, *El café amargo: los procesos de diferenciación y cambio social entre los chatinos* (Oaxaca: UABJO, Institututo de Investigaciones Sociológicas, 1987); and Greenberg, *Blood Ties*.

20. AHAO, DGC 1950–52, Cornelio Bourguet to Guillermo Álvarez, December 30, 1950, Cornelio Bourguet to Guillermo Álvarez, December 30, 1953, AHAO, DGC 1950–52; AHAO, DGC 1956, Cornelio Bourguet to Guillermo Álvarez, December 30, 1956; AHAO, DGC 1957, Cornelio Bourguet to Guillermo Álvarez, December 29, 1957; AHAO, DGC 1958, Cornelio Bourguet to Guillermo Álvarez, December 29,1958; and AHAO, DGC 1959, Cornelio Bourguet to Guillermo Álvarez, December 29, 1959.

21. For example, see AHAO DGC 1956, Cornelio Bourguet to Guillermo Álvarez, December 30, 1965; and AHAO DGC 1957, Cornelio Bourguet to Vicario General Guillermo Álvarez, December 29, 1957.

22. AHAO DGC 1959, Cornelio Bourguet to Canon Guillermo Álvarez, December 29, 1959.

23. AHAO DGC 1960–61, Cornelio Bourguet to Canon José Santa Cruz, January 17, 1960. Among the interesting revelations in this missive are Bourguet's claims that he cannot send 10,000 pesos immediately because it is all in small-denomination silver and copper coins. He said he dared not ship it by plane because of the potential scandal of sending such packages.

24. AHAO DGC 1959, Cornelio Bourguet to Archbishop Fortino Gómez León, September 3, 1959.

25. Ian Reader, *Pilgrimage in the Marketplace* (New York Routledge, 2016). See also Ian Reader, *Pilgrimage: A Very Short Introduction* (New York: Oxford University Press, 2015).

26. Rafael León, interview with the author, Juquila, Oaxaca, February 13, 2002.

27. Isidro Yescas Martínez, "El sacerdote que desafió la voluntad de Dios: El caciquismo de Cornelio Bourguet en Oaxaca," in *A Dios lo que es de Dios,* ed. Carlos Martínez Assad (Mexico: Aguilar, 1994), 184–94.

28. AHAO, DGC 1960–61, Aurelio León Fería to Archbishop Fortino Gómez de León, February 23, 1961.

29. AHAO, DGC 1962–64, Cornelio Bourguet to Guillermo Álvarez, December 3, 1962. See also Archivo Parroquial de Santa Catarina Juquila, Sacerdotes de la Aquidiocesis de Oaxaca, May 5, 1969, Libro número 7 de Providencias Diocesanas, 136–38.

30. Yescas, "El sacerdote que desafió la voluntad de Dios."

31. A series of articles appeared in the Oaxaca City newspaper, *Noticias,* related to the conflict centered on Bourguet: "El 15 del actual sadra Bourguet de Juquila," November 7, 1980; "El Juquila: los sacerdotes Barrita y Yescas subsistarán a Cornelio Bourguet," November 15, 1980; and Narciso Reyes, "Intervino la 23 de septiembre; el pueblo aceptó el mandato de Díos," November 18, 1980.

32. Sebastián, interview with the author, November 5, 2016.

33. Sebastián, interview with the author, December 2, 2022.

## Chapter Four

1. Reader, *Pilgrimage in the Marketplace.*

2. Valentín, interview with the author, August 21, 2016.

3. Reader, *Pilgrimage in the Marketplace.*

4. Ben Fulwider, "Driving the Nation: Road Transportation and the Creation of the Post-Revolutionary State, 1925–1960," PhD diss. (Georgetown University, 2004), 79–80.

5. Lalo, interview with the author, Acatzingo, Puebla, November 30, 2018.

6. Pilgrims of Tonameca, Oaxaca, interview with the author, Yolotepec, Oaxaca, November 11, 2017.

7. Samuel, interview with the author, Los Reyes Juárez, Puebla, August 16, 2016. For the town's pilgrimage, see José Luis Vázquez, "XXV Peregrinación al Santuario de la Virgen de Juquila (4a parte)," YouTube, March 12, 2013, https://www.youtube.com/watch?v=hTEq_bOJv8A.

8. Carlos, interviews with the author, August 27, 2016, and November 10, 2016.

9. Valentín, interview with the author, August 21, 2016.

10. Gobierno de México, Data México, San Salvador Huixcolotla, https://datamexico.org/en/profile/geo/san-salvador-huixcolotla.

11. Agustín, phone interview with the author, Acatzingo, Puebla, November 20, 2018.

12. Peter Gerhard, *A Guide to the Historical Geography of New Spain* (Norman: University of Oklahoma Press, 1993), 278–81. See also Stephen M. Perkins, "Macehuales and the Corporate Solution: Colonial Secessions in Nahua Central Mexico," *Mexican Studies/ Estudios mexicanos* 21, no. 2 (Summer 2005): 277–306; Juan Carlos Garavaglia and Juan Carlos Grosso, "Mexican Elites of a Provincial Town: The Landowners of Tepeaca (1700– 1870)," *Hispanic American Historical Review* 70, no. 2 (May 1990): 255–93; and Juan Carlos Garavaglia and Juan Carlos Grosso, "El comportamiento demográfico de una parroquia poblana de la colonia al México independiente, Tepeaca y su entorno agrario, 1740–1850," *Historia Mexicana* 40, no. 4 (April–June, 1991).

13. Diosey Ramón Lugo-Morín et al., "Redes sociales asimétricas en sistema hortícola del valle de Tepeaca, México," *Economía, Sociedad, y Territorio* 10, no. 32 (2010): 207–30.

See also Ezequiel Arivizu Barrón et al., "Análisis de producción y comercilización de hortalizas: Caso del mercado de Huixcolotla, Puebla," *Revista Mexicana de Ciencieas Agrícolas* 5, no. 4 (June–August 2014): 687–94.

14. Tania L. Montalvo, "Pemex pierde 90 mil litros diarios de combustible sólo en uno de sus ductos," *Animal Político*, December 12, 2016, https://www.animalpolitico.com/2016/12/pemex-robo-combustible.

15. "Puebla, encabeza decomisos de huachicol," *El Universal*, June 12, 2017, https://www.eluniversal.com.mx/articulo/nacion/seguridad/2017/06/12/puebla-encabeza-decomisos-de-huachicol; "Puebla, el epicentro del huachicol," *El Universal*, January 9, 2019, https://www.eluniversal.com.mx/nacion/puebla-el-epicentro-del-huachicol; "Cártel Jalisco Nueva Generación y 'Los bukanas' disputan el Triángulo Rojo, zona dorada del huachicoleo," *Vanguardia*, October 3, 2018, https://vanguardia.com.mx/articulo/este-es-el-triangulo-rojo-zona-del-huachicoleo-que-disputan-el-cartel-jalisco-nueva.

16. See Peregrinacion Ciclista de Huixcolotla A Juquila, Facebook, https://www.facebook.com/photo?fbid=1012346729648258&set=a.116521529230787.

17. Agustín, phone interview with the author, Acatzingo, Puebla, November 20, 2018.

18. See Peregrinacion Ciclista de Huixcolotla a Juquila, Facebook, https://www.facebook.com/photo?fbid=1012346729648258&set=a.116521529230787. The group posted an old photograph of the riders. The page also commemorates the passing of these pioneering riders: for example, Facebook, April 25, 2019, https://www.facebook.com/profile/100026188200070/search/?q=fallecimiento.

19. In general, pilgrimage groups announce their foundation on advertisements for each year's outing, on banners that accompany devotees on their way to the shrine, and on Facebook pages and YouTube videos. Often is it incorporated in their logos. See, for example, "66 Aniversario. Peregrinación a pie a la Basílica de Guadalupe Ciudad de México," YouTube, https://www.youtube.com/watch?v=WAtQXC86tQY. See also Peregrinación Ciclista de Huixcolotla a Juquila, Facebook, https://www.facebook.com/peregrinacion.ciclista.129?epa=SEARCH_BOX.

20. Violeta, interview with the author, Coscomatepec, Veracruz, August 27, 2016.

21. Jennifer Scheper Hughes, "The Niño Jesús Doctor: Novelty and Innovation in Mexican Religion," *Nova Religio: The Journal of Alternative and Emergent Religions* 16, no. 2 (November 2012): 4–28.

22. Norget, "Popular Indigenous Catholicism."

23. Carlos, interviews with author, August 27, 2016, and December 10, 2016.

24. Benito Juárez Ramírez, "Coscomatepec, principal exportador de chayote, pero el 'ganón' sigue siendo el coyote," *Alcalorpolítico*, July 27, 2016, https://www.alcalorpolitico.com/informacion/coscomatepec-principal-exportador-de-chayote-pero-el-ganon-sigue-siendo-el-coyote—208693.html#.XouaWC-ZNpgà.

25. Carlos, interview with the author, August 27, 2016.

26. José Luis Rosas, "Inicia éxodo de peregrinos: En autos, motocicletas, bicicletas y a pie, realizan su recorrido con la intención de visitar la Virgen," *El Imparcial*, November 24, 2014, http://imparcialoaxaca.mx/la-capital/1Js/inicia-%C3%A9xodo-de-peregrinos.

27. Marta, interview with the author, August 20, 2016.

# Chapter Five

1. Candy C., "Mañanitas a la Virgen de Juquila," YouTube, December 21, 2012, https://www.youtube.com/watch?v=IzTVF6EfFmY.

2. For example, see "Peregrinación Candelaria a Juquila," Tecali de Herrera, Puebla, YouTube, November 17, 2014, https://www.youtube.com/watch?v=USao7u1bjq0. See also "XXV al Santuario de la Virgen de Juquila, (2ª Parte)," YouTube, March 4, 2013, https://www.youtube.com/watch?v=8b4bik4rsxU; "Documental XIX Caminata de Fe Tlaxiaco Juquila 2015," YouTube, September 15, 2015, https://www.youtube.com/watch?v=N4cgLcAESN0.

3. This statement is based on a detailed analysis and comparison of online content on Facebook, YouTube, and Instagram: see Edward Wright-Ríos and Carlota Martínez-Don, "Posting the Journey," *Latin American Research Review* 59, no. 2 (2024).

4. Heidi Campbell, "Understanding the Relationship between Religion Online and Offline in a Networked Society," *Journal of the American Academy of Religion* 80, no. 1 (March 2012): 64–93.

5. Virgen de Juquila en Ti Confio, Facebook, https://www.facebook.com/groups/1624941937599366; Comunidad Virgen de Juquila en Facebook, Facebook, https://www.facebook.com/groups/1965835446888756; Pedido de Oraciones en comunidade a la "Virgen de Juquila," Facebook, https://www.facebook.com/groups/2003106043234188/?ref=pages_group_cta.

6. Virgen de Juquila, Facebook, February 20, 2020, https://www.facebook.com/profile.php?id=100071672556613.

7. See Santuario de la Inmaculada Virgen de Juquila, Facebook, https://www.facebook.com/Juquilaportaloficial/.

8. For example, on August 29, 2021, Magui Andrade shared Guatemalan singer Katy Calel's paean to Marian devotion from a different Facebook group, TV Católica Nazareth Estereo, September 16, 2020, https://www.facebook.com/groups/1624941937599366/permalink/4309537632473103/. This is an interesting choice, because Calel presents herself as a Maya Catholic singing in traditional dress. As in other instances, the associations of humility, piety, and cultural authenticity often linked to Indigenous groups appear to be in play.

9. "Bere Ramírez Is Feeling Blessed," September 1, 2021, shared on Oraciones a la Virgen de Juquila, Facebook, https://www.facebook.com/groups/1275226302676821.

10. Arllet Kelle Gavy, August 26, 2021, Facebook, https://www.facebook.com/groups/1624941937599366/search/?q=arllet%20kelle%20gavy.

11. See El Pedimento Virtual de la Virgen de Juquila (oficial), Facebook, https://www.facebook.com/groups/1072392366576931. Originally, "Con la fe de todos muy pronto la virgen te concederá tu petición."

12. Virgen de Juquila en Greensboro, Facebook, https://www.facebook.com/Virgen-De-Juquila-En-Greensboro-1205500932884282.

13. Caminando Juntos, Facebook, https://www.facebook.com/groups/551368188397710.

14. See, for example, Peregrinación Ciclista Nuestra Señora de los Dolores, Facebook, https://www.facebook.com/ciclistasacatzingojuquila; and Peregrinación Ciclista de Huixcolotla a Juquila, Facebook, https://www.facebook.com/peregrinacion.ciclista.129.

15. For example, see Peregrinacion a Pie al Santuario de Juquila, Facebook, October, 13, 2017, https://www.facebook.com/Peregrinacion-a-Pie-al-Santuario-de-la-Virgen-de-Juquila-348091905660917/.

16. For example, Peregrinación Ciclista Nuestra Señora de los Dolores, Facebook, October 30, 2018, https://www.facebook.com/photo/?fbid=266421554073538&set=a.105257163523312.

17. Peregrinación Ciclista Nuestra Señora de los Dolores, Facebook, https://www .facebook.com/ciclistasacatzingojuquila.

18. Peregrinación ciclista Santa Catarina—Juquila, Facebook, https://www.facebook .com/Peregrinacion-ciclista-santa-catarina-juquila-130455924414988/.

19. "Mary Mauricio Martinez Is with Peregrinación a Pie Tecamachalco La Villita," Facebook, October 15, 2022, shared on Peregrinación Ciclista de Huixcolotla a Juquila, www.facebook.com/peregrinacion.ciclista.129.

20. Morelos Bus Pilgrims, interview with the author, Juquila, Oaxaca, December 2, 2022.

21. Willy Jansen, "Old Routes, New Journeys: Reshaping Gender, Nation, and Religion in European Pilgrimage," in *Gender and Nation in European Pilgrimage*, ed. Willy Jansen, Catrien Notermans, and Ellen Badone (Burlington, VT: Ashgate, 2012), 1–18.

22. See, for example, Peregrinación Santiago Miahuatlán—Juquila, Oaxaca, Face-book, https://www.facebook.com/Peregrinaci%C3%B3n-Santiago-Miahuatl%C3%A1n -Juquila-Oaxaca-1794380457285330/.

23. For example, Caminando Juntos, Facebook, https://www.facebook.com/groups/ 551368188397710.

24. See posts from December 28, 2020, Peregrinación Santiago Miahuatlán—Juquila, Oaxaca, Facebook, https://www.facebook.com/Peregrinaci%C3%B3n-Santiago -Miahuatl%C3%A1n-Juquila-Oaxaca-1794380457285330/.

25. See posts from February 2, 2021, Peregrinación Ciclista Nuestra Señora de los Dolores, Facebook, https://www.facebook.com/ciclistasacatzingojuquila.

26. Reader, *Pilgrimage in the Marketplace*.

27. For example, Giovanni Miguel, "Peregrinación a Juquila," YouTube, January 19, 2008, https://www.youtube.com/watch?v=LqDlAGfv-Qw.

28. Mario Maple, "Peregrinación de Guelavia a Juquila 2009.wmv," YouTube, Febru-ary 26, 2011, https://www.youtube.com/watch?v=0n0ZgUy4lGk.

29. Reycondoy, "Peregrinación al santurario de la Virgen de Juquila 2," YouTube, Feb-ruary 1, 2008, https://www.youtube.com/watch?v=N9yvhXwUap4.

30. Huixcolotla's pilgrimage videos are posted by a business specializing in filming bike races, funerals, and festivals. The pilgrimage represents another job for this group. For example, see Play Turisloco, "Peregrinación Ciclista a Juquila Oaxaca 2018—Mariachi en San Pedro," YouTube, November 27, 2018, https://www.youtube.com/watch?v= _Q86wA2RQ-g&t=199s.

31. Rubial Garcia, *La santidad controvertida*.

32. Arrazador11010, "Pergrinación Candelaria a Juquila," YouTube, November 17, 2014, https://www.youtube.com/watch?v=USao7u1bjq0.

33. For example, groups often use songs by Los Guerreros del Sol, like "La historia de la Virgen de Juquila" and "Virgencita de Juquila," from the album *Buenos Días Virgencita* (2017).

34. For example, see CaminatadeFe, "2/10 Documental antropológico a pie ha-cia Juquila desde Tlaxiaco 2013 Introducción," YouTube, March 1, 2014, https://www .youtube.com/watch?v=8hBQoQTFABs.

35. CaminatadeFe, "18 Caminata de Fe Tlaxiaco-Juquila 10/12," YouTube, March 1, 2015, https://www.youtube.com/watch?v=Z7DvB4MuBrM.

36. CaminatadeFe, "Documental XIX Caminata de Fe Tlaxiaco Juquila 2015," You-Tube, September 3, 2015, https://www.youtube.com/watch?v=N4cgLcAESN0.

37. Videograpix Producciones Naidelyn, "Dron Juquila Oaxaca Noviembre 2019," You-Tube, April 18, 2020, https://www.youtube.com/watch?v=tCcuEUeWciQ. The comment section in this video includes a variety of these kinds of viewer posts.

38. Candy C., "Mañanitas ala Virgen de Juquila," YouTube, August 3, 2009, https://www.youtube.com/watch?v=m_c553R0a7A.

39. Gulaza, "6a Peregrinación al Santuario de la Virgen de Juquila del barrio 'El peñasco,' de Santiago Cuchilquitongo," YouTube, January 10, 2009, https://www.youtube.com/watch?v=vgZa6hp15TQ.

40. For example, see "Sobre Tierra Oaxaqueña, Sta. Catarina Juquila, Oaxaca, México," YouTube, December 31, 2017, https://www.youtube.com/watch?v=2nHiEEQgd6A&t=55s; Vive Oaxaca, "Conce Santa Catarina Juquila el nuevo 'Pueblo Mágico' de Oaxaca," YouTube, December 1, 2020, https://www.youtube.com/watch?v=DF96deJI76E.

41. Oaxaca Bonito, "Ruta de la Fe Juquila," YouTube, December 28, 2016, https://www.youtube.com/watch?v=tCPftMerSl8.

42. For example, Madommi Vlogs, "Aquí apareció la Virgen de Juquila," YouTube, March 29, 2020, https://www.youtube.com/watch?v=vjRPKK—lw8; and Traketin Tehuanga, "Viaje a Juquila," YouTube, December 15, 2020, https://www.youtube.com/watch?v=LlTyai6hkO8.

43. Cronos Audiovisual, "A la Virgen de Juquila. Los Borja. Vídeo Oficial 2017," YouTube, May 2, 2017, https://www.youtube.com/watch?v=4JXEo0AHDpI&list=RDwrzg66FHAAw&index=31.

44. Some, however, barely even allude to pious practices. For example, see bus company promotional videos: Chino Cruz, "Juquila 2014, Scania Irizar i6 4x2 Navani Turistica," YouTube, December 24, 2014, https://www.youtube.com/watch?v=rflSHWxf5iQ.

45. For example, see Arquidiócesis de Oaxaca, "Juquila 2015," YouTube, October 8, 2015, https://www.youtube.com/watch?v=jgn6MXwgBuA; "En vivo desde el Santuario de Juquila," YouTube, December 8, 2016, https://www.youtube.com/watch?v=NNAF7SYZDmo&t=4930s; and Arquidiócesis de Oaxaca, "Imaculada Virgen de Juquila, Bendición Solemne", YouTube, December 26, 2019, https://www.youtube.com/watch?v=7Z9BgAOPnsE.

46. Pilgrims of Tonameca, Oaxaca, interview with the author, November 11, 2017.

47. "Peregrinación a Juquila: Primer Día," YouTube, December 5, 2019, https://www.youtube.com/watch?v=ycz2UFpEL1o&t=1s. He includes another video where he interviews devotees, "40 Años de Peregrinar," YouTube, December 13, 2019, https://www.youtube.com/watch?v=YgYZfm3YoG8. As of August 4, 2021, his channel has thirty-six thousand followers.

48. Most of the Oaxacan archdiocese's links for the 2014 coronation's promotion are no longer active. This press release and digital poster from the archbishop remains: José Luis Chávez Botello, Arzobispo de Antequera Oaxaca, "Vivamos, disfrutemos, y proyectemos la coronación de la Virgen," October 5, 2014, http://www.arquioax.org/atrio/comunicado-de-prensa-domingo-5-de-octubre/. The poster explaining the newly crowned Juquila's iconographic makeover also remains accessible, http://3.bp.blogspot.com/-SpDluJOnPBs/VDYHjaUFp-I/AAAAAAAAAIc/XLiyUq41_1w/s1600/descripcion%2Bde%2Bla%2Bcorona%2Be%2Bimagen%2Bde%2Bla%2Bvirgen%2Bde%2Bjuquila.jpg.

49. For example, Aquidiócesis de Antequera Oaxaca, "Coronación Pontificia. Inmaculada de Juquila," YouTube, October 14, 2014, https://www.youtube.com/watch?v=R-wz9CQkUno.

50. Bypmexico, "Coronación de la Virgen de Juquila," YouTube, October 8, 2014, https://www.youtube.com/watch?v=R-wz9CQkUno.

51. Vive Oaxaca, "Celebración de la Coronación Pontificia de Nuestra Señora Inmaculada de Juquila," YouTube, October 9, 2014, https://www.youtube.com/watch?v=Fra-vaCI3eE&t=2245s.

52. Compare CaminatadeFe, "Documental XIX Caminata de Fe Tlaxiaco Juquila 2015," YouTube, September 3, 2015, https://www.youtube.com/watch?v=N4cgLcAESN0; Vive Oaxaca, "Celebración de la Coronación Pontificia de Nuestra Señora Inmaculada de Juquila," YouTube, October 9, 2014, https://www.youtube.com/watch?v=Fra-vaCI3eE&t=2245s.

53. Padre José de Jesús Aguilar Valdés, "La Virgen de Juquila—Historia de la Venerada Imagen y visita a su Santuario en Oaxaca," YouTube, June 2021, https://www.youtube.com/watch?v=fRub_mn-m_8.

54. Heidi Campbell, "Understanding the Relationship between Religion Online and Offline in a Networked Society," *Journal of the American Academy of Religion* 80, no. 1 (March 2012): 64–93; Campbell, *Digital Religion: Understanding Religious Practice in New Media Worlds* (London: Routledge, 2013); Campbell, "How Religious Communities Negotiate New Media Religiously," in *Digital Religion, Social Media, and Culture: Perspectives, Practices, and Futures*, ed. Pauline Cheong, Peter Fischer-Nielsen, Stefan Gelfgren, and Charles Ess (New York: Peter Lang, 2012), 81–96; and Campbell and Alessandra Vitullo, "Assessing Changes in the Study of Religious Communities in Digital Religion Studies," *Church, Communication, and Culture* 1, no. 1 (2016): 73–89.

55. Marc Loustau, Kristin Norget, and Eric Hoenes del Pinal, "Introduction: Locating Global Catholic Media," in *Mediating Catholicism: Religion and Media in Global Catholic Imaginaries*, ed. Eric Hoenes del Pinal, Marc Roscoe Loustou, and Kristin Norget (New York: Bloomsbury Academic, 2022). See also Kristin Norget, "Mediat(iz)ing Catholicism: Saint, Spectacle, and Theopolitics in Peru," *Journal of the Royal Anthropological Institute* 27 (2021): 757–79.

56. Coleman, *Powers of Pilgrimage.*

# Chapter Six

1. Javier, interview with the author, Zimatlán, Oaxaca, November 10, 2016.

2. They promoted their efforts on their Facebook page as they accomplished these tasks: see, for example, Peregrinación Ciclista Nuestra Señora de Dolores, Facebook, June 22, 2019, https://www.facebook.com/ciclistasacatzingojuquila?__tn__=%2CdC-R-R&eid=ARBALTRuWn67mQlYmQkDETZrGuKAzN7ABXTCIqQv20Z4GcTD-FisYuU4qYEf0UT11GRYN5zCr5IV_EMj&hc_ref=ARTAjSO2gWMO9GDjAxOJIK9m3soBHSh3DnGa4GlgMuX4wspZx_KT-5b8mQR7gDPFvjg&fref=nf.

3. Camila, interview with the author, Oaxaca, Oaxaca, July 12, 2016.

4. Joaquín, interview with the author, Sola de Vega, Oaxaca, December 2, 2016.

5. Santiago, interview with the author, Ayoquezco, Oaxaca, November 30, 2016.

6. Caminando Juntos, Facebook, https://www.facebook.com/groups/551368188397710. Before he left the group in 2018, Juan administered the page.

7. Santiago, interview with the author, Ayoquezco, Oaxaca, November 30, 2016.

8. Santiago, interview with the author.

9. Alicia, interview with the author, Zaachila, Oaxaca, November 29, 2016. Subsequent personal communication via Facebook direct message.

10. Juan, interview with the author, Oaxaca, Oaxaca, November 13, 2017.

11. Juan, interview with the author. Originally, "No comulgo . . . y allí se van, a la brevedad."

12. Juan, interview with the author. Originally, "No nos gusta servir. No nos gusta dejar nuestro libertinaje."

13. Wright-Ríos, *Revolutions*.

14. William A. Christian, *Visionaries: The Spanish Republic and the Reign of Christ* (Berkeley: University of California Press, 1996).

15. Originally, "Esto no es carrera. El chiste es llegar, y llegar todos juntos."

## Chapter Seven

1. Andrés, interview with the author, December 2, 2018. Originally, "Así empiezan las tradiciones."

2. "Female Cyclists in Mexico Rally for Their Rights in the Street," NBC News, You-Tube, August, 29, 2017, https://www.youtube.com/watch?v=eWNyiDBxSUY; Dani Cabezas, "Todo el machismo que sufre una mujer cuando circula en bicicleta," *Flooxer Now*, September 11, 2018, https://www.flooxernow.com/noticias/todo-machismo-que -sufre-mujer-cuando-circula-bicicleta_201809065b976f980cf2b0ecff39f0d8.html; Marcela Vargas, "La resistencia viaja sobre dos ruedas," *Corriente Alterna*, January 31, 2021, https://corrientealterna.unam.mx/galeria/mujeres-ciclistas-colectivas-cdmx/.

3. Play Turisloco, Facebook, November 23, 2023, https://www.facebook.com/profile .php?id=100044275441586.

4. Salomón, Domingo, Luis, and members of the Comisión, group discussion with the author, December 30, 2018.

5. Gobierno de México, Data México, Acatzingo, https://datamexico.org/es/profile/ geo/acatzingo#equidad. Demographic data cited by the government is from the 2020 census.

6. Patricia Plunket and Gabriela Uruñuela, "Recent Research in Puebla Prehistory," *Journal of Archeological Research* 13, no. 2 (June 2005): 89–127

7. Juan Manuel Márquez Murad, "Acatzingo: metamorfosis de la traza de un pueblo histórico," *Boletín de Monumentos Históricos*, tercera época, no. 11 (September–December 2007), https://revistas.inah.gob.mx/index.php/boletinmonumentos/article/view/ 2051/1980.

8. Garavaglia and Grosso, "Mexican Elites."

9. Gobierno de México, Data México, Acatzingo, https://datamexico.org/es/profile/ geo/acatzingo#equidad.

10. Samuel, interview with the author, Los Reyes Juárez, Puebla, August 16, 2016.

11. For example, Remigio, interview with the author, Juchatengo, Oaxaca, December 4, 2018.

## Chapter Eight

1. Tere, interview with the author, Oaxaca, Oaxaca, 9 November 2017.

2. Chema, interview with author, Huixtepec, Oaxaca, November 30, 2016.

3. Alicia, comment, November 29, 2016. Originally, "Es que veniste sin fe."

4. Alicia, interview with the author, Zaachila, Oaxaca, November 29, 2016.

5. Originally, "Gracias Virgencita por haber venido 50 meses consecutivos caminando a visitarte."

## Chapter Nine

1. Agustín, phone interview with the author, Acatzingo, Puebla, November 20, 2018.

2. Peregrinación Ciclista de Huixcolotla, November 12, 2019, https://www.facebook .com/photo/?fbid=399261927623411&set=pob.100026188200070.

3. Carlos, interview with the author, Coscomatepec, Veracruz, August 27, 2016.

4. Luis, interview with the author, Acatzingo, Puebla, December 1, 2018.

5. Luis, interview with the author, Tecomovaca, Oaxaca, December 2, 2018.

6. See Wright-Ríos, *Revolutions*, 73–82.

7. Photographer Alinka Echeverría produced a stunning artistic installation featuring stylized photographs of three hundred pilgrims traveling to the Virgin of Guadalupe's shrine carrying elaborate, decorative offerings on their backs. See Laura E. Pérez, "On the Road to Tepeyac, Guadalupe's Got Their Backs: Alinka Echeverría's Photographs of Religious Pilgrims Question What an Image Really Is," *Zócalo*, September 13, 2016, https://www.zocalopublicsquare.org/2016/09/13/road-tepeyac-guadalupes-got-backs/ viewings/glimpses. See also Alinka Echeverría, *Sur le chemin de Tepeyac* (Paris: Actes Sud, 2011).

8. Luis and Adriana, interview with the author, Juquila, Oaxaca, June 5, 2018.

9. Luis and Adriana, interview with the author.

10. Ernesto, interview with the author, Juchatengo, Oaxaca, December 4, 2018.

11. Ernesto, interview with the author. Originally, "Dios nos manda pruebas" and "Pero los doctores te dicen que no es verdad."

12. Ernesto, interview with the author. Originally, "No gastes."

13. Ernesto, interview with the author. Originally, "Yo le debo mucho a la Santísima Virgen y Diosito."

14. Domingo, interview with the author, Acatzingo, Puebla, December 1, 2018.

## Chapter Ten

1. Andrés Carrera Pineda, "El Pedimento, zona en disputa," *El Imparcial*, November 30, 2019, https://imparcialoaxaca.mx/los-municipios/380163/el-pedimento-zona-en -disputa/.

2. Santiago, interview with the author, Juquila, Oaxaca, December 2, 2022.

3. Lawrence Taylor, "Epilogue: Pilgrimage, Moral Geography, and Contemporary Religion in the West," in *Gender, Nation and Religion in European Pilgrimage: Old Routes, New Journeys*, ed. Willy Jansen, Catrien Notermans, and Ellen Badone (Burlington, VT: Ashgate, 2012), 209–20. See also Lawrence Taylor, "Moral Entrepreneurs and Moral Geographies on the US/Mexico Border," *Social and Legal Studies* 9, no. 3 (2010): 299–310.

4. Octavio Vélez, "Disputa municipio e Iglesia pedimento de Juquila," *NVI Noticias*, December 7, 2019, https://www.nvinoticias.com/nota/120538/ disputa-municipio-e-iglesia-pedimento-de-juquila?fbclid=IwAR0c_LZrG -BTtyUnqZG7IknRlk1KnnrDQSH1GuGtTcDUPByuIStA5dr7qW0.

5. Originally, "Virgen de Juquila, Concédame Casa."

6. Graziano, *Miraculous Images*, 113–54.

7. Originally, "Celebramos 6 años que nos has permitido llegar, te damos las gracias Virgencita de Juquila."

8. Originally, "La fe sobre reudas hacia ti."

9. Flor Hernández, "Incendian casetas y casas en El Pedimento, Juquila; acusan autoridades municipales omisión de gobierno de Oaxaca," *News Week Español*, February 4, 2019, https://newsweekespanol.com/2019/02/incendian-casetas-casas-pedimento -juquila-acusan-autoridades-municipales-omision-gobierno-oaxaca/. See "Policía de Oaxaca recupera pacíficamente El Pedimento de Juquila," *Milenio*, November 30, 2019, https://www.milenio.com/estados/policias-oaxaca-recuperan-pedimento-santa -catarina-juquila; Fernando Miranda, "Estalla conflicto entre 2 comunidades por tierras en Juquila, Oaxaca," *El Universal*, November 30, 2019, https://www.eluniversal.com.mx/ estados/estalla-conflicto-entre-2-comunidades-por-tierras-en-juquila-oaxaca; Miguel Maya Alonso, "Por la fuerza recuperan el Pedimento de Juquila," *El Imparcial*, December 1, 2019, https://imparcialoaxaca.mx/los-municipios/380417/por-la-fuerza-recuperan-el -pedimento-de-juquila/. See also on the attempt to reconstruct the police action and examine claims of death, Jorge Acevedo, "Crónica del desalojo del Pedimento en Juquila," *TVBUS Noticias*, https://www.youtube.com/watch?v=j-RmGN8DN9Y.

10. "Continúa trabado el conflicto del Pedimento en Juquila," *Panorama del Pacífico*, February 22, 2013, http://www.panoramadelpacifico.com/continua-trabado-el-conflicto -del-pedimento-en-juquila/; Andrés Carrera Pineda, "El Pedimento, zona en disputa," *El Imparcial*, November 30, 2019, https://imparcialoaxaca.mx/los-municipios/380163/ el-pedimento-zona-en-disputa/.

11. Reynaldo Bracamontes, "Llaman a terminar con la impunidad en el Pedimento de Juquila, Oaxaca," *NVI Noticias*, March 24, 2017, http://www.nvinoticias.com/nota/ 59893/llaman-terminar-con-la-impunidad-en-el-pedimento-de-juquila-oaxaca.

12. César Morales Niño, "La iglesia y los políticos de Juquila pelean por las jugosas limosnas del los peregrinos a la Virgen," *Noticias*, January 23, 2006; José Hannan Robles, "'Un atropello arrebatar al clero Pedimento de Juquila," *El Imparcial*, May 2, 2006; Maricruz Martínez, "Limosnas de Juquila, botín de muchos," *NVI Noticias* July 5, 2017, http://www.nvinoticias.com/nota/58499/limosnas-de-juquila -botin-de-muchos. See also Octavio Vélez, "Disputa municipio e Iglesia pedimento de Juquila," *NVI Noticias*, December 7, 2019, https://www.nvinoticias.com/nota/ 120538/disputa-municipio-e-iglesia-pedimento-de-juquila?fbclid=IwAR0c_LZrG -BTtyUnqZG7IknRlk1KnnrDQSH1GuGtTcDUPByuIStA5dr7qW0.

13. Pri Juquila, "Crecimiento Juquila," Facebook, June 1, 2013, https://www.facebook .com/photo/?fbid=494691780601020&set=ecnf.100001806088026.

14. Originally, "Santísima Virgen de Juquila te pido que me agas [sic] el milagro que la chosa se vende. . . . te pido con toda fe que mandes un buen cliente."

15. Originally, "Virgencita . . . te pido salud, amor y esperanza, te quiero mucho y te pido que me ayudes a conseguir mi sueño ser abogada, y quiero que me ayudes a olvidar lo que ha pasado, Amen."

16. Originally, "Virgencita: Se que no soy tu mejor hija, pero intento ser persona de bien, por esa razón me he tomado el atrevimiento de pedirte que no me dejes sola en la lucha de mi sueño de ser doctora y poder ayudar a mi prójimo ayúdame a cumplir mi sueño, a que se haga realidad, quiero ser doctora y nunca olvidar el motivo por lo que lo deseo."

17. Originally, "Virgen de Juquila: Gracias por haberme permitido seguir con mi familia después del descuido que tuve el día 17-Sep-12, gracias por tu milagro, José."

18. Originally, "Muchas Gracias Virgencita por darnos la salud y las herramientas para trabajar y llevar los alimentos a nuestra familia, Familia . . . , 04, diciembre, 2016, Pedimento."

## On My Skin and in My Heart

1. "Son tres años los que lleva cerrado el santuario de la Virgen de Juquila," Azteca Noticias, YouTube, December 6, 2022, https://www.youtube.com/watch?v=RTfjl__tW9o.

2. Felipe, interview with the author, Oaxaca, Oaxaca, December 7, 2022.

3. Alicia, interview with the author, Zaachila, Oaxaca, November 29, 2016. Subsequent personal communication, Facebook direct message.

4. Felipe, interview with the author, Oaxaca, Oaxaca, December 7, 2022.

5. Graziano, *Miraculous Images*, 128–36.

6. Gobierno de Oaxaca, "Oaxaca cuenta con un nuevo pueblo mágico," December 1, 2020, https://www.oaxaca.gob.mx/comunicacion/oaxaca-cuenta-con-un-nuevo-pueblo-magico-santa-catarina-juquila/. See also Laura Begley Bloom, "The 11 New Magical Towns of Mexico," *Forbes*, December 4, 2020, https://www.forbes.com/sites/laurabegleybloom/2020/12/04/revealed-the-11-new-magical-towns-of-mexico/?sh=94e63564fe62.

7. Juquila Pueblo Mágico, Facebook, September 24, 2022, https://www.facebook.com/JuquilaPuebloMagico.

8. Clicking through the photographs posted on the site reveals several of these kinds of posts, https://www.facebook.com/JuquilaPuebloMagico/photos. The cycling pilgrims of Huixcolotla, Puebla, are fond of sharing these posts and their wistful messages. For example, Peregrinación Ciclista de Huixcolotla a Juquila, Facebook, August 20, 2022, https://www.facebook.com/peregrinacion.ciclista.129.

9. For example, during Holy Week 2023, they shared a photograph of a pilgrim walking to the shrine of the Virgen de los Lagos in Jalisco from a group called "Caravana de la Fe," Peregrinación a Pie Tecamachalco La Villita, Facebook, April 4, 2023, https://www.facebook.com/profile.php?id=100015187783836.

# BIBLIOGRAPHY

Aguilar Ros, Alejandra. "Transcending Symbols: The Religious Landscape of Pilgrimage Studies in Mexico." In *New Pathways in Pilgrimage Studies: Global Perspectives*, edited by Dionigi Albera and John Eade, 142–62. New York: Routledge, 2016.

Arivizu Barrón, Ezequiel, Leobardo Jiménez Sánchez, Mercedes Jiménez Velázquez, Anibal Quispe Limaylla, Manuel Villa Issa, and José A. Ávila Dorantes. "Análisis de producción y comercilización de hortalizas: caso del mercado de Huixcolotla, Puebla." *Revista Mexicana de Ciencias Agrícolas* 5, no. 1 (2014): 687–94.

Barabas, Alicia M. "Cosmovisiones y etnoterritorialidad en las culturas indígenas de Oaxaca." *Antípoda*, no. 7 (2008): 119–39. https://doi.org/10.7440/antipoda7.2008.06.

Baskes, Jeremy. *Indians, Merchants, and Markets: A Reinterpretation of the Repartimiento and Spanish-Indian Economic Relations in Colonial Oaxaca, 1750–1821.* Stanford, CA: Stanford University Press, 2000.

Begley Gloom, Laura. "Revealed: The 11 New Magical Towns of Mexico." *Forbes*, December 4, 2020. https://www.forbes.com/sites/laurabegleybloom/2020/12/04/revealed-the-11-new-magical-towns-of-mexico/?sh=4d4ad4534fe6.

Blitzer, Jonathan. "Some Conservative Voters Rethink Trump's Immigration Agenda." *New Yorker*, April 19, 2018.

Bracamontes, Reynaldo. "Llaman a terminar con la impunidad en el Pedimento de Juquila, Oaxaca." *NVI Noticias*, March 24, 2017. http://www.nvinoticias.com/nota/59893/llaman-terminar-con-la-impunidad-en-el-pedimento-de-juquila-oaxaca.

Burkhart, Louise M. *The Slippery Earth: Nahua-Christian Moral Dialogue in Sixteenth-Century Mexico.* Tucson: University of Arizona Press, 1989.

Cabezas, Dani. "Todo el machismo que sufre una mujer cuando circula en bicicleta." *Floxer Now*, September 11, 2018. https://www.flooxernow.com/noticias/todo-machismo-que-sufre-mujer-cuando-circula-bicicleta_201809065b976f980cf2b0ecff39f0d8.html.

Campbell, Heidi. "How Religious Communities Negotiate New Media Religiously." In *Digital Religion, Social Media, and Culture: Perspectives, Practices, and Futures*, edited by Pauline Hope Cheong, Peter Fischer-Nielsen, Stefan Gelfgren, and Charles Ess, 81–96. New York: Peter Lang, 2012.

Campbell, Heidi. "Understanding the Relationship between Religion Online and Offline in a Networked Society." *Journal of the American Academy of Religion* 80, no. 1 (March 2012): 64–93.

Campbell, Heidi A., and Alessandra Vitullo. "Assessing Changes in the Study of Religious Communities in Digital Religion Studies." *Church, Communication and Culture* 1, no. 1 (2016): 73–89.

Campbell, Heidi, and Ruth Tsuria, eds. *Digital Religion: Understanding Religious Practice in Digital Media.* 2nd edition. Abingdon: Routledge, 2022.

Carrera Pineda, Andrés. "El Pedimento, zona en disputa." *El Imparcial*, November 30, 2019. https://imparcialoaxaca.mx/los-municipios/380163/el-pedimento-zona-en -disputa/.

Chassen-López, Francie R. *From Liberal to Revolutionary Oaxaca: The View from the South; Mexico, 1867–1911.* University Park: Pennsylvania State University Press, 2004.

Chemin, Eduardo. "Producers of Meaning and the Ethics of Movement: Religion, Consumerism and Gender on the Road to Compostela." In *Gender, Nation and Religion in European Pilgrimage: Old Routes, New Journeys,* edited by Willy Jansen and Catrien Notermans, 127–43. Burlington, VT: Ashgate, 2012.

Cheong, Pauline Hope, ed. *Digital Religion, Social Media, and Culture: Perspectives, Practices, and Futures.* New York: P. Lang, 2012.

Chowning, Margaret. *Catholic Women and Mexican Politics, 1750–1940.* Princeton, NJ: Princeton University Press, 2023.

Christian, William A. *Visionaries: The Spanish Republic and the Reign of Christ.* Berkeley: University of California Press, 1996.

Clendinnen, Inga. "Ways to the Sacred: Reconstructing 'Religion' in Sixteenth-Century Mexico." *History and Anthropology* 5 (1990): 105–41.

Coleman, Simon. "Do You Believe in Pilgrimage? Communitas, Contestation and Beyond." *Anthropological Theory* 2, no. 3 (September 1, 2002): 355–68.

Coleman, Simon. *Powers of Pilgrimage: Religion in a World of Movement.* New York: New York University Press, 2022.

Connaughton Hanley, Brian Francis. *Dimensiones de la identidad patriótica: religión, política y regiones en México, siglo XIX.* Mexico City: Universidad Autonoma Metropolitana, Unidad Iztapalapa, División de Ciencias Sociales y Humanidades, Departamento de Filosofia, 2001.

Eade, John, and Michael J Sallnow, eds. *Contesting the Sacred: The Anthropology of Christian Pilgrimage.* New York: Routledge, 1991.

Echeverría, Alinka. *Sur le chemin de Tepeyac.* Paris: Actes Sud, 2011.

Egan, Timothy. *Pilgrimage to Eternity: From Canterbury to Rome in Search of a Faith.* New York: Penguin Books, 2019.

*El Universal.* "Estalla conflicto entre 2 comunidades por tierras en Juquila, Oaxaca." November 30, 2019. https://www.eluniversal.com.mx/estados/estalla-conflicto-entre-2 -comunidades-por-tierras-en-juquila-oaxaca/.

*El Universal.* "Puebla, el epicentro del huachicol." January 9, 2019. https://www .eluniversal.com.mx/nacion/puebla-el-epicentro-del-huachicol/.

*El Universal.* "Puebla, encabeza decomisos de huachicol." June 12, 2017. https://www .eluniversal.com.mx/articulo/nacion/seguridad/2017/06/12/puebla-encabeza -decomisos-de-huachicol/.

Fedele, Anna. "Gender, Society and Religious Critique among Mary Magdalene Pilgrims in Southern France." In *Gender, Nation and Religion in European Pilgrimage: Old Routes, New Journeys,* edited by Willy Jansen and Catrien Notermans, 55–69. Burlington, VT: Ashgate, 2012.

Fulwilder, Benjamin. "Driving the Nation: Road Transportation and the Creation of the Post-Revolutionary State, 1925–1960." PhD dissertation, Georgetown University, 2004.

Garavaglia, Juan Carlos, and Juan Carlos Grosso. "El comportamiento demográfico de una parroquia poblana de la colonia al México independiente: Tepeaca y su entorno agrario, 1740–1850." *Historia Mexicana* 40, no. 4 (1991): 615–71.

Garner, Paul. "Federalism and Caudillismo in the Mexican Revolution: The Genesis of the Oaxaca Sovereignty Movement (1915–20)." *Journal of Latin American Studies* 17, no. 1 (1985): 111–33.

Gemzöe, Lena. "Big, Strong and Happy: Reimagining Femininity on the Way to Compostela." In *Gender, Nation and Religion in European Pilgrimage: Old Routes, New Journeys*, edited by Willy Jansen and Catrien Notermans, 37–53. Burlington, VT: Ashgate, 2012.

George, Michael. "Walking the Way." *National Geographic Magazine* 227, no. 5 (2015): 130–39.

Gerhard, Peter. *A Guide to the Historical Geography of New Spain*. Norman: University of Oklahoma Press, 1993.

Gobierno de México. "Acatzingo." Data México. Accessed March 8, 2024. https://www.economia.gob.mx/datamexico/en.

Gobierno de México. "San Salvador Huixcolotla." Data México. Accessed March 8, 2024. https://www.economia.gob.mx/datamexico/en.

Gobierno de México. "Santa Catarina Juquila." Data México. Accessed March 8, 2024. https://www.economia.gob.mx/datamexico/en.

Gobierno del Estado de Oaxaca. "Oaxaca cuenta con un nuevo Pueblo Mágico: Santa Catarina Juquila—Coordinación de Comunicación Social del Gobierno del Estado," December 1, 2020. https://www.oaxaca.gob.mx/comunicacion/oaxaca-cuenta-con-un-nuevo-pueblo-magico-santa-catarina-juquila/.

Graziano, Frank. *Cultures of Devotion: Folk Saints of Spanish America*. Oxford: Oxford University Press, 2007.

Graziano, Frank. *Miraculous Images and Votive Offerings in Mexico*. New York: Oxford University Press, 2015.

Greenberg, James B. *Blood Ties: Life and Violence in Rural Mexico*. Tucson: University of Arizona Press, 1989.

Hannan Robles, José. "Un atropello arrebatar al clero Pedimento de Juquila." *El Imparcial*, May 2, 2006.

Hernández Díaz, Jorge. *El café amargo: los procesos de diferenciación y cambio social entre los chatinos*. Oaxaca: Universidad Autónoma Benito Juárez de Oaxaca, Instituto de Investigaciones Sociológicas, 1987.

Hernández, Flor. "Incendian casetas y casas en El Pedimento, Juquila; acusan autoridades municipales omisión de gobierno de Oaxaca." *Newsweek en Español*, February 4, 2019. https://newsweekespanol.com/2019/02/04/incendian-casetas-casas-pedimento-juquila-acusan-autoridades-municipales-omision-gobierno-oaxaca/.

Hughes, Jennifer Scheper. "The Niño Jesús Doctor: Novelty and Innovation in Mexican Religion." *Nova Religio* 16, no. 2 (2012): 4–28.

Infobae. "Una cifra récord de peregrinos recibió la Basílica de Guadalupe para celebrar el Día de la Virgen." December 12, 2022, sec. México, América. https://www.infobae.com/america/mexico/2022/12/12/una-cifra-record-de-peregrinos-recibio-la-basilica-de-guadalupe-para-celebrar-a-el-dia-de-la-virgen/.

Jansen, Willy, and Catrien Notermans, eds. *Gender, Nation and Religion in European Pilgrimage: Old Routes, New Journeys*. Burlington, VT: Ashgate, 2012.

Jansen, Willy, and Catrien Notermans. "Old Routes, New Journeys: Reshaping Gender, Nation and Religion in European Pilgrimage." In *Gender, Nation and Religion in European Pilgrimage: Old Routes, New Journeys*, edited by Willy Jansen, and Catrien Notemans, 1–18. Burlington, VT: Ashgate, 2012.

Jordan, Miriam. "The Town Fought Back." *New York Times*, June 26, 2018.

Juárez Ramírez, Benito. "Coscomatepec, principal exportador de chayote, pero el 'ganón' sigue siendo el 'coyote.'" *Alcalorpolítico*, July 27, 2016. https://www.alcalorpolitico.com/informacion/coscomatepec-principal-exportador-de-chayote-pero-el-ganon-sigue-siendo-el-coyote—208693.html.

Kaufman, Suzanne K. *Consuming Visions: Mass Culture and the Lourdes Shrine*. Ithaca, NY: Cornell University Press, 2018.

Knight, Alan. *The Mexican Revolution*. Lincoln: University of Nebraska Press, 1986.

Kurlantzick, Joshua. "21st-Century Religious Travel: Leave the Sackcloth at Home." *New York Times*, April 29, 2007.

Larkin, Brian R. *The Very Nature of God: Baroque Catholicism and Religious Reform in Bourbon Mexico City*. Albuquerque: University of New Mexico Press, 2010.

Loustou, Marc, Kristin Norget, and Eric Hoenes del Pinal. "Introduction: Locating Global Catholic Media." In *Mediating Catholicism: Religion and Media in Global Catholic Imaginaries*, edited by Eric Hoenes del Pinal, Marc Loustou, and Kristin Norget. New York: Bloomsbury Academic, 2022.

Lugo-Morín, Diosey Ramón, Javier Ramírez-Juárez, José Arturo Méndez-Espinoza, and Benjamín Peña-Olvera. "Redes sociales asimétricas en el sistema hortícola del valle de Tepeaca, México." *Economía, Sociedad y Territorio* 10, no. 32 (2010): 207–30.

Luque Agraz, Elin. "Análisis de la evolución de los exvotos pictóricos como documentos visuales para describer 'la otra historia,' de México." PhD dissertation, Universidad Nacional de Educación a Distancia, 2012.

Márquez Murad, Juan Manuel. "Acatzingo: metamorfosis de la traza de un pueblo histórico." *Boletín de Monumentos Históricos*, tercera época, no. 11 (December 2007).

Martínez, Maricruz. "Limosnas de Juquila, botín de muchos." *NVI Noticias*, July 5, 2017. http://www.nvinoticias.com/nota/58499/limosnas-de-juquila-botin-de-muchos.

Martínez Vásquez, Víctor Raúl, and Francie R. Chassen-López, eds. *La Revolución en Oaxaca, 1900–1930*. Oaxaca de Juárez, Oax: Instituto de Administración Pública de Oaxaca, 1985.

Maya Alonso, Miguel. "Por la fuerza recuperan el pedimento de Juquila." *El Imparcial*. Accessed March 8, 2024. https://imparcialoaxaca.mx/los-municipios/380417/por-la-fuerza-recuperan-el-pedimento-de-juquila/.

Meyer, Jean A. *El conflicto religioso en Oaxaca (1926–1938)*. Oaxaca: IAGO, 2006.

Milenio. "Policía de Oaxaca recupera pacíficamente El Pedimento de Juquila." November 30, 2019, sec. Estados. https://www.milenio.com/estados/policias-oaxaca-recuperan-pedimento-santa-catarina-juquila.

Montalvo, Tania. "Pemex pierde 90 mil litros diarios de combustible sólo en uno de sus ductos." *Animal Político*, December 12, 2016. https://animalpolitico.com/2016/12/pemex-robo-combustible.

Morales Niño, César. "La iglesia y los políticos de Juquila pelean por las jugosas limosnas del los peregrinos a la Virgen." *Noticias*, January 23, 2006.

Morales Sánchez, Antonio. *Romería de Juquila*. Oaxaca: Sedetur, 1997.

Norget, Kristin. *Days of Death, Days of Life: Ritual in the Popular Culture of Oaxaca.* New York: Columbia University Press, 2006.

Norget, Kristin. "Mediat(iz)ing Catholicism: Saint, Spectacle, and Theopolitics in Lima, Peru." *Journal of the Royal Anthropological Institute* 27, no. 4 (2021): 757–79.

Norget, Kristin. "Popular-Indigenous Catholicism in Southern Mexico." *Religions* 12, no. 7 (July 14, 2021): 531–49.

Orth, Maureen, and Diana Markosian. "The World's Most Powerful Woman." *National Geographic Magazine* 228, no. 6 (2015): 30.

*Panorama del Pacífico.* "Continúa trabado el conflicto del pedimento en Juquila." February 22, 2013. http://www.panoramadelpacifico.com/continua-trabado-el-conflicto-del-pedimento-en-juquila/.

Perkins, Stephen M. "Macehuales and the Corporate Solution: Colonial Secessions in Nahua Central Mexico." *Mexican Studies* 21, no. 2 (2005): 277–306.

Plunket, Patricia, and Gabriela Uruñuela. "Recent Research in Puebla Prehistory." *Journal of Archaeological Research* 13, no. 2 (2005): 89–127.

Rath, Thomas. *The Dread Plague and the Cow Killers: The Politics of Animal Disease in Mexico and the World.* New York: Cambridge University Press, 2022.

Reader, Ian. *Pilgrimage: A Very Short Introduction.* New York: Oxford University Press, 2015.

Reader, Ian. *Pilgrimage in the Marketplace.* London: Routledge, 2016.

Rodríguez, Oscar. "Francisco concede coronación pontificia de La Virgen de Juquila." *Milenio*, September 2, 2014. https://www.milenio.com/estados/francisco-concede-coronacion-pontificia-virgen-juquila.

Rosas, José Luis. "Inicia éxodo de peregrinos: En autos, motocicletas, bicicletas y a pie, realizan su recorrido con la intención de visitar La Virgen." *El Imparcial*, November 24, 2014. http://imparcialoaxaca.mx/la-capital/1Js/inicia-%C3%A9xodo-de-peregrinos.

Rubial García, Antonio. *La santidad controvertida: hagiografía y conciencia criolla alrededor de los venerables no canonizados de Nueva España.* Mexico City: Fondo de Cultura Económica, 2015.

Ruiz Cervantes, Francisco José. *La revolución en Oaxaca: el movimiento de soberanía, 1915–1920.* Mexico City: Fondo de Cultura Económica y Instituto de Investigaciones Sociales, 1986.

Ruiz y Cervantes, Joseph. *Memorias de la portentosa imagen de Nuestra Señora de Xuquila.* Mexico City: Felipe de Zúñiga y Ontiveros, 1791.

Sánchez Silva, Carlos. *Indios, comerciantes y burocracia en la Oaxaca poscolonial, 1786–1860.* Oaxaca: Instituto Oaxaqueño de las Culturas, 1998.

Sarmiento Zúñiga, Mario Carlos. "Un portento milagroso en época de reformas: La imagen de la Inmaculada Concepción de Juquila en la configuración de una devoción secular." *Estudios de Historia Novohispana* 56, no. 56 (2017): 26–39.

Taylor, Lawrence J. "Epilogue: Pilgrimage, Moral Geography, and Contemporary Religion in the West." In *Gender, Nation and Religion in European Pilgrimage: Old Routes, New Journeys*, edited by Willy Jansen, Catrien Notermans, and Ellen Badone, 209–20. Burlington, VT: Ashgate, 2012.

Taylor, Lawrence J. "Moral Entrepreneurs and Moral Geographies on the US/Mexico Border." *Social and Legal Studies* 19, no. 3 (2010): 299–310.

Taylor, William B. *Theater of a Thousand Wonders: A History of Miraculous Images and Shrines in New Spain.* New York: Cambridge University Press, 2016.

Thomases, Drew. *Guest Is God: Pilgrimage, Tourism, and Making Paradise in India*. New York: Oxford University Press, 2019.

Turner, Victor W., and Edith L. B. Turner. *Image and Pilgrimage in Christian Culture: Anthropological Perspectives*. New York: Columbia University Press, 1978.

Univision. "'Mi hija es un milagro que me concedió la Virgen': Millones ya peregrinan hacia la Virgen de Guadalupe." Accessed December 10, 2022. https://www.univision .com/noticias/america-latina/peregrinacion-virgen-de-guadalupe-2022-ciudad-de -mexico-fotos.

Van Young, Eric. *The Other Rebellion: Popular Violence, Ideology, and the Mexican Struggle for Independence, 1810–1821*. Stanford, CA: Stanford University Press, 2001.

Vanderwood, Paul J. *The Power of God against the Guns of Government: Religious Upheaval in Mexico at the Turn of the Nineteenth Century*. Stanford, CA: Stanford University Press, 1998.

vanguardia.com.mx. "Cártel Jalisco Nueva Generación y 'Los bukanas' disputan el Triángulo Rojo, zona dorada del huachicoleo," October 3, 2018. https://vanguardia.com .mx/noticias/nacional/este-es-el-triangulo-rojo-zona-del-huachicoleo-que-disputan -el-cartel-jalisco-nueva-CNVG3416352.

Vargas, Marcela. "Mujeres ciclistas: la resistencia viaja en dos ruedas." *Corriente Alterna*, January 31, 2021. https://corrientealterna.unam.mx/galeria/mujeres-ciclistas -colectivas-cdmx/.

Vélez, Octavio. "Disputa municipio e Iglesia pedimento de Juquila." *NVI Noticias*, December 7, 2019. https://www.nvinoticias.com/nota/120538/ disputa-municipio-e-iglesia-pedimento-de-juquila?fbclid=IwAR0c_LZrG -BTtyUnqZG7IknRlk1KnnrDQSH1GuGtTcDUPByuIStA5dr7qW0.

Wright-Ríos, Edward. *Revolutions in Mexican Catholicism: Reform and Revelation in Oaxaca, 1887–1934*. Durham, NC: Duke University Press, 2009.

Wright-Ríos, Edward. *Searching for Madre Matiana: Prophecy and Popular Culture in Modern Mexico*. Albuquerque: University of New Mexico Press, 2014.

Wright-Ríos, Edward, and Carlota Martínez-Don. "Posting the Journey to Juquila: Pilgrimage, Digital Devotion, and Social Media in Mexico." *Latin American Research Review* 59, no. 2 (2024).

# INDEX

Page numbers in italics refer to figures, and references to plates are specified.

Wars of Independence, 44, 46, 52
Washington State, 128
WhatsApp, 168, 174

Yaitepec (Mexico), 153–54; votive
  chapel, seized control of, 169–70
Yolotepec (Mexico), 130, plate 10
YouTube, 12, 79–80; digital entrepre-

neurs, 86–87; Juquila's followers
  on, 85; pilgrimages, 86–91, 93, 113,
  186n19

Zapata, Emiliano, 52
Zavaletas family, 59–60
Zimatlán, Oaxaca (Mexico),
  34, plate 7